1001 QUESTIONS ANSWERED ABOUT BIRDS

BY ALLAN D. CRUICKSHANK
AND HELEN G. CRUICKSHANK

*With photographs by Allan D. Cruickshank
and drawings by James MacDonald*

DOVER PUBLICATIONS, INC.
NEW YORK

Dedicated to

Farida A. Wiley and George T. Hastings

distinguished naturalists and inspiring teachers

Published in Canada by General Publishing
Company, Ltd., 30 Lesmill Road, Don Mills,
Toronto, Ontario.
Published in the United Kingdom by Constable
and Company, Ltd., 10 Orange Street, London WC 2.

This Dover edition, first published in 1976, is an
unabridged and unaltered republication of the
work first published in 1958 by Dodd, Mead &
Company, New York.

International Standard Book Number: 0-486-23315-4
Library of Congress Catalog Card Number: 75-41881

Manufactured in the United States of America
Dover Publications, Inc.
180 Varick Street
New York, N.Y. 10014

PREFACE

Since man first took his place among the animals of the earth he has watched birds and wondered about them, he has envied their powers of flight and their freedom of movement across the skies. This interest has not died with the growing sophistication of civilized man. Kings, presidents, prime ministers, lawyers, doctors, merchants, coal miners, schoolboys and teachers today all share a common interest in observing birds. In fact, there is scarcely a level of present-day society where bird watchers are not found.

Today guides to the identification of birds in both North America and Europe are numerous and excellent. Field recognition has been raised to a level undreamed of a few decades ago. Innumerable week-end explorers, each with a pair of binoculars suspended from his neck, carry guides to bird identification in their pockets, and spend long hours searching for birds and studying them.

Life histories of individual birds and publications concerned with the birds within the borders of the various states contain excellent material on ornithological subjects. In addition, research projects as well as a vast number of entertaining and informational books which are first and foremost recreation reading about birds provide a varied fare for all readers. Such books answer questions about the identification of the various species or the lives of individual birds.

In easily used form this book answers the questions most frequently asked about birds in general: their structure, distribution, annual cycles, migration, their sizes, numbers and why they behave as they do. It is hoped that those interested in birds will find here the answers to their own questions about these strange and curious feathered creatures.

ALLAN D. CRUICKSHANK
HELEN G. CRUICKSHANK

Rockledge, Florida

CONTENTS

PHOTOGRAPHS

(Following page 144)

Saw-Whet Owl
Magnificent Frigate-Bird
Wild Turkey
Arctic Loon
Sooty Tern
Mute Swan
Ruby-Throated Hummingbird
Roseate Spoonbill
Ring-Billed Gull
Lesser Yellowlegs
Leach's Petrel
Black Vulture
Ducks
American Egret
Brown Pelican
Ducks on a U.S. Fish & Wildlife Service Refuge

1001 QUESTIONS ANSWERED ABOUT BIRDS

I. THE CLASSIFICATION OF BIRDS

1. Sometimes birds are referred to as animals. Is this correct?
Everything in the world is placed in one of three kingdoms: mineral, vegetable or animal. Scientists are not always sure whether some of the more primitive forms of life are animal or vegetable. There is no such uncertainty about the higher forms of life. A bird is not a mineral. It is not a member of the plant world. Therefore it must belong to the animal kingdom.

2. What is the distinctive characteristic of birds? Birds are vertebrate chordates. This means they have backbones made up of a series of vertebrae that form the chief support of their bodies. Birds alone make up the class Aves. Birds, and only birds, have feathers. Therefore any animal that grows feathers must be a bird.

3. What are the nearest relatives, biologically speaking, of birds?
Birds are derived from the reptiles. Though birds have advanced far beyond the most highly developed reptiles, their kinship, reaching back more than a hundred million years, remains.

4. Where was the most ancient fossil of a bird discovered? The earliest fossil of a bird, named Archaeopteryx by scientists, was discovered in 1851 in a slate quarry in Bavaria. This creature so closely resembled a lizard that the presence of feathers alone proved that it was a bird.

5. What geological era produced Archaeopteryx? The fossil remains of Archaeopteryx were found in Mesozoic rocks estimated to be about 150 million years old.

6. Have many bird fossils been discovered? The delicate bones of birds are crushed easily. Their flesh is eaten by other animals. Feathers also are eaten, particularly by insects. Therefore comparatively few bird fossils have been discovered.

While no modern species of bird dates back as far as the Eocene, during that period most modern families except the passerines or perching birds were represented in North America. Fossil loons, grebes, herons, ducks, grouse, sandpipers, cranes and owls have all been found in Eocene deposits located in many western states and along the east coast of the United States.

7. How many fossil birds have been found in North America? More than 350 species of fossil birds have been found on the North American continent.

8. Do representatives of any of those fossil species still live? Less than half of the 350 species of fossil birds are modern forms that still exist on earth.

9. What is the total number of fossil species found in the world? Dr. Alexander Wetmore of the Smithsonian Institution has estimated that almost 800 species of fossil birds have been found in the entire world.

10. When did modern birds appear on earth?   While fossil remains reveal the fact that birdlike creatures occurred during the Cretaceous era, it was not until the Eocene (after the disappearance of the dinosaurs) that modern birds became well established. At that time some birds, very much like certain species living today, were numerous.

11. How are birds named?   Birds have two names: a common name and a scientific or technical name, this latter being in Latin. *Robin* is the common name for a familiar North American bird. *Turdus migratorius* is the scientific name of the American robin.

12. How were the common names of birds given to them?   The common name of a bird is usually given to it by the people of the country it inhabits. The same bird may be given different names in different places. Even in one area, a bird is sometimes called by several names. For instance, the flicker has received more than 125 names in America. Before the advent of Europeans, the names given the flicker by the various Indian tribes were almost as numerous. It is evident that many names applied to a single species of bird leads to vast confusion as to what species is under discussion.

13. How is the scientific name of a bird established? The scientific naming of a bird follows rigid rules. Each species is given two Latin names. The first name refers to the genus to which the bird belongs. This first name is shared by other birds in the same genus. The second name indicates the species of the bird. It is restricted to that particular species. North American orioles belong to the genus Icterus. An orchard oriole is *Icterus spurius,* a Baltimore oriole is *Icterus galbula* and a Bullock's oriole is *Icterus bullocki.* Orioles may be called by various common names in different parts of the continent, but when a scientist reads the technical name, he knows precisely which bird is meant.

14. Occasionally three Latin words are used in the name of a bird. Why is this? When a third Latin name is given to a bird it indicates not only the genus and species of the bird but also that this particular bird varies slightly from the type species. The scientist calls such birds subspecies or races. Since subspecies (or races) seldom can be distinguished in the field they are of interest only to the laboratory scientist.

For instance, a small warbler, the yellowthroat (*Geothlypis trichas*), occurs from the Atlantic to the Pacific and from southern Canada to the Gulf of Mexico. Wherever a bird student may go in this area, if he sees or hears a yellowthroat he recognizes it as a familiar friend. Nevertheless, scientists have discovered that measurements of the bill, tarsus and other parts of the yellowthroat vary slightly in different parts of its great range. Therefore a third name (subspecies or race name) has been given to the yellowthroat wherever consistent variations occur. Thus we find the Maryland yellowthroat named *Geothlypis trichas trichas,* the Northern yellowthroat called (for short) *G. t. brachidactylus,* the Florida yellowthroat called *G. t. ignota,* and so on. The field student pays no attention to the third name of the yellowthroat for he cannot distinguish one race from another in the field.

15. Are there any birds still unnamed by scientists? Certainly there are no known unnamed species of birds in the United States. It may be that in remote areas of the earth a few species of birds have not yet been discovered by scientists.

16. Should a new species be discovered, how would it be named?
In the United States the Committee on Nomenclature of the American Ornithologists' Union (A.O.U.) settles all questions about the names of birds in the country. Similar committees exist in many other countries. These groups often confer. Should a new bird be discovered in a remote part of the earth, the scientist who first described it would have the privilege of naming the bird, subject to the rules of nomenclature accepted by the ornithologists of the world.

17. On what basis do scientists separate birds into groups?
Many groups of birds lack sharply defined and obvious characteristics found in many groups of animals. Many of the groups are divisions made more for convenience than because of distinguishing features. The divisions are based largely on internal differences such as the structure of the palate and the arrangement of skull bones.

18. Are there external characteristics that may be recognized by a beginner?   If a beginning bird student knows the outstanding characteristics of each group of birds, he can usually determine which order it belongs to. There is great variation in the birds of most orders but a few external characteristics shared by all may be recognized. For instance, birds in the order of Procellariiformes range from almost pure black to almost pure white, and from a tiny least petrel scarcely as large as a barn swallow to the largest of all sea birds that has the greatest wing spread of any species, the wandering albatross. Whatever their size or color, all birds in this order share the characteristic of a tube-nose. Moreover, all species are alike in ejecting from their bills a reddish-orange oily liquid when disturbed. No matter what they feed on, this oily substance smells alike in all species and the scent clings to old skins that have lain for years in museum trays.

19. What are the terms used in the breakdown of the class Aves?
        Class Aves (birds)
          Order
            Family
              Genus (plural: genera)
                Species
                  Subspecies (or race)

20. What is meant by an order? Biologically speaking, an order of birds is a large group of birds sharing certain internal characteristics.

21. What is a family? Birds in a family show the characteristics of the order to which they belong, but in addition, each family unit shares some features not present in the entire order. For instance, the outstanding external characteristic of the order Apodiformes is tiny feet. This order is represented in North America by two of its three families: the swifts and the hummingbirds. Both have the tiny feet characteristic of the order Apodiformes. But all members of the swift family have small bills and mouths that gape widely. Birds in the hummingbird family all have long needlelike bills.

Therefore swifts and hummingbirds are both members of the large order Apodiformes, but belong to different families: Apodidae (swifts) or Trochilidae (hummingbirds).

22. What is meant by a genus? Sometimes birds within a family show a group characteristic not shared by all members of the family. For instance, in the United States the family Sylviidae includes gnatcatchers and kinglets. It is easy for even a beginning student to distinguish between these two groups of birds. Though they belong to the same family, each is in a different genus.

23. What is a species? Birds that look alike, act alike and interbreed are called species.

24. What is a subspecies or race? A subspecies or race usually is a geographical population distinguished from the type specimen by a subtle difference in measurements, color or song. The variations seldom can be recognized in the field but are discovered by careful study in the laboratory. Subspecies interbreed on the edges of their ranges.

25. What is a type species? The species of a genus upon which the generic name depends is called the type species. Theoretically this is the species which most perfectly exemplifies the characters of the genus. If a genus originally contained but one species, that is the type species.

Today if a scientist describes a new genus, he designates a type species. Failure to do so in the past has resulted in much disagreement among authors.

26. What is a type specimen? The specimen or individual on which a scientist bases his description of a new species or subspecies is called the type specimen. Today these are carefully labeled and preserved in museum collections. Unfortunately the vast majority of specimens on which the original descriptions of birds were based are lost forever.

27. Do birds ever hybridize? This rarely happens in nature though blue-winged and golden-winged warblers interbreed frequently enough so that their offspring, distinguishable in the field, are given specific names. Some ducks hybridize, but this happens most frequently among captive individuals.

28. Are there variations among birds of a given species? Usually all birds of a species look alike and act alike as far as the observer can determine. Close acquaintance often reveals slight differences among the individuals of a single nest. This becomes more apparent when several young wild birds from a single nest are reared in captivity. Then the birds which appear superficially identical show individual traits. Occasionally a bird may show unusual bill development, a patch of color not quite like others of its species, or behavior which varies from the normal for its relatives. It may be that just such subtle or unusual variations from the average played a part in the rise of the great contrasts found among the birds of the world today.

29. How many orders of birds are there in the world today? There are 27 orders of birds in the world.

30. How many of these orders are represented in North America? Nineteen orders of birds are found at present in North America.

31. Is the number of orders stationary in North America? Early in this century the sole representative in North America of the parrot order became extinct when Carolina parakeets disappeared forever. However, the discovery that trogons come into the mountains of southern Arizona has kept the total number of orders at 19. Though an order was lost, a different one was gained.

32. How many families of birds are found in the world? The number of families recognized by most authorities is 163.

33. How many families of birds are found in North America? Sixty-eight.

34. How many species of birds are there in the world? Because all scientists do not agree on the precise definition of the term *species,* there is disagreement as to the number in the world. It is about 8,600. (See Question 797.)

35. How many species of birds are found in North America? For the reason given above, the total varies with individual scientists. Some group species together. Others split them apart. Most agree that the total number lies in the region of 650 species. (See Question 798.)

36. Why are the names of birds arranged as they are instead of alphabetically? It is customary to arrange the orders, families, genera and species in relation to their development. The most primitive birds come first, with the others placed successively in accordance with their development. The most highly developed birds come last. It might be said that the most primitive birds are placed on the bottom step of evolution, while each bird climbs toward the top as it becomes less like its ancestors.

37. Among the orders of birds represented in North America, which is most like its remote ancestors? The order of loons comes first, for in this order the birds are the most primitive. Their bones and other characteristics are the most nearly like those of ancient fossil birds of any on this continent.

38. What birds in North America show the highest development? The order of perching birds (usually called passerine birds) is placed last or at the top of the stairway of evolution. Passerine birds are the most highly developed birds and least like the primitive birds that lived long ago.

39. Are the present arrangement and nomenclature permanent?
As scientists learn more and more about birds, facts may come to light which prove previous classification wrong. Moreover, scientists regularly devise new ways for testing relationships. Sometimes these upset previous beliefs. At times they bring about a permanent change in the classification of birds, while occasionally they are accepted for a while and then discarded.

Nothing can be more fluid than the classification of birds. This is confusing to the student who learns a certain classification only to have the whole arrangement changed. But the student should not be dismayed by any changes in either the arrangement of birds or their names. He must recognize the change as growth in knowledge and understanding of birds.

40. Do ornithologists throughout the world accept the same arrangement of orders and families that is used in the United States?
There is a difference of opinion as to which birds are most primitive and which are most highly developed. This difference is reflected in the ornithological literature of different countries. For instance, in Great Britain, the crows, ravens, jays and magpies are placed at the top of the evolutionary scale instead of sparrows as in the United States. The unfamiliar arrangement makes it necessary to consult the index of a bird book from a foreign country, but the scientific names of the species will be the same as in American books.

41. What are the orders of the birds of the world?

42. Where is each placed in the evolutionary scale of development?

43. What are the families of the birds of the world?

44. How many species of birds are there in each family?

45. Which families are represented in North America north of the Rio Grande?

46. What is the general range of the various bird families of the world?

(In the following section, which answers the questions above, the range given is very general. Orders with representatives in North America are indicated in parentheses, as (1–N.A.) following the world number of the order. The common names of the orders and families with representatives in North America are shown in italics.)

ORDERS, FAMILIES, NUMBER OF SPECIES IN EACH FAMILY AND GENERAL RANGE OF BIRDS OF THE WORLD AND OF NORTH AMERICA

1. Ostriches (Struthioniformes)
   1 family: ostrich (1 species). Africa and Arabia.
2. Rheas (Rheiformes)
   1 family: rhea (2 species). South America.
3. Cassowaries (Casuariiformes)
   2 families: 1. cassowary (6 species). New Guinea, adjacent islands and North Queensland.
   2. emu (1 species). Australia.
4. Kiwis (Apterygiformes)
   1 family: kiwi (3 species). New Zealand.
5. Tinamous (Tinamiformes)
   1 family: tinamou (51 species). Mexico through South America.
6. Penguins (Sphenisciformes)
   1 family: penguin (17 species). Antarctic north to the Galápagos Islands.
7. (1–N.A.) *Loons* (Gaviiformes)
   1 family: loon (4 species). Circumpolar.
8. (2–N.A.) *Grebes* (Colymbiformes)
   1 family: grebe (18 species). All continents and larger islands.
9. (3–N.A.) *Tube-nosed swimmers* (Procellariiformes)
   4 families: 1. *albatross* (14 species). Breed mostly in Southern Hemisphere but range widely over the seas.
   2. *shearwater, fulmar* (62 species). Oceans, coasts and islands of the world.
   3. *storm petrel* (24 species). Oceans, coasts and islands throughout the world.

4. diving petrel (5 species). Southern Hemisphere.

10. (4–N.A.) *Totipalmate swimmers* (Pelecaniformes)
6 families: 1. *tropic-bird* (3 species). Tropical oceans.
2. *pelican* (8 species). World-wide except for polar areas.
3. *booby, gannet* (9 species). Nearly worldwide.
4. *cormorant* (29 species). World-wide.
5. *anhinga* or *snakebird* (4 species). Mostly tropics of the world.
6. *frigate-bird* or *man-of-war bird* (5 species). Tropical and temperate oceans.

11. (5–N.A.) *Long-legged waders* (Ciconiiformes)
7 families: 1. *heron, egret, bittern* (66 species). Worldwide.
2. Boat-billed heron (1 species). New World tropics.
3. whale-headed stork (1 species). Africa.
4. hammerhead (1 species). Africa.
5. *wood ibis,* stork, jabiru (17 species). Nearly world-wide.
6. *ibis, spoonbill* (31 species). Nearly worldwide.
7. *flamingo* (6 species). Tropics of the world.

12. (6–N.A.) *Waterfowl* and screamers (Anseriformes)
2 families: 1. screamer (3 species). South America.
2. *duck, goose, swan* (167 species). Worldwide.

13. (7–N.A.) *Diurnal birds of prey* (Falconiformes)
5 families: 1. *New World vulture* (6 species). New World.
2. secretary-bird (1 species). Africa.
3. *kite, hawk, eagle,* Old World vulture, harrier (220 species). World-wide.
4. *osprey* (1 species). Nearly world-wide except for New Zealand.
5. *caracara, falcon* (60 species). World-wide.

14. (8–N.A.) Megapodes, *gallinaceous birds,* hoatzin (Galliformes)

7 families: 1. mound bird or megapode (18 species). Australia, New Guinea and many of the East Indies.

2. curassow, guan, *chachalaca* (45 species). Southeast Texas through South America.

3. *grouse, ptarmigan* (19 species). Throughout most of land areas north of the Tropic of Cancer.

4. *New World quail*, Old World partridge, pheasant, jungle fowl, peacock (183 species). Most members of this family belong in the Old World.

5. guineafowl (7 species). Africa, Arabia, Madagascar.

6. *turkey* (2 species). United States and Mexico.

7. hoatzin (1 species). South America.

15. (9–N.A.) *Marsh Birds* (Gruiformes)

12 families: 1. roatela, monia (3 species). Madagascar.

2. bustard-quail (14 species). Africa, New Guinea, islands of the East Indies, Australia.

3. plain-wanderer (1 species). Australia.

4. *crane* (14 species). All continents except South America.

5. *limpkin* (1 species). Southern United States through South America.

6. trumpeter (3 species). South America.

7. *rail, coot, gallinule* (129 species). Worldwide.

8. sun-grebe (3 species). Tropical lands around the world.

9. kagu (1 species). New Caledonia.

10. sun-bittern (1 species). Central and South America.

11. cariama (2 species). South America.

12. bustard (24 species). All Old World continents.

16. (10–N.A.) *Shore birds, gulls, terns, alcids* (Charadriiformes)

16 families: 1. *jacana* (7 species). Tropical lands of the world.

2. painted snipe (2 species). Tropical lands of the world.
3. *oystercatcher* (4 species). All continents.
4. *plover, turnstone, surfbird* (61 species). World-wide.
5. *sandpiper and allies* (80 species). World-wide.
6. *avocet, stilt* (7 species). All continents.
7. *phalarope* (3 species). Breeds north of the Tropic of Cancer, winters chiefly in Southern Hemisphere.
8. crab-plover (1 species). Along shores of Indian Ocean.
9. thick-knee (9 species). All continents except North America.
10. pratincole, courser (17 species). All Old World continents but most species found in Africa.
11. seed-snipe (4 species). South America.
12. sheath-bill (2 species). Islands of the African and South American coasts.
13. *skua, jaeger* (4 species). Colder oceans of both hemispheres.
14. *gull, tern* (85 species). World-wide.
15. *skimmer* (3 species). Tropics of the world.
16. *auk, murre, puffin* (22 species). Oceans of the northern hemisphere.

17. (11–N.A.) *Pigeons, doves and sand-grouse* (Columbiformes)
　　2 families: 1. sand grouse (16 species). Africa, Eurasia.
　　　　　　　 2. *pigeon, dove* (302 species). World-wide. (The extinct dodo belonged to this family.)

18. Parrots, lories, macaws (Psittaciformes)
　　1 family: parrot, lory, macaw (326 species). Tropics of the world.

19. (12–N.A.) *Cuckoos* and plantain eaters (Cuculiformes)
　　2 families: 1. plantain eater (20 species). Africa.
　　　　　　　 2. *cuckoo, ani, roadrunner* (129 species). All continents.

20. (13–N.A.) *Owls* (Strigiformes)

      2 families: 1. *barn owl,* grass owl (10 species). Nearly world-wide.

               2. *owl* (133 species). World-wide.

21. (14–N.A.) *Goatsuckers and allies* (Caprimulgiformes)

      5 families: 1. oilbird (1 species). Northern South America.

               2. frogmouth (12 species). Australia and adjacent islands.

               3. potoo (5 species). American tropics.

               4. owlet-frogmouth (7 species). Australian region.

               5. *goatsucker* (70 species). All continents.

22. (15–N.A.) *Swifts, hummingbirds* (Apodiformes)

      3 families: 1. *swift* (74 species). World-wide.

               2. crested swift (3 species). East Indies.

               3. *hummingbird* (327 species). Western Hemisphere.

23. Mousebirds or Colies (Coliiformes)

      1 family: mouse-bird (6 species). Africa.

24. (16–N.A.) *Trogons* (Trogoniformes)

      1 family: *trogon* (34 species). Tropics of the world.

25. (17–N.A.) *Kingfishers,* todies, motmots, bee eaters, rollers, hoopoes, hornbills (Coraciiformes)

      10 families: 1. *kingfisher* (88 species). World-wide.

               2. tody (5 species). West Indies.

               3. motmot (8 species). New World tropics.

               4. bee-eater (24 species). Old World tropics.

               5. roller (11 species). Old World tropics.

               6. ground-roller (5 species). Madagascar.

               7. cuckoo-roller (1 species). Madagascar and adjacent islands.

               8. hoopoe (1 species). Eurasia and Africa.

               9. wood-hoopoe (6 species). Africa.

             10. hornbill (46 species). Africa, Southern Asia, nearby islands.

26. (18–N.A.) Jacamars, puffbirds, barbets, honey guides, toucans, *woodpeckers* (Piciformes)

      6 families: 1. jacamar (16 species). New World tropics.

               2. puffbird (33 species). New World tropics.

               3. barbet (78 species). Tropics of the world.

4. honey-guide (13 species). Africa.
5. toucan (41 species). New World tropics.
6. *woodpecker,* piculet, wryneck (214 species). World-wide.

27. (19–N.A.) *Perching birds* (Passeriformes)
69 families:
1. broadbill (14 species). Philippines, Malaysia.
2. woodhewer (63 species). New World tropics.
3. ovenbird (209 species). South America.
4. ant-thrush (238 species). Central America to Argentina.
5. ant-pipit (12 species). New World tropics.
6. tapacolo (28 species). Central America to Argentina.
7. *cotinga* (90 species). Arizona to Argentina.
8. manakin (59 species). Mexico to Argentina.
9. *tyrant flycatcher* (365 species). New World.
10. sharpbill (1 species). Costa Rica to Brazil.
11. plant-cutter (3 species). South America.
12. pitta (23 species). Africa, Australia, southeastern Asia.
13. New Zealand Wren (4 species). New Zealand.
14. asity (2 species). Madagascar.
15. lyrebird (2 species). Australia.
16. scrub-bird (2 species). Australia.
17. *lark* (74 species). One North American species; remainder are chiefly in Old World.
18. *swallow* (75 species). World-wide.
19. cuckoo-shrike (58 species). Africa, Asia, Australia.
20. drongo (20 species). Africa, southern Asia to Australia.
21. Old World oriole (32 species). Old World.
22. *crow, magpie, jay.* Nearly world-wide.
23. bell magpie, Australian butcherbird (13 species). Australia.
24. magpie-lark (2 species). Australia.
25. bowerbird (17 species). Australia.
26. bird of paradise (43 species). New Guinea.

27. parrotbill (18 species). Eurasia.
28. *titmouse* (65 species). Chiefly north of the Tropic of Cancer throughout the world.
29. *nuthatch* (22 species). Same as titmouse but chiefly Old World.
30. coral-billed nuthatch (1 species). Madagascar.
31. *creeper* (17 species). Chiefly Old World north of the Tropic of Cancer.
32. *wren-tit* (1 species). Oregon to Lower California.
33. babbler (261 species). Old World tropics.
34. bulbul (109 species). Old World tropics.
35. *dipper* (5 species). Nearly world-wide.
36. *wren* (63 species). Mainly New World tropics.
37. *mockingbird* (30 species). New World.
38. *thrush* (303 species). World-wide.
39. wren-thrush (1 species). Costa Rica and Panama.
40. Old World warbler (378 species). Old World.
41. *kinglet, gnatcatcher* (20 species). Old and New World.
42. Old World flycatcher (378 species). Old World.
43. accentor, hedge sparrow (12 species). Europe and northern Asia to Alaska.
44. *pipit,* wagtail (48 species). Nearly world-wide.
45. *waxwing* (3 species). Around the world north of the Tropic of Cancer.
46. *silky flycatcher* (4 species). Southern United States through Central America.
47. palm-chat (1 species). Santa Domingo.
48. wood-swallow (10 species). Africa, Asia, Australia.
49. vanga shrike (11 species). Madagascar.
50. *shrike* (72 species). Old and New World.

51. wood-shrike (13 species). Old World.
52. pepper shrike (2 species). New World tropics.
53. shrike-vireo, greenlet (3 species). New World tropics.
54. wattled crow, saddleback (3 species). New Zealand.
55. *starling* (103 species). Old World only until introduced into New World.
56. honey-eater (160 species). Australia, New Zealand.
57. sunbird (106 species). Old World tropics.
58. flowerpecker (54 species). Asia, Australia.
59. white-eye (80 species). Africa, Asia and islands to New Zealand.
60. *vireo* (41 species). New World.
61. honey-creeper (36 species). New World tropics.
62. Hawaiian honey-creeper (22 species). Hawaii.
63. *wood warbler* (109 species). New World.
64. *weaver-finch* (263 species). Old World— introduced into New World.
65. *blackbird, troupial* (88 species). New World.
66. swallow-tanager (1 species). Brazil.
67. *tanager* (197 species). Chiefly in the tropics of the New World.
68. plush-capped finch (1 species). Northern Andes.
69. *grosbeak, finch, bunting, sparrow* (426 species). World-wide except Australia.

II. THE DISTRIBUTION OF BIRDS

47. What is meant by bird distribution? This involves many factors. Distribution of birds in geological time is largely confined to the study of fossils and their distribution in the rocks over the earth. Geographical distribution is concerned with the areas of the earth where various birds occur. Finally there is the distribution of birds according to ecology or habitat.

48. What is meant by the range of a bird? While most species of birds can fly and many of them are capable of flying tremendous distances, they are, nevertheless, generally confined to particular areas called ranges.

49. Why do birds, free to fly wherever they choose, limit their movements to these ranges? This long has been a subject investigated and debated by scientists. Many factors have brought about the present-day distribution of birds. Some of these factors were lost in geological time when continents were shaped, when glaciers pressed forward and receded, and climates changed radically. Examination of the scanty fossil material discovered has helped this study.

At present, climate, mountain ranges, deserts, oceans and so on are controlling factors in the movements of birds. Food of course is vital and those birds which have developed specialized food habits must limit their ranges to the places where that food is available.

50. How big is the range of a bird? Some species of birds are cosmopolitan and range over the entire world. Others have an extremely restricted range of but a few miles. There is every possible variation in size between these extremes.

51. What are some cosmopolitan birds? Ospreys have been recorded on every continent and many of the large islands of the world. Marsh hawks also range the continents of the world. Short-eared owls have been found on every continent. Herring gulls may be found near water throughout most of the Northern Hemisphere.

52. What are some of the extremely limited ranges of birds in the United States?   Kirtland's warblers nest only in a jack pine area about 100 miles by 60 miles in Michigan. In the United States the Everglades kite is found in a very limited area in Florida. About 60 of these birds were believed alive in 1958, and most of these were concentrated along the southwestern part of Lake Okeechobee. Wherever they occur, large quantities of the fresh-water snail, *pomacea caliginosa,* also are found, for this is almost the sole food of the Everglades kite.

53. Do the ranges of birds, once established, remain the same indefinitely?   Throughout the existence of life on this world there has been a constant change in most forms. Usually changes are exceedingly slow and frequently can be detected only through study of fossils. On this continent, changes have been accelerated greatly since the settlement by Europeans. Sometimes the changes have increased the size of a bird's range because man has created more favorable habitats for a species, while the ranges of other species have decreased because of destruction of their habitat.

54. What are some species with increased ranges due to human activities?   Cardinals, house wrens and robins have all enlarged their ranges since colonial days. Chestnut-sided warblers, which demand low, fairly dense shrubby areas interspersed with open fields, have not only increased their range but have also created a sharp rise in the total population of their species. Purple sandpipers once were restricted in their wintering range to the rocky shores of the North Atlantic. As man built more and more large stone breakwaters, these sandpipers followed southward as fast as suitable food in the form of marine life developed on the breakwaters. Now this once northern species winters as far south as central Florida.

55. What species have suffered a diminished range because of man?   Marsh reduction by drainage has forced ducks, rails, herons and other marsh birds to leave areas once densely populated by them. Destruction of vast forests has brought the ivory-billed woodpecker to the verge of extinction and was an important factor in the end of the passenger pigeon.

The range of other species has diminished in extent because the race itself has been persecuted by man until few individuals remain. At one time whooping cranes were found throughout the interior of the North American continent. Now they are restricted in the United States to a small wintering range on the Texas coast. They maintain a small breeding range in northern Canada. Trumpeter swans that once enjoyed a great range are now restricted to a few areas in Wyoming and adjacent states, Alaska and western provinces of Canada.

56. What is the geographical range of a bird? The geographical range of a bird covers the entire area where a species has been recorded, whether as a breeding bird, a wintering bird, a transient or merely a wandering individual. (See Question 67.)

57. What is a breeding range? A breeding range includes the entire area wherein a species nests.

58. What is a wintering range? The wintering range of a species of bird is the area where it occurs in winter.

59. What is meant by seasonal distribution? During the year certain birds nest in an area. These may leave once the nesting season ends, though some may stay in the same area throughout the entire year. Birds not seen at other times of the year may be present during spring and fall migration, while a new population may move in to spend the winter. Seasonal distribution has particular interest in a study of local birds.

60. How many types of seasonal distribution are there? In the United States there are five easily recognized types:

          (1) Permanent residents
          (2) Summer residents
          (3) Summer visitants
          (4) Transient visitants or migrants
          (5) Winter visitants

61. What are permanent residents? These are species which have representatives present throughout the year in a given area. (See Question 126.)

62. What are summer residents?   Summer residents are the birds which nest in an area, but leave it in winter. (See Question 127.)

63. What are summer visitants?   These birds visit an area in summer but do not breed there. (See Question 128.)

64. What are winter visitants?   Winter visitants are birds which spend the winter in an area but do not remain there to nest in summer. (See Question 130.)

65. What are transient visitants or migrants?   Transient visitants or migrants are birds that travel through an area as they move to and from their breeding grounds and their winter homes. These birds do not remain in the area either for breeding or for wintering. (See Question 129.)

66. What are accidental birds?   Birds which do not fit into any of the seasonal categories are called accidental, casual, or straggler birds. Even in the clearly stated seasonal distribution groups there is some overlapping. But birds referred to as accidentals usually belong to a completely different region. Sometimes a storm carries a bird far outside its normal range. Occasionally a migrating bird may follow a ship, using it when tired as a temporary resting place, and arrive at a land that is distant from its known range. It is believed that physiological factors sometimes go awry and cause birds to migrate in the wrong direction to places beyond their normal range.

67. What is ecological distribution?   This is the distribution of birds according to environment. While the geographical distribution of meadowlarks spans the United States and spills into Mexico and Canada, they are not found everywhere within that area. They are confined to the grasslands and fit into this specific niche among the varied organisms of that environment.

68. What is a biotic community?   A biotic community includes all the plant and animal life of a given type of habitat. Biotic communities are usually determined by the dominant plants of an environment and ordinarily are named for those plants.

69. What are the chief types of biotic communities of the world?
Land or terrestrial, fresh-water, and marine or salt-water.

70. Which of these biotic communities is most important to birds?
Though many birds have become well adapted to one or both of the
water biotic communities, the land or terrestrial is most important.
The most aquatic of birds seek land to lay their eggs and incubate
them.

**71. On what basis have scientists divided North America into
biotic communities?** Each of the nine major biotic communities of
the North American continent is typified and named for the climax
growth of the area.

**72. What are the major biotic communities of the North American
continent?** Tundra, coniferous forest, deciduous forest, grassland,
southwestern oak woodland, pinyon pine-juniper woodland, chaparral, sagebrush, and scrub desert.

**73. Does all the land of the continent fit within one of these cate-
gories?** Many areas are in a transitional state, sometimes because
man has wrought a change by some such means as cutting down
a forest, by drainage, or in other ways. Certain areas are transitional
because of natural forces such as lightning-caused fire, or floods. In
other areas the transitional state is progressing naturally with the
slowness of a geological period. Moreover, at the edges of the various
biomes, overlapping of the adjoining biotic communities occurs. Such
overlaps are called ecotones.

74. What are seral communities? When an area within a major
biotic community shows one or several stages leading toward the
climax biotic community, it is called a seral community.

75. What are the most common natural seral communities?
Shores, fresh-water marshes and salt-water marshes, swamps, savan-
nas and wet or riparian woodlands.

76. What is altitudinal distribution? It has been estimated that
250 feet of altitude on a mountain slope corresponds roughly to one

degree of latitude or about 69 miles of northward progression. On mountain slopes, biotic communities succeed one another to conform to the climatic changes brought about by altitude. Birds are distributed accordingly.

Assuming that a climber began at an altitude of one mile, upon reaching the summit of 14,110-foot Pike's Peak at about latitude 39 degrees, he would have passed through the equivalent of 35.3 degrees of latitude, or approximately 2,215 miles north. If this distance northward were actually traversed a traveler would reach about the 74th degree, which is well within the Arctic Circle.

77. What is a habitat?   A habitat is the environment which a species normally demands within its geographical range. The habitat of a bird plus all the many organisms that occupy the same habitat make up the biotic communities discussed before.

78. Why is knowledge of habitat preference virtually essential to the bird student?   The distribution of most species of birds is governed quite rigidly by their habitat preference. Within that habitat they carry on their vital activities of finding food and shelter, of laying their eggs and rearing the young. In order to know the bird it is necessary to be acquainted with its habitat requirements.

79. What is a territory?   The territory of a bird is any area which it defends against other individuals of its own species.

80. Why is it essential for a bird to maintain a territory?   The territory has several useful functions. Among many species joint defense of the territory establishes a strong sexual bond. It insures essential cover, food for the pair and their young, and ample nesting material. The male by defense of the territory protects his partner and young from other males of the species.

81. Do all species of birds have a territory?   It is believed that almost all birds have some kind of a territory. Among some species it is limited to a tiny area to which the male attracts the female for mating purposes and that accomplished, the territory is then abandoned. Some species of ducks defend a sunning place. Except for a comparatively small percentage, birds maintain a territory for nesting purposes, or for feeding, or both.

82. What are the chief kinds of territories defended by birds?
Breeding territories and nonbreeding territories are the chief types.

83. Do breeding territories differ?   The majority of passerine birds have a territory which is used for mating, nesting and for feeding both the adults and young.

The territories of some passerine birds are used only for mating and nesting. Swallows, swifts and frequently such blackbirds as redwings and grackles nest in fairly compact groups but feed at a distance from the nesting area.

Some male birds defend only a mating area which may be far from the nest. A nest cared for only by a female is not considered a true territory. Male hummingbirds, prairie chickens, and the ruff of Europe have mating areas which they defend. The two latter species display in arenas where they mate with any females which visit them.

Very small mating and nesting areas are found among colonial birds such as swifts, swallows, terns, murres, gannets and gulls. These and many other colonial species defend only the distance they can reach while sitting on their nests. Such birds feed away from the nest.

84. What are nonbreeding territories?   Some birds, such as the belted kingfisher, often defend feeding territories away from the breeding territory. A kingfisher may defend as much as a mile of brook for feeding while its nest is in a bank a half mile or more from the brook.

A winter territory may be the same one occupied during the breeding season by a permanent resident in an area. Winter residents frequently establish feeding territories which are defended strongly against others of its own species. Spotted sandpipers and house wrens that winter in Florida are particularly militant in this respect and there is much noisy conflict until the territories are firmly established.

85. How large is a territory?   This varies with the species, with the amount of food and cover available, with the dominance of an individual and to a certain extent on the size of the bird.

Colonial birds which feed away from their nests usually have the smallest territories. They defend an area about the distance they can reach while incubating their eggs. When food and shelter are abundant the sizes of territories among most species may be small but the less food available and the more scanty the shelter, the larger the territorial demands will be. For instance, on one island off the Maine coast, warblers have an average territory of .60 acre, while during an outbreak of spruce budworm in Ontario, Kendeigh found warblers averaging but .37 acre to a territory, while a few actually defended but .1 an acre. Probably this is as small as any territory ever defended for the triple purpose of breeding, nesting and feeding of young and adults. A pair of bald eagles or other large predatory birds may defend many square miles. (See S. Charles Kendeigh, "Bird Population Studies in the Coniferous Forest Biome during a Spruce Budworm Outbreak," *Biol. Bull.*, No. 1, 1–100; Ontario, Canada.)

86. Do birds maintain the same-size territory throughout the nesting period? Changes in the amount of food available may cause birds to acquire and defend a larger territory or permit their boundaries to shrink. Mourning doves, however, quite consistently start the season by defending large territories which gradually shrink as nest duties increase. American coots and common gallinules often begin the season with rather small territories but extend the limits of these as the season advances.

III. BIRD FLIGHT

87. How are birds adapted for flight? Most birds have wonderfully designed wings which are moved by highly developed flight muscles. The body is streamlined to offer the least resistance to the air. The skeleton is strong yet light. In addition a surprisingly rapid, well organized metabolism permits quick consumption and economic utilization of food, and respiration is aided by a marvelous system of air sacs.

88. What is meant by different types of flight? Anyone who carefully studies birds in flight will notice at least five major types of movement. There are considerable variations in each type, and often borderline cases between two types which defy exact classification. The most common type is ordinary flapping, the second gliding, the third soaring, the fourth fluttering, and the fifth hovering. Many species of birds regularly use two of these types, while some use all five.

89. What are some examples of gliding flight? When a ruffed grouse is flushed it starts out with a whirr of flapping wings, but once sufficient velocity is reached it shifts into long glides through the trees. A flock of Canada geese may flap over a lake, but if they decide to land, the birds frequently bank and descend in long impressive glides. The length of these glides is governed by the velocity of the bird at the beginning of the act, the weight and sail surface of the individual, the wind direction, and the amount of rising air at that time and place.

90. What are some examples of soaring flight? Nearly everyone in North America has seen either large turkey vultures with uptilted motionless wings circling across the sky, or herring gulls riding in suspended animation on the updrafts of a ferry. Thus two entirely different types of wings seem to be best fitted for soaring: the wide expansive wings of vultures and hawks, or the long narrow wings of gulls and albatrosses.

But note that both these types of wings give their owners a very extensive sail area in proportion to their body weight. Soaring may be called gliding on rising air currents.

91. What are some examples of flapping? The great majority of birds use flapping flight. A robin flying across a garden, a crow hurrying across a corn field or a heron coming over a lake regularly demonstrates this type of flight. The wings appear to beat up and down in unison and to the human eye resemble the motion of oars in rowing.

92. What is meant by fluttering flight? Fluttering flight generally refers to a bird in stationary flight over one spot without the aid of a headwind. The hummingbirds do this with perfection as they hang suspended before a flower. Kinglets and many warblers regularly flutter at the tip of a branch while picking off insects gathered there, and flycatchers habitually flutter while catching their prey. Moreover, some species such as skylarks, purple finches and white-winged crossbills often give the most ecstatic part of their flight songs in fluttering flight.

93. How does fluttering flight differ from hovering? The two are rather similar but hovering requires aid from a fresh headwind. In hovering, the tail usually is fanned and pointed downward, the rear of the body tilted downward, and the speed and angle of the wing-beats regulated to support the bird yet prevent the wind from pushing it backward. The osprey, rough-legged hawk, Bonaparte's gull, common tern and belted kingfisher regularly give excellent demonstrations of hovering.

94. How rapidly does a flying bird flap its wings? This varies considerably from species to species, sometimes from individual to individual and even from occasion to occasion. In a single bird the rapidity of its wing-beats depends to some degree on the air conditions of the moment as well as on the *attitude* of the bird. Is the bird pursued, in pursuit, or is it simply moving from one place to another? Under most conditions a wood ibis has one or two wing-beats per second, an American crow from 3 to 5, a domestic pigeon from 3 to 8, and most passerine birds from 12 to 16.

95. Which birds have the fastest wing-beats? Hummingbirds, the tiniest feathered creatures in the world, have wing-beats so fast that they appear as hazy as an airplane propeller in motion. Analysis of slow-motion pictures indicate that these wing-beats may be as fast as 50 to 75 times per second.

96. Do all birds flap both wings together? Study the flight of a loon, heron, goose, duck, gull, crow or any other large bird and it will be obvious that both wings beat in unison. It is more difficult to see that a thrush, waxwing, blackbird, sparrow or any other passerine bird does likewise but careful research indicates that they do.

One bird that appears to break this rule is the chimney swift. There has been much controversy as to whether or not these birds beat their wings alternately. Some have maintained that it was only the erratic banking, veering and stalling type of flight that gave this illusion. Slow-motion pictures indicate that while both wings do beat together, the various parts of each wing may move at different speeds and angles and add to this illusion. This unique manner of flight is no doubt necessary because of the lack of tail or steering gear in a chimney swift.

97. Does a bird always start its flight into the wind? All birds prefer to take off into the wind and with some it is a necessity. Approach down wind toward a flock of Canada geese in a field, a flock of herring gulls on a beach, or a group of coots on a pond and they will at first fly toward you, then swerve. The heavier the bird the more necessary this is. The need to take off into the wind causes a great many turkey vultures to meet their death along the highways. They drop to feed on some creature killed by a passing car, but having to make a running start into the wind in order to take off, they in turn are struck by the next speeding car, especially one coming down wind.

98. Does this mean that birds generally fly against the wind? The take-off is the only movement demanding an into-the-wind direction. Thereafter birds fly mostly into or with the wind. Their chief concern seems to be a strong crosswind. During a crosswind some birds tack slightly into the wind to maintain a straight course. Others may avoid tacking, allow themselves to be blown slightly off course, and then make the last part of their journey directly into the wind in order to reach a specific goal.

99. How important is the tail in flight?   The tail of a bird is of great importance in flight, aiding considerably in balancing, in steering, and in regulating the amount of sail surface. A soaring bird adds to its sail surface by fanning its tail, and often changes direction simply by tilting it slightly. Loons, grebes, ducks and other birds with very small tails are handicapped for making quick turns and generally have to fly in a relatively straight course.

100. How fast do birds fly?   As in many aspects of bird behavior, this varies considerably from species to species, from individual to individual and from occasion to occasion. A bird that is pursuing a meal, eluding a predator or flying at leisure adjusts its speed to the situation. A turkey vulture may hang almost motionless in a stiff breeze one minute, then turn and glide at 60 miles per hour the next.

The majority of small land birds travel at speeds between 20 and 30 miles per hour, geese and ducks usually range from 40 to 55 m.p.h., while some shorebirds on extended flights regularly reach 40 to 60 m.p.h.

101. Which birds fly the fastest?   Much work needs to be done clocking birds in flight before an unequivocal answer can be given to this question. Swifts in Mesopotamia have been timed at the almost incredible speed of 200 m.p.h. A peregrine falcon pressed by an airplane went into a dive at 180 m.p.h., while a golden eagle attacked by a peregrine traveled 120 m.p.h. A flock of red-backed sandpipers overtook and passed an airplane moving at 90 m.p.h., and the pilot estimated that these little birds were traveling more than 110 m.p.h.

102. What is the difference between air speed and ground speed? The air speed of a bird is its progress through the air without help or hindrance from the wind, while its ground speed is its actual progress through space. A bird with an air speed of 45 miles per hour flying with a tail wind of 15 m.p.h. would have a ground speed of 60 m.p.h. The same bird fighting a head wind of 15 m.p.h. would have a ground speed of only 30 m.p.h.

103. What advantage do many birds gain by flying in V-formation? As a bird flaps its wings it disturbs the air and leaves whirling eddies behind. Some gregarious species take advantage of the upward sections of these whirls and each bird in the V-formation stations itself at the correct place so the inner wing obtains support from the wake of the bird immediately ahead. Thus every bird in the flock except the leader saves energy by using the V-formation type of flight. (See Question 138.)

104. How can a flying bird alight without tumbling forward? Everyone knows that a vehicle going at great speed cannot stop abruptly without destruction. Likewise landing by a bird requires considerable skill and care. The heavier the bird and the faster the speed the greater the caution needed. Before landing a bird may decrease its speed by gliding. It may brake by fanning its tail and tilting it downward, throwing its body into an upright position, and making a few rapid forward wing-strokes. In many species the wings are extended wide until the body is perfectly balanced. At the moment of landing much of the impact is absorbed by the long legs and strong springy leg muscles. Some species such as hawks and shrikes use the surplus movement to glide up to a high perch. In many water birds no great effort is made to slow down, the bird simply coasting on top of the water in a long graceful slide. Birds, like airplanes, make use of the wind as a brake when landing by heading into it.

105. Why do many French Canadians say a cormorant cannot fly without dipping its tail in reverence to God? Is there any basis for this belief? A cormorant is a very heavy bird and its wings are small in proportion to its weight. Therefore when it takes off from a perch it loses altitude before gaining enough momentum to rise. Since cormorants frequently perch on buoys or low posts they regularly dip their tails in the water in the process of beginning flight. If the perch is high, however, the cormorant will not dip its tail. If the wind is strong a cormorant even on a low post need not wet its tail on the take-off.

106. Why do so many water birds run across the water before taking flight? Many water birds run across the water before taking flight for the same reason a seaplane taxies along before the take-off—to gain momentum. The take-off requires more power than ordinary flying and special effort is required to build up sufficient speed to rise. All birds which do this have relatively small wings in proportion to their body weight. Those with the least sail area in proportion to weight have to run the farthest. Loons, grebes, swans, geese, diving ducks, coots and others regularly patter along the surface each time they have to fly. The stronger the headwind the quicker the take-off.

107. Do all ducks run across the surface of the water to take off?
Ducks are divided into two major types, the diving ducks which regularly dive beneath the surface to obtain food, and the dabbling ducks which usually hunt for food in shallow water by tipping up. Diving ducks such as scaup, canvasback and scoters with their relatively small wings and their feet situated far back on the body must run along the surface before the take-off.

Dabbling ducks such as mallards, widgeon and teal have comparatively large wings in proportion to their weight and their feet occupy a more forward position. These birds can rise straight out of the water, and often use a fluttering type of flight to mount rapidly.

108. Why do so many small birds have an undulating flight?
This undulating type of flight, prevalent in most passerine birds, generally is found in species which are light and relatively weak. It is most noticeable in birds such as goldfinches which habitually bound roller-coaster-fashion back and forth above the meadows and fields. It is produced by quickly alternating flapping flight with gliding. The bird gives a few rapid flaps, thus bounding upward and forward, whereupon it uses the momentum so generated to glide forward and downward. Since the frontal resistance in small light birds is comparatively greater than in large heavy birds, the small bird conserves energy by gliding through the air with the wings folded much of the time.

109. What is meant by the aspect ratio of a wing? This is the ratio between the length and width of a wing. The albatross has an aspect ratio of 11 to 1, the condor 8 to 1, while rails may be less than 2 to 1.

110. Are hummingbirds the only birds that fly backward? While hummingbirds are probably the champions of backward flight they are by no means the only birds that can fly in this way. When two herons or egrets fight, periodically one of them caught at a disadvantage in the dispute will flutter backward. Occasionally warblers fluttering at the tip of a branch as they pick off insects will flutter backward to a better position. Flycatchers regularly flutter backward when they overshoot some flying insect. It is probable that any bird which uses fluttering flight can move backward when pressed to do so.

111. Can any bird fly upside down? Very few birds fly upside down. Periodically during courtship performances or in play such birds as the bald eagle, red-shouldered hawk, marsh hawk, swallow-tailed kite and wood ibis roll over on their backs and sail for a short distance upside down. Some may even take two or three flaps in this position. Ravens have been observed flying briefly upside down, usually in the courting season and when the wind is strong.

112. Do birds that fly ever lose the ability to do so? During the postnuptial molt most birds shed their flight feathers rather synchronously one or two at a time from each wing, and new feathers quickly replace the lost ones so that the birds at all times are able to fly. This is essential in most cases to prevent the birds from starving or falling prey to predators. Ducks, rails and coots, however, shed all of their flight feathers at once and may be flightless for a month or more. At that time rails, coots and dabbling ducks become very secretive and seldom leave the protective thickets of the swamp. Diving ducks venturing out on open water take every precaution to stay out of danger and dive to escape from birds of prey.

IV. THE MIGRATION OF BIRDS

113. What is meant by migration? In its broadest sense any regular mass movement of animals between two areas is called migration. Therefore one might say that the morning and evening flights of herons, crows and starlings between their feeding grounds and favored nocturnal roosting areas are migrations. In ornithology, however, the term is used most commonly in reference to the mass movements of birds between the widely separated areas they occupy at different seasons. In North America this migration generally is to and from northern breeding grounds and southern wintering grounds.

114. Do animals other than birds migrate? Unquestionably bird migrations are the most conspicuous and spectacular. Nearly all orders of flying birds include species that are migratory. But birds are by no means the only animals that migrate. To mention a few others: mammals (lemmings, reindeer, caribou, some bats), fish (alewives, salmon, herring, eels) and insects (some dragonflies, butterflies, grasshoppers) have migrations just as amazing and fascinating as those of birds.

115. When was bird migration first noticed? Undoubtedly bird migrations were noticed from time immemorial and have been correlated with the changing seasons ever since the Pleistocene. The movements of some nomadic tribes were governed by bird migrations. Months in the Persian calendar were based on or named after birds or bird migrations dominant at that time of year. The same was true among many savage tribes. Numerous references to migration are found in the Bible and in the writings of Homer. The earliest recorded observations of migration are apparently in the Old Testament in the book of Exodus (16:13) and again in the book of Numbers (11:31). The first recorded observation of migration recognized as such is probably when Job (39:26) says: "Doth the hawk fly by thy wisdom, and stretch her wings toward the south?" Homer in the *Iliad* described the Trojan advance as being "like the cranes which flee from the coming winter and sudden rain, and fly with clamor towards the streams of the ocean."

116. When was the first recorded observation of bird migration made in the New World? On October 9 or 10, 1492, Captain Martín Alonso Pinzón, who was in command of the *Pinta*, observed a movement of land birds far at sea. He induced Columbus to shift his course to the southwest. If Columbus had maintained his original westward course he would have landed on the mainland of North America instead of on San Salvador.

117. Is it true that ancient man, unable to explain the phenomena of migration, created many fantastic theories? Apparently the movements of large birds which could be readily observed have been generally understood. Man could conceive of large species undertaking great flights. But the sudden disappearance and appearance of small birds puzzled him. Numerous theories to explain this phenomenon arose. It is impossible to discuss all of these at length here. Four major explanations were:

1. *Transportation.* According to this theory, small birds were carried across the Mediterranean on the backs of large species.

2. *Hibernation.* Rails, swifts and swallows were thought to bury themselves in the mud or hide in caves and hollow trees and hibernate as do some mammals, reptiles, amphibians, fish and insects.

3. *Transmutation.* Some people believed that one species merely turned into a different species for a period of the year. Even Aristotle stated that the European robin changed into a European redstart for the summer.

4. *Trip to the moon.* An anonymous treatise published in London in 1703 propounded the theory that birds migrated to the moon for the winter. The author even gave details, stating that the journey took 60 days, and that the birds in a semihibernating state flew with terrific speed through the rarefied atmosphere on this remarkable journey.

118. Do any birds hibernate? Since some mammals, reptiles, amphibians, fish and many lower forms of animal life hibernate, it was logical to assume that some birds might do likewise. Centuries ago the hibernation theory was used to explain the disappearance of many birds, including rails and swallows. The examples given proved to be false and many writers subsequently ridiculed the hibernation idea. Recent studies, however, indicate that some boatsuckers, swifts and hummingbirds may enter a torpid or hibernating condition. The body temperature drops to a level near that of the surrounding air, breathing is slow and often indiscernible, and reactions are either very slow or entirely lacking. In 1949 Dr. Jaeger studied a poorwill in a state of hibernation for a known period of 85 days. (See Dr. Edmund C. Jaeger, "Further Observations on the Hibernation of the Poorwill," *Condor,* No. 51, 105–09. See also Question 286.)

119. Why do birds migrate?   No single answer can adequately cover this subject. There are numerous theories, none of which is satisfactory for all examples of bird migrations. One might say it is an inherited rhythm of behavior adopted by birds in ancient times. But one must not assume that bird migration has developed along a strict narrow line, and that there must be one basic answer to explain all of these movements. The thinking of people living in the temperate zones of the world may be influenced by the fact that many species in both the Northern and Southern Hemispheres engage in mass movements away from both poles as temperature, day length and food supplies diminish. One might conclude, therefore, that temperature and food are the all-important factors. These are indeed important considerations. Even the most rugged water birds are forced to move when inland waters freeze. But some birds migrate long before there is any marked change in temperature and while food still is abundant. In fact, many birds in New England start south in August when temperature, vegetation and food are increasing, and before these reach a maximum for the year. Many birds pass by areas of abundant food supply. Moreover, it has been proved that many long-distance migrants can be kept in captivity and maintained out of doors even during severe weather as long as adequate food is supplied. Of all living creatures birds are best adapted to withstand extremes of temperature as long as they have sufficient food.

Before accepting any one theory as the all-inclusive explanation, bear in mind that many species migrate other than north and south, that some species confined the year around to tropical regions have distinct migrations, and that the migrations of some species are governed by rainfall or drought. Remember, too, that in certain species some populations migrate while others do not, and that there are species that do not migrate at all.

120. What are some of the theories used to explain bird migration?
Some ornithologists have suggested that the migration of birds in the northern part of the Northern Hemisphere can be attributed to the ice age. According to this theory the birds originating in these northern lands were forced southward by the advance of the giant glaciers, but due to an instinctive attachment to their homeland, the birds returned to nest in those sections of the northern areas which subsequently opened in summer.

Other ornithologists say that all birds originated in the tropics. Some species looking for better feeding grounds on which to raise a family moved northward. After the breeding season they were forced south by the severity of winter, but due to the success on the summer breeding grounds they moved north again the following spring.

There are other theories. Each concept is seemingly sufficient to explain the migration of a limited number of species, but each concept breaks down when applied as a single unequivocal explanation of migration as a whole.

121. Why has man failed to formulate a satisfactory, indisputable explanation? No one statement explains everything about bird migration. The answer may lie in a complex combination of numerous theories. Most birds are filled with wanderlust and stationary birds are an exception. Species with little wanderlust have to endure local extremes and undoubtedly many stationary species have been wiped out in the past. Those species with wanderlust were more successful in surviving and this trait, acted upon by natural selection in varying circumstances, created the migratory routes. One must remember always that birds have been migrating for an incalculable time and the whys and wherefores are not necessarily explainable by present conditions. The original causes for migration and for routes existing today may have vanished from the earth long ago.

122. What is diurnal migration? Some birds migrate chiefly or entirely by day and their movements are usually conspicuous or even spectacular. As a general rule birds which migrate in the daytime are strong fliers, those which normally range over wide open areas. Most of them capture their food on the wing or fly great distances in the course of finding it. Day migrants include swifts and swallows, which

feed as they fly, and herons, geese, ducks and hawks, which are
strong fliers and on the average day cover wide areas in search of
food.

Some of these birds such as loons, ducks and shorebirds may
show little preference for diurnal migrations and make many long
journeys at night. Typical conspicuous examples of diurnal migration
are (1) the V's and skeins of cormorants, geese and ducks seen flying overhead each spring and fall, (2) the whirling masses of broad-
winged hawks on their southward journey, and (3) thousands upon
thousands of swallows rushing northward up a river valley during
a single spring morning.

123. What is nocturnal migration?   Many species of birds migrate
only or chiefly at night. As a general rule, most night migrants are
either weak-flying, secretive or shy. Some suggest that these birds feel
safer moving across wide open spaces under cover of darkness.
Strictly speaking, the migrations of many of these birds are not
entirely nocturnal, for some may cover long distances during the
day, feeding as they move across the countryside in the desired direction. The major part of their great journeys, however, is undertaken at night. Nocturnal migrants include most bitterns, rails,
cuckoos, creepers, wrens, thrashers, thrushes, vireos, warblers, tanagers and sparrows.

**124. What is the best explanation offered for the development of
nocturnal migration?**   Food is probably the major factor. Long
diurnal flights of birds unable to feed as they go would result in their
landing in the evening with their stomachs empty. The evening might
be stormy and cold, preventing sufficient feeding before the coming
of night. By feeding all day and migrating at night the birds arrive for
breakfast and have the entire day to alternately rest and gather
food. (See Question 285.)

125. What is altitudinal migration?   Some birds, nesting on high
mountains, instead of engaging in long migratory flights, merely
descend to lower slopes and valleys as winter approaches. In a
descent of several thousand feet they accomplish what other birds of
the same species do in their latitudinal migration of hundreds or even
thousands of miles from north to south. In the space of a few minutes

they may be on favorable wintering grounds which their more northern and sometimes arctic cousins may take a week to reach. In winter, in the lowlands of Colorado, water pipits which nested on the highest plateaus of the state probably feed side by side with water pipits which nested on arctic tundras. Likewise, other species, such as chickadees, juncoes and siskins may descend in a brief space of time from the snow-covered conifers at 8,000 feet to warm open creek bottoms only a couple of miles below in the valleys. (See Question 76.)

126. What is meant by permanent residents?   This group of birds includes all species that regularly have representatives present in the suitable habitat of a region throughout the year. Some species such as the ruffed grouse, bobwhite and house sparrow are virtually stable, the same individuals being present all year. Others, such as the American crow, blue jay and song sparrow generally are migratory, the individuals in some areas during winter being different from those in summer.

127. What are summer residents?   It seems wise to preface this explanation with advice that a species may fall into different categories depending on the region under discussion. In order that one definite region may be in mind, it is assumed in this and the next three categories that birds around New York City are being discussed. Summer residents are those species not normally present in winter. They arrive from the South, nest within the New York region, and then retire to the South again. The length of stay on the breeding grounds varies considerably from species to species. Some, such as the woodcock, may arrive around New York as early as March and linger until November or even December. Others, such as the orchard oriole, are not to be expected until May, and most of them depart for the South before the end of August.

128. What are summer visitants?   This term refers to those species which do not breed in an area but merely visit it in summer. Around New York City the summer visitants fall into two major groups. Many southern herons have postnuptial wanderings. After the breeding season they move north and some of them regularly reach the northeastern states every summer. Other species, such as the Wilson's petrel, the greater shearwater and the sooty shearwater, breed in the southern part of the Southern Hemisphere. They migrate north to get away from their winter and occur on the North Atlantic during its summer months. They never breed in the Northern Hemisphere; they merely visit it.

129. What are transient visitants?   This group includes all of those species which normally breed to the north of the region under discussion, winter south of it and occur in the region chiefly during migrations. Around New York City typical examples would be the Swainson's thrush, bay-breasted warbler and Lincoln's sparrow. In northern Maine all three of these species are summer residents because they breed there.

130. What are winter visitants?   Those species that breed north of a region but come south into it to spend the winter fall into this category. Typical examples in the New York City region are the pine siskin, tree sparrow and snow bunting. Some species, such as the goshawk, snowy owl, white-winged crossbill and redpoll, often are absent for several years at a time and thus are referred to as irregular winter visitants.

131. At what altitude do birds migrate?   The old conception was that most birds migrated above 15,000 feet, most from 30,000 to 40,000 feet. Recent studies indicate that in most lowland areas few birds reach 5,000 feet, that the bulk of migrants rarely fly above 3,000 feet, and that most movements, especially at night, are at less than half that height. Naturally the topographical features of the country beneath and the sky conditions above affect the altitude at which birds migrate on any particular day or night. Many birds migrate just above the waves when crossing extensive water areas. This applies not only to water birds and shorebirds, but also to passerine species as well. On numerous occasions off the Florida coast warblers, vireos, sparrows and even hummingbirds have been seen barely clearing the waves as they flew by fishing boats on an invisible but well defined course.

132. What are the highest records of birds in flight?   Judging from aviators' observations, pelicans, geese and ducks sometimes travel as high as 8,000 to 9,000 feet, several species of shorebirds reach 12,000 feet; and storks occasionally fly at 20,000 feet. Great elevated land masses, of course, often force birds passing over to fly at heights far above normal. On the Mount Everest Expedition of 1921, Dr. Wollaston recorded a lammergeier (bearded vulture) at 24,000 or 25,000 feet, and identified curlews and godwits passing over at 20,000 feet. Other explorers in the Himalayas have been astonished to hear the calls of large flocks of nocturnal migrants flying over in the frigid temperatures at 18,000 to 20,000 feet. In the *Field* (December 18, 1920, p. 876) it is stated that an observer while making photographic observations of the sun at Dehra Dun in India obtained a picture of geese flying at an estimated altitude of 29,000 feet.

133. At what speed do birds migrate? Formerly it was conceived that birds on migration flew at a great height at very fast speeds. Both of these contentions have proved false. Recent studies indicate that the majority of birds travel between 20 and 40 miles per hour. There is great variation. Herons may move at less than 20 miles per hour, small land birds generally travel between 20 and 30 m.p.h., while most geese and ducks fly from 40 to 55 m.p.h. These speeds, of course, depend to some degree not only on weather conditions, but also on the attitude of the birds concerned. Some birds, such as ducks, jaegers, certain hawks and swifts, are capable of attaining much higher speeds, but few ever surpass 100 m.p.h.

134. How many miles does the average bird cover in one day during migration? Here again there are great extremes. Some birds may fly only a short distance one day, then cover many times that distance the next. Even birds which travel at only 20 miles per hour can cover 160 miles during an eight-hour sustained flight. A mallard banded at Thief Lake, Minnesota, was taken two days later at Meredosia, Illinois, suggesting a speed of 322 miles a day. A lesser yellowlegs banded at Cape Cod, Massachusetts, was recovered six days later on the island of Martinique in the West Indies. If one assumes that it took the bird five of the six days to travel the 1930 miles between the two points, then it averaged 386 miles per day. But such rates are unusual. The lesser yellowlegs is a powerful flier, and since most of the journey undoubtedly was over a wide expanse of water, the bird was forced to take an unusually sustained flight.

Records indicate that most migration is unhurried. Few birds travel every day, and it is doubtful that many birds make sustained flights exceeding eight to ten hours. A Lincoln's sparrow banded at Jamestown, North Dakota, averaged only 49 miles per day in flying 540 miles to Midway Park, Saskatchewan. Statistics show that the rate of travel increases as the breeding grounds are approached, and that the late migrants average much longer distances per day than early migrants.

135. Is mortality great among birds during migrations? If so, what are the major causes?   Naturally any mass movement of birds over great distances is a dangerous adventure. Each year thousands upon thousands of migrants fail to reach their destination. Storms or abrupt, unseasonable changes in weather often have disastrous effects. After an extremely severe March snowstorm in Minnesota, Dr. Roberts reported that 750,000 Lapland longspurs were found dead on the ice of two lakes. Many birds crossing extensive bodies of water become exhausted, especially during storms and periods of strong head winds. On several occasions the authors have seen birds trying to reach a boat far at sea drop into the ocean and disappear beneath a large curling wave. Small, weak fliers, or even tired normally strong fliers, are vulnerable to predation while crossing wide open areas. Peregrine falcons have been seen snatching mourning doves circling above an Army transport off Long Island, New York, and jaegers have been seen seizing passerine birds migrating off the Florida coast. Annually birds crash into lighthouses, bridges, tall buildings, wires and other man-made structures. Since their inception in 1946, airport ceilometers with visible beams have caused the death of numerous birds. At times many birds are attracted to the light and fly back and forth through it. Some kill themselves in collision with other birds, or by striking buildings, or occasionally by crashing onto the ground. ("The Birds of Minnesota" by T. S. Roberts.)

136. It has been said that destruction of migrating birds around European lighthouses has been much greater than at American stations. Is there any basis for this contention?   Formerly this was true. Numerous European lighthouses are situated on the main migratory routes or flyways for that continent and consequently in the days of fixed white beams lured many migrants to death. But in the eastern United States, for instance, most migratory routes are inland from the coast, thus by-passing the lighthouses. Very heavy flights of night migrants along the coast usually occur only during strong westerly winds and under such conditions skies are normally clear, lighthouses readily visible, and the blinding effect of the beam sharply reduced.

On the other hand, during easterly winds which bring most drizzles and fogs, when the blinding effect of the beam would be disastrous, few night migrants are traveling along the coast. Regardless of geographic location, however, this destruction can be virtually stopped by illuminating the lighthouse itself on the outside and by changing from fixed white lights to those which are either red, revolving or flashing. Most modern lighthouses have beams which revolve or flash, and annual destruction therefore is comparatively light.

137. Do species when migrating mix readily or do they separate themselves into flocks made up entirely of their own species?
There are great differences in the flocking habit. Birds such as falcons, hummingbirds and kingfishers normally travel in solitary style. With most day migrants the birds seem to separate themselves according to feeding habits, roosting requirements, speed, and manner of flight. Some species, such as nighthawks and chimney swifts, normally travel in groups consisting exclusively of their own species. Various kinds of shorebirds and blackbirds regularly form tremendous mixed flocks.

With nocturnal migrants the composition of the flocks is difficult to ascertain. Some authorities say that at night the birds are not in flocks, but uniformly distributed across the sky. These authorities say that since the birds are moving under cover of darkness there is no advantage to be gained by flocking. This, however, should not be given as an unequivocal answer. The authors frequently have seen V's of geese and shorebirds coming across the sky at the first hint of dawn. They recall one group of passerine night migrants which apparently were caught over the extensive New York City region at dawn and had to traverse miles of steel and concrete canyons before landing. By the time they reached the northern edge of New York City, it was light enough to see these nocturnal migrants (tanagers, orioles, and mixed warblers) come down in one closely knit flock. Of course, the birds could have formed the flock when it became light.

138. Are Canada geese the only birds that fly in V-formation?
By no means, for many species of birds habitually travel in V- or wedge-shaped formation. To mention a few: numerous species of cormorants, ibis, swans, geese, ducks, shorebirds and gulls regularly arrange themselves in the V-pattern. One of the most stirring sights the authors ever saw was four large flocks of marbled godwits in separate V's traveling along the California coast against a flaming sunset.

Around New York City in April large V-shaped flocks of double-crested cormorants annually are seen high in the sky heading eastward along the coast or northward up the Hudson River. At that time one invariably hears uninformed observers exclaiming about the spectacular V's made by the migrating "geese." (See Question 103.)

139. Does the oldest, most experienced bird always lead the flock? Anyone with a critical eye can settle this question for himself by carefully checking flocks of migrating birds. Frequently the flock breaks formation and reassembles a short distance beyond with a different individual at the head of the flock.

140. Many birds breeding in North America go to the Southern Hemisphere for the winter. Do any birds that breed in the Southern Hemisphere spend part of the year in the Northern Hemisphere? Very few birds nesting in the Southern Hemisphere visit the United States or adjacent waters. Outstanding examples of annual visitants are species such as the Wilson's petrel, greater shearwater and sooty shearwater, which nest in the southern part of the Southern Hemisphere, yet regularly spend the summer (their winter) on the waters off North American shores.

141. Do migratory birds return to the same nesting territories year after year? Banding data indicate that young birds do not show a special tendency to return to the exact area where they were born. On the other hand, once birds have nested they tend to return to their nesting territories year after year. Banding has shown that house wrens, robins and bluebirds frequently return to the identical nesting site year after year, yet rarely is one of the young found back in the area where it hatched. (See Question 851.)

This general rule does not hold for birds which nest in colonies. In colonial species young birds also tend to return to the colony where they hatched. This is probably due to the highly specialized nature of their nesting requirements, and the fact that they are more or less gregarious throughout the year.

142. Do migrating birds winter in the same areas year after year?
Indications are that they frequently do. Observers who do intensive field work often note that partially albinistic birds which can be identified readily frequently appear in the same area each autumn for several years in a row. This contention is substantiated by numerous banding records. White-throated sparrows banded at Thomasville, Georgia, returned for several successive winters to the very clump of bushes where they originally had been captured. At Lake Merritt in Oakland, California, about 50 per cent of the ducks caught in a single winter were wearing bands attached there in previous years.

143. What is a flyway? Strictly speaking, there is probably no area in the United States over which some birds do not travel in their latitudinal migration from their northern breeding grounds to their southern wintering grounds. There are, however, lanes which are most heavily traveled and where the greatest flights occur. These are known as flyways.

144. What are the major flyways in the United States? Some authorities recognize as many as seven major flyways:

(1) *Atlantic Coast Flyway.* This follows the eastern coast or coastal plain and is used by most birds breeding in eastern North America and migrating to, from, or through the West Indies.

(2) *Appalachian Flyway.* Many impressive hawk movements and great passerine flights follow this route along the Appalachian Mountains and ridges. Some of these birds take great trans-Gulf flights to and from Yucatán, Central America and South America.

(3) *Mississippi Flyway.* This includes all flights up and down the great Mississippi River valley. It is probably the most heavily traveled flyway in the United States.

(4) *Great Plains Flyway*. Many birds follow this preferred habitat up and down the Great Plains to and from Mexico.

(5) *Sierra Nevada Flyway*. This is the western counterpart of the eastern Appalachian Flyway and is the major route used by the majority of passerine birds traveling between western Canada and Mexico.

(6) *Pacific Coast Flyway*. This lane follows the Pacific coast and is used by many species nesting in Washington, Oregon and California en route between their breeding grounds and Mexico.

(7) *Cross-country Flyway*. This is a great curving lane which many ducks and other birds follow on their journeys between western and central Canada and the southeastern United States.

145. How far do birds migrate?   The length of the migration route is variable, sometimes even in individuals of the same species. Some mountain breeders such as water pipits and Oregon juncoes may merely drop into the valleys for the winter. Some species such as the song sparrow and American robin may travel only a short distance south of the breeding grounds. Others like the red-eyed vireo and American redstart may breed as far north as Canada, yet journey to South America. Many shorebirds (sandpipers and plovers) which breed in the arctic regularly winter in the southern part of South America. Some birds nest in the arctic tundras of Siberia and migrate to Australia and New Zealand.

146. Why are there such amazing differences in the distances traveled by migrants?   This is another one of those puzzling questions awaiting a satisfactory answer. In many cases the length of the journey seems to be correlated with food requirements. Thus insect-eaters usually travel farther than seed-eaters. But this is by no means a complete, all-inclusive explanation. The bobolink, which can and does eat quantities of seeds, migrates from Canada and northern United States across the tropics and way down into Argentina. Yet the golden-crowned kinglet, essentially an insect-eater, may spend the severest winter in the snow-draped woodlands north of Maine. Furthermore, one well might ponder why so many birds pass by apparently ideal habitats with an abundance of food north of the equator and proceed far south of the equator to spend the winter. Size, strength or flying ability seem to have little correlation with the length of the journey taken by a migrant. Some small weak-flying species travel much farther than many large, powerful fliers.

147. Which is the champion long-distance flier of the world?
The species generally mentioned first is the arctic tern. Some of these birds nest as far north as open land is found, sometimes within 450 miles of the North Pole. Most of them winter in the southern part of the Southern Hemisphere and some reach antarctic waters. Their round-trip flight undoubtedly exceeds the circumference of the earth. They probably see more hours of daylight than any other creature, since some live in the land of the midnight sun on both breeding grounds and winter home.

But there are many great migrants and wanderers among the sea birds and when more information comes to light some of these may well rival the arctic tern. A wandering albatross banded on the Kerquelen Islands in the antarctic south of Africa was shot 12 days later 3,150 miles away. Another was recovered 6,000 miles from its breeding island.

148. Are all long-distance migrants large birds with wings especially adapted for long sustained flights? This is by no means true. Many small passerine birds undertake amazing journeys. As mentioned before, the bobolink, a bird smaller than an American robin, may migrate from Canada to Argentina, a distance of 6,000 to 7,000 miles. Most black-poll warblers travel from 3,500 to 8,000 miles each way. Some breed as far north as Alaska, yet winter as far south as Brazil.

149. Do birds always return north by the same route they used going south? Most species seen going south through an area may be expected to pass through that area again during the northward journey. There are exceptions. The golden plover and Connecticut warbler are recorded regularly during their southward flights across New England in late summer, yet are accidental in this area in spring. Their normal northward migration routes are west of the Appalachian Mountains.

150. Is it true that golden plovers take non-stop flights from Nova Scotia to South America? When late summer comes, thousands of

golden plovers breeding in the great arctic tundras head southeastward to Newfoundland and Nova Scotia. From there they are reported to fly non-stop to South America and are recorded on the
eastern seaboard of the United States chiefly when wild easterly storms
tire the weaker individuals and blow them shoreward. The golden
plover is such a powerful flier that it is easy to place credence in this
remarkable journey. However, the authors often have seen flocks of
shorebirds far at sea trotting over and feeding across great rafts
of floating marine algae, and it is possible that many, if not most,
migrating sandpipers and plovers regularly pause to rest and feed in
this manner.

**151. Some people say that great migratory flights of birds are not
astonishing feats of endurance but are merely the activity of
everyday life concentrated on one unswerving aim. Is this sound
reasoning?**   It is true that birds probably are the most active of all
animal classes and that they use a great amount of energy every day.
In birds such as terns, swifts and swallows, which fly a large part of
the day, it is obvious that by merely straightening out the miles
traveled during a day of normal activity, the distance would be great.
It is estimated that the European swift when feeding its young covers
as much as 500 miles a day.

However, many birds do relatively little sustained flying during the
average day, and the distance covered by these birds on migration is
truly amazing. Consider birds such as the least bittern, sora and
Virginia rail, which normally creep through dense swamp vegetation
and seldom fly unless flushed, and even then flutter weakly only for
a few yards before dropping back into the protective cover of the
marsh. The flights of such birds from New England to Florida, the
West Indies and even farther south are almost unbelievable.

**152. Do birds on migration find their way by following topo-
graphical features?**   Since many major flyways in North America
run up or down a mountain ridge, valley, river or coastline some people say that migrating birds find their way by following visible routes.
In many instances, however, birds follow routes across extensive
prairies and wide oceans without distinct topographical features to
guide them. Consider the golden plovers that fly from Nova Scotia
across the open ocean to South America, or those that hop across the

Pacific from Alaska to Hawaii. The ever-changing ocean would show few stable features to guide a migrating bird. In 1953 a Manx shearwater, removed from its burrow on the island of Skokholm off Wales, was taken by airliner to Boston and released. It returned to its burrow on Skokholm 12 days and 13 hours later, having traveled about 250 miles a day to cover the 3,200 miles back to its nest. Certainly there were no topographical features on the Atlantic to guide it.

153. Do old, experienced birds lead the young ones on migration and teach them the routes to follow? In some birds such as geese, which usually migrate in families or flocks consisting of several families, it is possible that the young learn the migration routes by accompanying the older, more experienced birds. Field observations, however, indicate that the young of many species fly southward for the first time without any adult birds to show them the route. Careful experiments substantiate these field observations. Young crows were kept at Edmonton, Canada, until all adult crows had departed south of that region. When released, the young birds migrated south as though traveling over a familiar route. On the Baltic coast of East Prussia young white storks were banded and released after all adults had departed for their wintering grounds. Most of these young traveled southeastward toward the Black Sea, following without adult help the ancestral migration route of white storks from that Baltic area.

154. If neither topographical features of the landscape nor guidance by old experienced birds explains how migrants find their way, how can these remarkable uncharted journeys be explained? At present there is no adequate answer to explain the amazing ability of birds to find their way. Some scientists have suggested that it is just random searching, but the rapidity with which many birds when taken across the ever-changing oceans for hundreds of miles from their nests return home indicates that this theory is not a satisfactory answer. Other scientists have suggested theories involving guidance by the angle to the sun, one of the magnetic poles, knowledge of astronomy and inherited memory. Unable to find a satisfactory answer, man often has explained the phenomenon by the use of ambiguous phrases such as a "homing instinct" or a "sense of direction." Actually all one can say is that birds have an inherited migration instinct, with a definite sense of the route to follow and

the goal to reach. Much experimenting and study is needed to explain
this fascinating and perplexing problem of how birds determine their
direction even when traveling through darkness, fog and across wide
bodies of water they have never before traversed.

**155. If a bird is captured and taken to a place where it has never
been before, can it find its way home?** Many experiments have
proved that birds have an amazing and at present inexplicable direc-
tion-finding ability. One of the most frequently mentioned of these
experiments involved sooty and noddy terns which were nesting on
the Dry Tortugas Islands about 60 miles west of Key West, Florida.
These species from tropical seas are seldom seen farther north. Some
of these birds were captured, marked for easy identification and
released at various points. Five individuals were released as far north
as Cape Hatteras, North Carolina, a place they certainly had never
been. Three of the five returned quickly to their nests. The two
sooty terns were back on their nests 1,000 sea miles away in five days.

In another experiment two Manx shearwaters taken from their
burrows on the island of Skokholm off Wales were released at Venice,
Italy where the species does not occur. One of these birds was back
on Skokholm two weeks later. As the Manx shearwater is strictly a
marine species, it undoubtedly took the long sea route westward
across the Mediterranean past Gibraltar and then northward to its
nesting burrow, a distance of some 3,700 miles.

**156. Has this amazing ability of birds to find a definite course and
quickly reach a definite goal been put to use by man?** Immediately one thinks of the pigeon corps used for decades in military
intelligence and communication systems. During World War I tens
of thousands of domestic pigeons were used. In the Meuse-Argonne
offensive alone 442 pigeons belonging to the United States Army de-
livered 403 messages over distances of 20 to 50 kilometers without
losing one important dispatch. From Pliny it is learned that Roman
knights took swallows with them to races in Rome and immediately
after the event, stained the birds with colors of the winning chariot.
The released swallows quickly flew back to their homes and carried
the news of victory. In the Gilbert and Marshall Islands of the South
Pacific, frigate birds are trained and used to carry messages from one
island to another.

157. How do birds know when to migrate?   Although migration is generally synchronized with changes in day length, air temperature, moisture conditions, wind direction and air flow, it does not occur until the bird attains a special physiological condition. Fat generally is accumulated in preparation for the special energy required on a long flight. In most cases reproductive glands become either enlarged or shrunken. Just what causes these physiological changes to occur with cyclic regularity no one can explain. Nor is the exact relationship between the internal and external factors clearly understood. Once this condition is reached some simple stimulus or "release" is required to start the bird on its way. Just what the release may be cannot be stated unequivocally. It may be merely an abrupt change in temperature. The entire subject is complex and much research must be carried on before a clear, satisfactory explanation is reached. Caged birds, even though provided with plenty of food and kept under comfortable temperatures in closed laboratories, are affected by a migratory fever. At the normal migration season for their free wild relatives they too become restless, hop nervously about their cages day and night and are obviously urged to move by some internal impulse.

158. Is the degree of development and condition of the sexual organs the entire stimulus?   In some species it seems quite obvious that the migratory impulse is linked closely with the reproductive cycle. Banding records support observations that storks, gulls and other birds which take several years to attain a breeding condition do not return regularly to northern breeding grounds until full sexual maturity is reached. In the Northern Hemisphere most birds on their northward migration have enlarged sexual organs increasing in activity, while the sexual organs of southbound migrants are small and inactive. In the nonbreeding season the sex organs may shrink to $\frac{1}{25}$ their usual size and become so small that careful dissection and study are necessary to determine the sex.

As an experiment, research workers took a number of departing migrants in autumn and by artificial light subjected these birds to long days of activity. After a few weeks eggs formed in the ovaries and the migratory impulse abated. On the other hand, scientists have studied the behavior of castrated birds. Gulls, crows, and European robins from which the gonads had been removed not only migrated to their wintering grounds, but many of them returned to their breeding grounds the following spring. Some students have interpreted this to mean that neither swelling gonads nor the appearance of sex hormones in the blood could have been the driving stimulus. It must be remembered, however, that sex hormones may be distributed by the adrenal glands.

The prevailing belief today is that the reproductive cycle and migratory pattern, though closely and complexly correlated, are distinctly independent.

159. Could increasing light and temperature be the factors that inform a bird of the time to migrate north?   In some cases there is close correlation between increasing light and temperature and consequently many people have accepted the theory that those factors inform a bird when to migrate north. But consider the migratory shorebirds wintering in South America. They start north in March and April at a time when light and temperature are decreasing, not increasing, in that part of South America. Consider also the warblers that winter near the equator where changes in light and temperature conditions from season to season are negligible. It is obvious that in March, April and May these birds headed into the northern United States and Canada are progressing into a land of lower not higher temperatures.

160. What is reverse migration?   From time to time birds are observed making extended mass movements in the opposite direction from which they should be going. In most instances these movements are into a head wind. During such movements at Point Pelee on the north shore of Lake Erie dozens of species of birds have been observed flying south into a southerly wind even though it was spring and they should have been headed north.

161. What causes reverse migration?   As yet there is no satisfactory explanation. Some scientists have suggested that many species of birds may have an instinctive response to wind direction. At certain times under special circumstances this impulse is so irresistible that the migration flight assumes an abnormal direction.

162. European ornithological publications contain numerous records of essentially American passerine species. Why do so few

European land birds stray to North America? At first this does seem a perplexing problem, since the distance west or east across the Atlantic is identical. However, it must be remembered that the prevailing winds in this part of the earth are westerly. American wanderers are helped eastward by the prevailing winds while European species headed westward have to struggle against the eastward air currents. Moreover, tropical disturbances often trap migrating birds off or along the North American coast before whirling on their normal northeastward course across the ocean toward Europe.

163. Every spring newspapers carry stories about the arrival of swallows at the Mission of El Capistrano in California. What species of swallows are these? The cliff swallow, a bird that originally nested on the sides of cliffs, but in many areas now nests under bridges and under the eaves of buildings. In fact, in many sections the species is so closely associated with buildings that it is called the eaves swallow.

164. Is it true that these swallows arrive at the mission on the same day each year? These swallows arrive with considerable regularity each spring, but certainly not always on a specific date, as often stated. Some years they may be a week or so early, some years a week or so late.

165. Do any birds migrate with clocklike regularity? Most birds accomplish their migratory journeys during very definite periods each year. In many cases their date of arrival may be predicted with surprising accuracy. But the use of the term "clocklike regularity" is an exaggeration. Even in the case of the most regular migrants there often is a variation of several days in the time of arrival from one year to the next. As a general rule early migrants which are more affected by extreme weather conditions are less dependable. But the date of arrival for the late migrants may be predicted quite accurately. For instance, one can be fairly sure that American redstarts, ovenbirds, scarlet tanagers and rose-breasted grosbeaks will arrive around New York during the first week in May each year. Such a degree of accuracy is astonishing when one considers the length of the trip undertaken by these species from their tropical wintering grounds.

166. What is meant by irregular migrations? This term is used for those birds with erratic migrations which do not follow any regular seasonal pattern. Some call it migration without periodicity. There are numerous examples, but two will suffice. Periodically there are great mass movements of snowy owls south of their normal range. Some scientists correlate these explosive movements with the lowest points in the population of arctic lemmings and hares on which snowy owls normally feed. There are somewhat similar unpredictable mass movements of both red and white-winged crossbills. At such times these northern conifer dwellers appear in large flocks far south of their normal range. These movements probably are correlated with great failures in the cone crops of pines, firs and spruce, at which times the birds are forced to seek food elsewhere.

167. Why is the migration of land birds on the Atlantic side of the United States much more spectacular than that on the Pacific Coast? Since the climate on the Pacific Coast is much more uniform than that on the Atlantic Coast, migration is much less spectacular. Moreover, a large number of birds on the west coast are permanent residents. There are many winter visitants but these birds arrive and depart gradually both in autumn and spring. Even those migrants which winter in the tropics trickle in with slow, even regularity and the tremendous waves so characteristic of the east are lacking.

168. Why are the spring waves of migratory birds more spectacular in the northern ⅔ of the eastern United States than in the southern third? The southern climate is normally mild and uniform, so migratory birds trickle through every day, gradually and steadily. In the North the large spectacular waves are the result of a variable climate. A cold wave or a chilly, wet northeaster dams up all migrants at its southern edge for several days. Then, when the wind again becomes southerly and the temperature moderates, the swarm of birds checked by the storm rushes forward in a tremendous mass movement.

169. Is it true that some birds in the United States move north, not south, after the breeding season? In many species of birds there are great dispersals after the breeding season, some young scattering in all directions from their breeding grounds. Not only do a great many young wander north but many adults engage in postnuptial wanderings. Herons, egrets and eagles banded in Florida may be recorded in New England. Cormorants, herons, ducks, gulls and others banded on their New England breeding grounds regularly are recorded in late summer and early autumn in New Brunswick, Nova Scotia and Quebec.

170. Do small species ever hitchhike by riding on the backs of large birds? The young of loons, grebes and ducks often climb on the backs of their parents as they swim about and are transported in that manner. However, the reports of hitchhiking adult birds are creations of the imagination. In years gone by, man believed that it was impossible for small passerine birds to migrate across the Mediterranean. Therefore it was thought that storks and cranes stopped on the shores of this large body of water and allowed small species to climb aboard before crossing. Annually, even today, one reads in newspapers stories of eagles and geese transporting small birds, but investigations of all such reports always prove erroneous.

171. Do any birds navigate by means of a built-in sonar system? The oilbirds of northern South America find their way in the total darkness of the breeding caves by means of a "sonar system." That is, by uttering frequent high-pitched notes which are echoed by the cave walls or other objects about them, these birds avoid obstacles in the same manner that bats do. Oilbirds are capable of many squawks and clucks but these are not used for guidance. For navigation in total darkness, they utter clicking sounds with a duration of about 2/1000 of a second, having a frequency of about 7,000 cycles per second. This is well within the range of human hearing. These sounds bounce or echo from obstacles and warn the birds of their presence. Navigation by sound is called sonar guidance.

V. THE INTERNAL BIRD

THE SKELETONS OF BIRDS

172. What are the outstanding characteristics of a bird's skeleton?
Extreme lightness of the framework together with strength are characteristic of the bones of birds. The light, strong bones show considerable fusion to adjacent bones, making a rigid yet elastic skeleton.

173. How is the lightness attained? Many bones of birds are pneumatic, that is, they are filled with air, whereas the same bones of mammals may be solid or filled with marrow. Many of the hollowed bones are pared to extreme thinness.

174. Is strength lost when bones become hollow? Engineers have discovered that hollow girders are stronger than solid ones of the same weight. This holds true for the bones of birds. Moreover, the larger hollow bones supply more surface for the attachment of muscles, a distinct advantage among birds that fly.

175. Why is this combination of lightness, strength and elasticity essential to these flying creatures? Aerial acrobatics cause great and sudden stresses and only a frame engineered to perfection could withstand them. The bones of many soaring birds have in their fused finger bones internal trusslike supports very much like the struts inside airplane wings. Similar struts support some of the larger bones of the wings and legs.

176. It is sometimes said that for each bone in a mammal there is a similar bone in a bird. Is this true? Yes, though the fusion of many bones and great changes in others to adapt them for flight create a difficult problem of identification for the layman. The keen, skilled eye of the scientist can correlate most of the bones in birds with those that are found in mammal skeletons.

177. What is the general form of a bird's skeleton? The bones of a bird's sacrum and hip girdle are molded into a tubelike, thin structure which is both light and strong. The shoulder girdle and breastbone form an exceptionally rigid unit. The backbone, composed of from 10 to 22 vertebrae, is coalesced to form one solid rod which supports the back. The ribs are beautifully long, thin and flat. They permit considerable movement for breathing and flying while being very strong and light. Each rib overlaps its neighbor, thus giving resilient strength which has been compared to that of a woven basket.

The wings are attached to the solid and powerful thorax by a three-jointed support. They can pull away from the thorax and strike against it without causing any yield in its rigid construction.

178. What is the keel of a bird?   The breastbone or sternum is found in both mammals and birds. Among flightless birds such as the ostrich this is flat. But in all flying birds there is a mid-ridge called the keel on the breastbone. The most important flight muscles are attached to the keel.

179. Among birds of flight, is there any difference in keel development?   Birds that fly with powerful strokes of their wings or with swiftly beating wings, such as falcons, swallows and hummingbirds, have big keels and large flight muscles.

Birds that soar a great deal, such as the albatrosses, vultures and condors, and which depend on buoyancy and a large wing area to keep them aloft, have a much smaller or more shallow keel and also smaller flight muscles than falcons, hummingbirds and so on.

180. Is any part of a bird's skeleton flexible?   Though the skeleton of a bird is mostly rigid, the neck is an exception. Birds have extremely flexible necks which to some degree compensate for the hands which they lack. Owls can turn their heads almost completely backward.

Because of the flexible neck, birds are able to reach, stab quickly in any direction, preen their feathers easily and peer at objects they wish to examine. Some birds, such as herons, even fold their necks when in flight or at rest.

181. What makes possible the unusual flexibility of a bird's neck?
The large number of vertebrae in the neck give it great flexibility.

All mammals, even the giraffe, have but seven neck vertebrae. The average number of neck (or cervical) vertebrae of birds is about 14. Swans have 23 such vertebrae. The neck of a bird surpasses that of a snake in freedom of motion.

182. What is the relation between the weight of the skeleton and the rest of a bird's body?   The relation between skeleton weight and body weight varies with each species. The bones of an ostrich form a much greater proportion of the total weight than is true among birds that fly. Birds that habitually soar, such as the wandering albatross, have a skeleton proportionally much lighter to total body weight than is true of birds that fly with powerful wing-beats as do falcons.

A brown pelican soars easily and also flaps strongly. The average weight of one of these big birds with a 6½-foot wingspread is 8 pounds. The dried skeleton of a brown pelican weighs only 9 ounces. Dr. Robert Cushman Murphy reported that the skeleton of a magnificent frigate bird with a wingspread of 7 feet weighed only 4 ounces. That is less than the weight of its feathers.

183. To what part of the human body does the wing of a bird correspond?   The bones of a bird's wing correspond to the upper arm, forearm and hand of man. Birds can fold their wing bones into a compact Z. When stretched, the wings move in but one plane. In this way the wing obtains its essential rigidity.

184. In what way does the skull differ from the human skull? Unlike the human skull, that of a bird has extremely thin and light bones. Nevertheless they are strong. The bones are fused together, with few exceptions. The ornithologist Elliott Coues wrote that a bird skull is a poem in bone and its architecture is frozen music.

185. What bones in the skull of a bird are not fused together? The tongue bones are separate from the skull bones. The lower jaw moves freely. Otherwise most of the skull bones are fused into a rigid, smooth whole.

THE MUSCLES OF BIRDS

186. Which muscles of birds show the greatest development?   The breast muscles. In birds these are known as flight muscles and usually are very large and well developed.

187. Is there variation among birds in the development of flight muscles?   Birds with deep keels, or those that fly with powerful wing movements, have enormous flight muscles. Falcons, hummingbirds, swallows and nighthawks all exhibit well-developed flight muscles.

188. Is there any difference in development between muscles that raise the wings and those that lower them?   In most birds the muscles that control the powerful downstroke are larger than those that raise the wings. Sometimes the depressor muscles are ten times as large as the muscles that elevate the wings. Dr. William Beebe discovered that in some pigeons the weight of these great pectoral muscles equals ⅕ the weight of the entire bird.

189. Do any of our familiar birds reverse this customary muscle development?   Among hummingbirds the upstroke is about as strong as the downstroke. Therefore their elevator and depressor muscles are about equally developed.

190. The apparent size of a bird often changes because it fluffs or tightens its feathers. Is this done by muscular activity?   Birds have an enormous number of muscles in their skin. For instance, a Canada goose is said to have 12,000 skin muscles. These are used for fluffing the feathers, to draw them tight against the body, to shake them after a water or dust bath, to part the feathers for incubation, to lift the plumes in ceremonial acts, and for certain complicated feather movements in flight. Owls, turkey gobblers and prairie chickens often fluff their feathers until their bulk is almost tripled.

191. Do the feeding habits of birds affect any of their muscles?   The muscles controlling the jaws of birds show considerable variation. These adaptations have usually evolved so the birds can maintain efficient feeding.

192. What are the muscles that close the jaws called? Adductor muscles.

193. In which birds are the adductor muscles well developed? The adductor or closing muscles are particularly well developed among seed eaters that crush hard seeds before swallowing them. Grackles, blue jays and cardinals all shell or crush seeds before swallowing them. Birds of prey such as hawks and shrikes that tear their food apart also have well developed adductor muscles.

194. What are the muscles called that open the jaws? Protractor muscles.

195. Which birds have well-developed protractor muscles? Nighthawks, chimney swifts and other insect-eaters that catch insects and swallow them without first crushing them have well-developed protractor or gaping muscles.

196. What muscles control perching? Several leg muscles assist in the perching of birds but this is chiefly controlled by tendons leading to the toes.

197. The feet and toes of birds appear to be nothing but skin and bones. Are there any muscles in them? All the muscles in the feet of birds are like tendons in form. This helps conserve body heat in these generally featherless areas. (See Question 488.)

198. What muscles enable a woodpecker to use its bill as a hammer or chisel? Strong neck muscles make it possible for a woodpecker to drill or drum. These are aided by a strong bill and also by thick head bones (unusual in birds) which act as shock absorbers.

199. Why do some birds have white breast muscles while these are dark in other species? Unless adequate blood supply reaches the breast to enable a bird to fly well, its breast muscles are white. Lack of blood vessels in the breasts of domestic chickens and turkeys explains their white breast muscles and also the reason why they fly weakly and for very short distances. If a ruffed grouse is flushed several times in succession, it becomes so fatigued that it can be picked up. It does not have sufficient blood vessels in its flight or breast muscles to bring in adequate fuel and remove the wastes generated by flight.

Birds that fly for long distances have dark breast muscles due to the concentration of blood vessels in them. Large breast muscles are not enough to support sustained flight. Adequate blood must course through them if the muscles are to sustain prolonged flight.

200. Do dark leg muscles give a clue to the activity of birds?
Birds that run, walk and scratch habitually have dark leg muscles because of the abundance of blood vessels in them.

201. What kind of bird has the largest breast muscles in proportion to its body? Tiny hummingbirds with their small wings fly with an almost incredible expenditure of effort. Their breast muscles are estimated to be about four times as large, proportionately, as those of a pigeon. (See Question 188.)

BIRD BRAINS

202. Is the slang term "bird brain," indicating a light brain or a brainless person, an apt one? On the contrary, the brain of a bird is very large and heavy in proportion to the weight of its body.

203. Which parts of a bird's brain are most highly developed?
The optic (sight) lobes are highly developed in birds. The section of the brain concerned with hearing is also well developed. The cerebellum, which controls and co-ordinates muscular activities concerned with movement and flight, are particularly well developed.

204. Are any parts of a bird's brain poorly developed? The olfactory lobes, concerned with the sense of smell, as well as those connected with the sense of taste, are poorly developed.

The cerebrum is large in birds but it is fairly smooth and unfissured. This part of the brain is believed to control voluntary thought and reasoning. Therefore, it is believed that birds do little reasoning and that their movements are largely instinctive, not the result of conscious thought.

205. Are birds able to think at all?   Scientists believe most bird behavior is the result of instinctive reaction. Nevertheless, it appears that birds do depart occasionally from the instinctive pattern and act in a way that indicates a certain amount of reasoning. The fact that herring gulls take advantage of cement highways and parking fields when they drop clams on them, thus breaking them open, is frequently cited in this respect. The authors have watched an American egret at Lake Eola in Orlando, Florida, take note of the fact that bread thrown to the ducks attracts fish. The egret repeatedly picked up bread dropped on the shore and put it in the water. It then watched intently until fish nibbled at the bread, whereupon the egret speared the fish.

206. Is there any difference in the brain development of the various orders?   The brain development of birds does not follow the systematic order as originated by man. Under the man-made (American) system, the loons should have the least development of the brain and the sparrows should show the greatest development.

Actually the family of crows, ravens, magpies and jays shows the greatest brain development of any. Next in development is the brain of parrots. The species mentioned also show a very high degree of adaptability and resourcefulness.

207. Aren't the large brains of birds a handicap to creatures in which lightness contributes to ease of flight?   While the brains of birds are large, they are encased in an extremely thin, light skull. Its long axis is almost transverse with the spinal column. Moreover, the brain is crowded to the back of the skull, which aids in the balance of the bird in flight.

208. Are the cranial nerves of a bird as numerous as those of man?   Birds have 12 pairs of cranial nerves, as do mammals. This is the highest number of cranial nerves found in vertebrates.

THE HEARTS OF BIRDS

209. Is the heart of a bird like that of the reptiles from which it evolved?   The heart of a bird shows a definite advance over the heart of a reptile. It is like that of a mammal in that it has four completely separated chambers. These permit a double circulation; that is, the blood flows through the lungs, where it is purified before being circulated through the body again. It is large, thick-walled and powerful, and the beat is rapid.

210. How does the heart of a bird differ from the human heart? The aortic arch which carries pure blood to the body turns to the right in birds but to the left in man and other mammals.

211. What proportion exists between a bird's heart and its body weight? The heart of all birds is proportionally large but this proportion varies with the species. The smaller the bird, the larger is its heart in comparison to its body. It is largest in the hummingbirds. In these smallest of birds the heart varies from 19 to 22 per cent of the total body weight.

212. Is the relation between weight and heart size the same in mammals as in birds? As in birds, the smaller the mammal, the larger is its heart in proportion to its size. But the increase in heart size is infinitely larger in birds than in mammals. In man the heart is but .5 per cent of his weight.

213. Why is a large, powerful heart essential for birds? Their rapid metabolism, high temperatures, rapid heartbeats and ceaseless activity as well as their sudden climbs into the sky or abrupt plunges earthward all make fantastic demands on the heart. The heart must be large and powerful to sustain the pace maintained by birds.

214. Does the blood of a bird differ radically from that of man? While the blood of birds is not significantly richer in hemoglobin than that of mammals, it has more red blood corpuscles per ounce than any other animal in the world. The concentration of sugar in their blood averages about twice as much as in man.

215. What are the phagocytes found in the blood of birds? These are mobile amoeboid cells which are able to leave the blood completely and migrate into the tissues. There they overwhelm microbes, devour dead tissue, help repair injuries and even carry material from one area to another.

216. Is the blood pressure of birds and man alike? The blood pressure of birds is higher than that of normal humans. Using mercury scaled in millimeters, a pigeon will average 145 and a hen 180, while man averages 120.

217. How fast does the heart of a bird normally beat? This varies with different species and also with their activities. However, the larger, more primitive birds, such as loons, pelicans and cormorants, have a slower heartbeat than the quick, active passerine birds such as thrushes, warblers and hummingbirds.

218. How fast does the heart of a chicken beat? About 300 times a minute.

219. Do any birds have a faster heartbeat than the chicken? In comparison to some species of birds, a chicken may be said to have a slow heartbeat. The heart of a black-capped chickadee beats about 400 times a minute when asleep, but about doubles this when active or excited. The heart of a hummingbird beats about 615 times a minute, while that of a sparrow beats about 800 times a minute. A contented canary's heart may beat but 514 times a minute, but if it is excited it may speed up to more than 1,000 beats a minute!

220. Why do birds apparently unhurt often die if picked up after hitting a window? While not seriously injured by the accident, a bird is often so frightened when picked up that it dies of heart failure. Probably the blood vessels, placed under too great a strain, rupture.

HOW BIRDS BREATHE

221. What are the chief organs connected with a bird's respiration? The external and internal nares (the latter opening directly into the pharynx); a slitlike opening, the glottis (leading to the windpipe or trachea); two lungs which are rather small and inelastic; and an amazing system of air sacs are the chief organs of respiration.

On the upper part of the trachea is the larynx but this lacks the vocal cords found in mammals. At the lower end of the trachea is the syrinx or voice box. (See Question 567.)

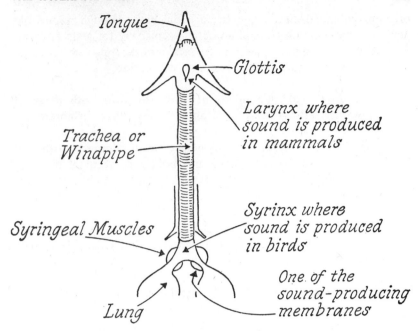

Respiratory and Vocal Organs of a Bird

222. How many air sacs do birds have?   There are five or more pairs of air sacs. These are connected with the lungs and spread throughout the body. Branches from the air sacs extend into the hollow bones, sometimes even reaching into the small toe bones.

223. Of what advantage to the bird are the air sacs?   Not only do the air sacs contribute to the lightness of a bird but they also add to the efficiency of respiration. They play an important part in the cooling system of a bird which has a rapid, hot metabolism.

224. What proportion of air intake by birds is used for cooling? Probably at least half of the air intake is used for cooling a bird. According to estimates, a flying pigeon uses only ¼ of its intake of air for breathing and ¾ for cooling.

225. How does the air move through the sacs?   It is believed that the various connections between the air sacs and the lungs permit the air to circulate in a one-way pattern, so there is a constant stream of clean, unmixed air flowing through the bird. Though nature has never produced in any animal an outlet exclusively for stale air comparable to that of a jet engine, the air sacs in birds approach this ideal more closely than any other vertebrate adaptation.

226. How do the oxygen needs of birds compare with those of other animals?   Birds need more air than any other vertebrate.

227. How does the respiratory system of man compare with that of birds?   In man the lungs make up about 5 per cent of his body volume. In a duck, the respiratory system (lungs and air sacs) make up about 20 per cent of the body volume.

228. Why are the oxygen needs of birds so high?   A combination of high body temperature, rapid metabolism and excessive activity makes heavy oxygen demands in birds.

229. How much of the large air intake is expelled with each breath?   Unlike mammals, which do not completely empty their lungs, birds expel all the air from their lungs with each breath.

230. Is all of the air expelled from the air sacs also with each breath?   Scientists say the pigeon not only expels all the air from its lungs but also from its air sacs, when in flight. Probably this is true for some other species of birds. However, though pigeons expel all air from both their lungs and air sacs in flight, they expel it only from the lungs when at rest.

231. The large air sacs in a bird lend it buoyancy, which is helpful in flight or swimming on the surface. But isn't this buoyancy a handicap when a bird dives?   Dabbling ducks such as mallards and black ducks undoubtedly find the extra air in the air sacs helpful while feeding in shallow water. But ducks that feed on the bottom of deep water, loons, cormorants, grebes and other deep divers are believed to squeeze the air from their feathers and to empty to a considerable degree the air from their lungs and air sacs before diving.

232. How long can diving birds stay under the surface?   Average dives are of short duration, perhaps averaging less than a minute.

However, diving birds not infrequently stay down as much as three minutes.

233. Do birds breathe the same way mammals do? Unlike mammals, the active phase of the breathing cycle is in exhaling, not the inhaling. In flight their wing-strokes compress the rib cage and help expel the air. Birds fly into breath instead of running out of breath.

234. Do birds have a fairly steady rate of breathing? On the contrary, the breathing of birds is most irregular, varying not only with the species but also with individual birds. In each species it varies according to their activity, body temperature and temperature of the air.

235. What are some striking examples of slow breathing? Hummingbirds cannot eat enough during the day to sustain themselves through the night at their daytime rate of metabolism. Therefore at night their breathing becomes so slow that they are almost in a state of hibernation.

236. Does temperature affect the rate of a bird's breathing? If a bird becomes so chilled that its body temperature is lowered, its breathing slows, sometimes dramatically. Under laboratory conditions the temperature of a house wren was lowered to 74 degrees. When this happened, its rate of breathing slowed to 28 times a minute. The same species was subjected to extremely high temperatures and its breathing rate speeded up to a maximum of 350 times a minute.

237. Of what value to a bird is the change of breathing rate according to temperature? By slowing its breathing a bird can conserve body heat. By breathing rapidly in high temperatures, a bird pumps fresh, cool air through its system, which prevents its body from becoming overheated. Moreover, water vapor passes into the air sacs from the blood and is quickly discharged.

238. Is the average breathing rate under different conditions known for any species? Common pigeons are often the subject of scientific inquiry. It has been learned that pigeons breathe 450 times a minute in flight, slow to 180 breaths a minute while walking, and at rest breathe but 29 times a minute.

HOW BIRDS DIGEST THEIR FOOD

239. In what way does the digestive system of birds assist them as creatures of flight? Foods of high protein content and easily digested foods are demanded by birds. These are digested with great rapidity and efficiency. (See Question 273.)

240. Do birds utilize the food efficiently? In growing birds about 33 per cent of the food intake is utilized. The average growing mammal can utilize only about 10 per cent of its intake of food.

241. How does the mouth of a bird differ from that of mammals? The bill of a bird, corresponding roughly to mammal lips, is hard and dry. In no living bird are teeth present.

242. How can the digestion of a bird work efficiently without teeth? Substituting for teeth is a powerful gizzard which grinds food when necessary. The gizzard is located near the bird's center of gravity.

243. Is it an advantage to a bird not to need teeth? Lack of teeth eliminates the need for heavy jaws and jaw muscles. This helps to lighten a bird's head, which is a definite advantage in flight. The skull of a pigeon weighs only $\frac{1}{5}$ of 1 per cent of its body weight. A comparable proportion exists between the skull and body weight of most birds of flight.

244. Do birds have glands in their mouths similar to those of mammals? In general, saliva glands, mucus glands and taste buds are largely absent or poorly developed. There are some striking exceptions to this generality, however. The gluelike saliva on the tongue of insect-eating woodpeckers assists them in gathering food, if not in digesting it. The nests of swiftlets (see Question 657) are formed from the saliva of these birds.

245. Is there a reason for the brilliant colors lining the mouths of many species of birds? The bright colors in the mouths of young birds assist in their feeding by guiding the parent birds. Usually brilliant colors in the mouths of adult birds play a part in courtship ceremonies. Black guillemots, cormorants and mergansers are among the birds that open their bills to display the colors within when courting.

246. Do the tongues of birds differ from those of mammals? The tongues of many species of birds are extremely specialized for the acquisition of their particular kind of food. Therefore there is much more variation in the design of the tongue among birds than among mammals.

247. What are some of the remarkable adaptations among the tongues of birds? The tongue in some woodpeckers is rather like a fishhook. In some species the tip is hard and needlelike with barbed hooks at the sides. The tongue may be as much as five times as long as the bill. At the back, the tongue divides into two cartilaginous processes. When the long tongue is drawn in, these processes lie around the cranium. In certain species the processes come together again on the forehead and eventually end in one of the nostrils, in which case the tongue is compressed like an accordion when drawn inside the bill. As mentioned before, the tongues of some woodpeckers, particularly those that feed often in ant hills, are as sticky as the tongues of anteaters.

The tongue of some species of hummingbirds is grooved or tubelike for ease in obtaining nectar. The tip is fringed and in this respect it resembles the tongue of bees and butterflies. Lories (members of the parrot family) which eat nectar, and keas, which lap blood from mammals, also have brushlike growths on the tip of the tongue.

The tongues of most parrots are delicate organs of touch and with them the birds daintily pick up food. It is thought that their tongues are of value in making the many sounds which parrots are capable of producing.

The tongues of most waterfowl (except mergansers) are thick, fleshy, and fringed along the sides for sifting fine bits of food from the ooze on the bottom.

248. What lies between the mouth of a bird and its stomach? The esophagus.

249. What is the crop and where is it?   The crop is an enlargement on the side of the esophagus about halfway between the mouth
and the stomach. This is largely a storage place for birds that must
have a large amount of food daily, yet have stomachs too small to
digest rapidly the food required to maintain life. The crop is not
present in all species of birds. It is of great importance to those
species which have set periods of feeding instead of feeding quite
continuously, as swallows do. The crop is not a digestive organ,
though a certain amount of saliva from the mouth follows the food
into the crop and may help to soften it.

250. How does the crop help birds with their feeding problems?
The crop enables birds such as grouse, bobwhites and other members
of the gallinaceous family which prefer to feed heavily twice daily
to collect quantities of food, store it, and then pass it gradually into
the stomach for digestion while sleeping or resting.

   Birds which regurgitate food for their young (pelicans, herons,
waxwings, goldfinches and so on) often carry food for considerable
distances in the crop or distended esophagus.

251. What is "pigeon milk"?   Degeneration of the cells which
line the crop produces in pigeons (and some species of parrots) a
thick, cheesy secretion called "pigeon milk." On this the young birds
are fed until they are old enough to eat the seed diet of the adults.

252. Does only the female pigeon produce this "milk"?   Both
the male and female produce the milk during the breeding season.
It is extremely rich, containing about 35 per cent fat. The milk of
most cows seldom has more than 5 per cent fat content.

253. Do birds that eat chiefly insects have a crop?   The esophagus
of insect-eating birds is capable of considerable distention. If an
unusually large concentration of insects is discovered, advantage is
taken of the situation and the prey may be held in the esophagus for
leisurely digestion. However, insect-eaters feed almost continuously
throughout the day and thus do not need, generally, to store food
as do birds that feed less frequently.

**254. Hawks and owls that often feed on rather large mammals
cannot catch them very frequently. How do they handle their food**

needs? Vultures sometimes fill their crops so full of carrion that they cannot rise from the ground for some time after feeding. The crops of caracaras become so filled when the birds gorge themselves that they hang over the chest like stuffed pockets. Hawks fill their crops with all the food they can get, for they may not make another catch for hours or even a day or more. Owls sometimes swallow so many mice or rats that the crop cannot hold them all and the tail of the last one may hang out of the bill until some of the first swallowed have been digested. In all of these birds the food is passed gradually from the crop into the stomach for digestion, thus maintaining the flow of food needed for their high rate of metabolism.

255. Is the stomach formed like a pouch as in mammals? The stomach may be a simple sac but more often it is two-chambered. It is most often hard and rather lens-shaped as if two millstones lay one on top of the other. The first chamber is called the proventriculus. This is fairly soft and glandular. Here the gastric juices are secreted and the breakdown of the food begins.

The second part of the stomach is known as the gizzard. This is very thick-walled and muscular. The thick, ridged and horny grinding surface is usually assisted by pebbles or sand grains in breaking down food.

256. Are the stomachs of all birds quite alike? As there is variation in the crops, so is there variation in the stomachs of birds. Birds that eat very hard foods usually have large gizzards. Birds that eat largely insect food or soft fruits do not need a powerful gizzard. In them the first part of the stomach is of the greatest importance. Flesh-eaters have much less need for a gizzard than do seed-eaters and they usually have glands scattered over the entire stomach. In them much of the breaking down of food is by chemical and bacterial action.

In some birds there is a seasonal change in the stomach. Herring gulls have a hard stomach in summer when they eat much fruit and grain, and a soft one in winter when their chief food is fish. A similar change occurs in the stomachs of other species which consistently eat one type of food part of the year and then change to another kind of food at another season.

257. Do any birds lack a stomach (both the proventriculus and gizzard)? Some of the fruit-eating birds of the tropics have a nearly straight digestive tube with almost no distinctive features. Digestive processes are carried on quite continuously throughout the tube.

258. Is the sand or gravel in a bird's gizzard essential to the grinding up of the food? About this there is considerable controversy. Whether or not the gravel is essential, it probably does help to grind the food. Moreover, it may add important minerals such as phosphorus and calcium to the diet of birds.

259. Is the gravel swallowed accidentally or deliberately? Seed-eating birds apparently swallow gravel deliberately. Shorebirds and other species that probe in the earth or in ant hills may swallow much of the grit accidentally.

260. Aside from the addition of gravel, does the gizzard ever have strange characteristics? Anhinga gizzards have hairlike processes which form a sieve that prevents fish bones from passing into the small intestine. Some of the tropical fruit-eating pigeons have many hard conelike projections on the lining of the gizzard. Perhaps the strangest of all adaptations of the gizzard is found in the male hornbill. Before passing food to the imprisoned female, the male wraps it in a tough skin secreted by his gizzard walls.

261. Are the gizzard walls comparable in strength to the teeth of mammals in grinding power? The walls of a seed-eater's gizzard are so strong that they can bend a steel needle without being perforated. Moreover, a turkey gizzard can crush a whole walnut and that of a hen can crush a hazelnut.

262. What digestive step follows that taking place in the stomach? From the gizzard the food enters the small intestine, where digestion is consummated. Bile from the liver and pancreatic enzymes are added to complete digestion.

263. Is the small intestine of all birds alike? Animal-eating birds have fairly short, coiled small intestines. Vegetable-eaters, as well as those that eat both animal and vegetable food, have longer, looped small intestines.

264. What bird has the longest small intestine? Probably the ostrich, which eats little but vegetable matter. Its small intestine is 46 feet long.

265. What bird has the shortest small intestine? The ruby-throated hummingbird, which eats insects, spiders and nectar, has a small intestine only two inches long. If any species of bird has a shorter one, it is doubtless one of the smaller relatives of this tiny bird.

266. What is the final stage in the digestive system of a bird? In both vegetable and animal feeders, the food is well digested by the time it reaches the large intestine. Efficient utilization of the food results in a minimum of waste and indigestible matter. In all species of birds, the large intestine is markedly reduced in comparison to that of mammals. Frequently it is but an inch long.

267. Aside from the small residue left after digestion, how have birds further reduced the function of the large intestine? Hawks and owls form pellets in the fore part of the stomach. Fur, teeth, bones and feathers are formed into hard balls and ejected through the mouth. Gulls often eject pellets of fish bones and scales in the same manner.

Crows, jays, thrushes and grosbeaks often spit out the husks of seeds and the pits of small fruits instead of passing them through the intestine.

268. How often are pellets formed? This depends on the species of bird. Owls usually regurgitate pellets, perhaps as many as three or four, once a day. Hawks, which tear their food apart, do not swallow as much indigestible material that cannot be passed through the small intestine. Therefore they may not eject a pellet for several days in a row. Passerine birds that eat hard insects pass the chitinous material as pellets either after each meal or several times daily.

269. Why is the regurgitation of pellets necessary? Only small, soft material can pass through the small intestine of a bird. Therefore coarse or bulky material must be regurgitated. An exception to this rule is found among fruit-eating birds which are able to pass the seeds and stones of berries and fruits through their entire digestive system.

270. Why are pellets of interest to scientists? Bird pellets, being formed from the food eaten, are valuable in studying the food habits of birds. This is particularly true with owls, since all of their food is swallowed whole and the bulky parts are regurgitated. By collecting all of the pellets regurgitated by an owl it is possible not only to tell what it ate but how much it ate.

271. Has the trait of passing seeds unharmed through the digestive tract had any effect on vegetation? Many seeds and small fruits are widely disseminated by birds. It might almost be said that the sweet coating on the seeds of berries and fruit were developed so birds would scatter the germs of new plant life for those species without winged or hooked seeds.

272. Does the large intestine (or rectum) of a bird have any function not demanded of that organ by mammals? Among birds the only outlet from the body is the cloaca at the end of the large intestine or rectum. Not only does it excrete waste from the digestive tract, but from the kidneys also. In contrast to mammals, there is little water content in birds and most of the urine is made up of slightly soluble white uric acid. The reproductive organs of both male and female birds open at the cloaca.

The large intestine of birds is very short. Often this is no more than an inch in length.

273. How long does digestion require? This varies with the species and the food it eats. It is most rapid among passerine birds. Fruit in particular is digested rapidly. The stone of a cherry may be excreted by a robin 20 minutes after it is swallowed.

274. Is there any reason why birds should digest food so rapidly? Their high body temperatures can be maintained only by constant replenishment of their food supply. Food is the fuel which enables them to maintain their swift, intense way of life.

METABOLISM AND TEMPERATURE

275. How does the metabolism of a bird compare with that of mammals? All birds have a high rate of metabolism. Probably some of the smallest hummingbirds have the highest rate of metabolism of any creatures. An Allen's hummingbird, by no means the smallest species, uses about 80 cubic centimeters of oxygen per gram of body weight per hour when hovering. Even when it rests, its metabolic rate is more than 50 times as fast as that of man.

276. How do birds support this high metabolic rate? By eating enormous quantities of food. Even the food that birds select conserves weight. Their foods are high in calories and rich in energy. Robins are said to eat as much as 14 feet of earthworms in a single day. Most young passerine birds eat their weight in food daily and many adult birds eat almost as much.

277. Does the high rate of metabolism result in high body temperature? Birds have evolved the highest operating temperatures of any animal. Birds live at such an intense rate that most songbirds survive less than two years.

278. What body temperatures result from this intense living? Sparrows average about 107 degrees, while some thrushes have a temperature as high as 113 degrees Fahrenheit.

279. Are temperatures higher among the higher orders of birds than among the lower orders? Ostriches, which belong to the order now at the foot of the evolutionary ladder, have a temperature of 104 degrees, while the kiwi, on the fourth step, has a temperature of only 100 degrees. However, the highest temperatures found among birds are in the passerine group at the top of the ladder of evolution.

280. Do arctic birds have a lower temperature than those that live in the tropics? The temperatures of birds do not appear to be affected by either arctic cold or equatorial heat. The lowest temperatures are found among the more primitive birds. Passerine birds have the highest temperatures, whether they live in the tropics or the arctic.

281. Are birds able to endure as great cold as mammals? Penguins, snow petrels and arctic terns are able to live nearer the poles than any mammal. To be sure, at the present time man has established outposts near both poles but he survives there only because his supplies are brought from warmer climates.

282. Do birds perspire when it is hot? Birds have no sweat glands in their skin. Heat and water are "perspired" into the air sacs, carried to the lungs and discharged through the nose or mouth. When birds are very hot, they open their mouths and breathe fast to provide an escape for excess heat.

283. Have birds any other means of cooling themselves in hot weather? Birds usually look thinner in hot weather than in cold because they hold their feathers close to the body, pressing out the insulating air and permitting body heat to dissipate.

284. How do birds protect themselves against cold? Plenty of food that can be turned into body heat is the first requirement. In cold weather birds fluff their feathers until their bulk is almost trebled. This insulates them against the cold and at the same time prevents the loss of body heat.

285. How often must young birds be fed in order to maintain their rapid growth and high metabolism? The frequency of feeding increases with the age of the nestlings. Among primitive birds the intervals are longer between feedings than among the most highly developed birds. For instance, a grebe may be fed only five to ten times an hour while sparrows, chickadees and wrens may be fed from 30 to 70 times or more an hour. (See Question 124.)

286. Is the high state of metabolism constant among birds? A few years ago in California a poorwill (a member of the goatsucker family) was discovered in a state of hibernation. It was repeatedly visited by scientists while in this torpid state. Its breathing was scarcely measureable. However, such isolated instances of bird hibernation in no way revive the ancient belief in mass hibernation of birds. (See Question 118.)

287. In recent years newspapers have had accounts of torpid, sleeping swallows being flown across the Alps, then released in a warmer climate. Were these birds hibernating? When swallows, dependent on flying insects for food, are caught by a cold snap that kills their food, they cluster by the hundreds in holes, caves or hollow trees where they sleep pressed close together to conserve body heat. If the cold lasts long they die from lack of food. In recent years cold snaps have overtaken swallows several times. Then these birds were gathered up, flown by planes to warmer places across the Alps and released where ample food was available. The torpid swallows were not hibernating but their life processes were retarded and their reactions became slow and labored.

THE UROGENITAL SYSTEM OF BIRDS

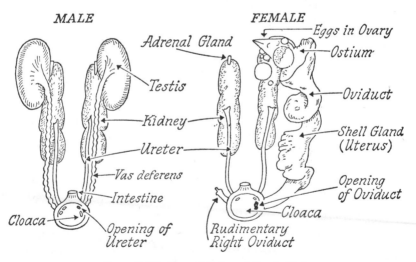

Urogenital Systems of Male and Female Birds

288. What do the kidneys of birds consist of? Each of the two kidneys is three-lobed and each lobe in turn is subdivided into smaller lobes. They are made up of a most complicated mass of circulatory vessels that are divided into innumerable smaller vessels, capsules and tubules. These number from about 30,000 in passerine birds to 200,000 in domestic fowls. Birds usually have almost twice the number found in mammals of comparative size.

289. Why is such a complicated set of kidneys required in birds? Birds have an almost perfect system for purifying and using again their body liquids. The kidneys regulate the salts and liquids in the body. The kidneys discharge the uric acid in a nearly solid form of whitish guano together with the solids from the digestive tract.

290. Since birds have no bladder, what happens to the water content filtered from body wastes? This is almost completely reabsorbed through the walls of the cloaca. It is this system of reabsorption of the water which gives birds an almost perfect system of water usage and conservation.

291. Drinking of ocean water is fatal to thirsty sailors. How do oceanic birds survive for long periods of time far from fresh water? It is believed that some oceanic birds, because of the efficiency of their kidneys, can drink salt water without harm. However, because of this efficiency, which permits reuse of water filtered and purified by the kidneys, it is possible that oceanic birds seldom need to drink. Certain land birds, such as the red crossbill, have been seen drinking from oceanic tide pools. In spite of the efficiency of the kidneys of birds and the belief that at least some species are able to drink salt water without harm, too much salt in their diet will kill most land birds.

292. When do birds reach breeding age? Most passerine birds arrive at a breeding condition in the first spring before they are a year old. Some large birds such as game birds, herons and a few species of hawks also breed in their first year. One exception to this among passerine birds is the crow, which does not begin breeding until the second year. This is true of most of the small gulls and peregrine falcons.

Large gulls such as the herring gull and great black-backed gull do not breed until their third or fourth year. Some bald eagles do not breed until their fifth year. Thus it is apparent that there is considerable variation in the age of first breeding among birds.

293. What are the female organs or ovaries of a bird like? Birds usually have two ovaries, but among most species only the left one develops. In many species the right ovary has shrunk until it is difficult to find, while in a few species it has disappeared altogether. The ovaries of hawks and owls are usually paired and show nearly equal development. Each appears capable of producing eggs or ova.

294. Can birds lay unfertilized eggs? Domestic fowl frequently lay unfertilized eggs. Among wild birds this happens but rarely, for not only do the reproductive organs of both male and female develop at the same time of year but most females can find a mate.

295. What happens to the egg or ovum as it develops? The egg begins development within a follicle. When released from the follicle, the egg passes from the ovary into the oviduct. There it is fertilized if this is to take place. Next the egg, which is mainly yolk, receives a thick covering of albumin from glands in the middle part of the oviduct.

In the lower part of the uterus the shell gland adds a shell. If the bird lays colored eggs, the pigment is added at this place. The egg is then ready to be laid.

296. Once an egg has started on its journey from the ovary, how long before it will be laid? From the time the egg is released from its follicle it is about 4½ hours until it reaches the uterus of a domestic hen. It remains in the uterus about 18 to 20 hours. The pigment is added during the last five hours of its stay in the uterus. The egg is pushed from the uterus through the vagina, into the cloaca and out of the anus. It is not held any length of time in these final areas.

297. Is there a seasonal change in the ovaries? When the breeding or reproductive season approaches, the ovaries become greatly swollen and enlarged. After this season has ended, the ovaries shrink until they are so small it is almost impossible to detect them. This is another instance of the efficiency of a bird's body. When the ovaries are not in use, they do not add weight to these creatures of the air.

298. How many ova does a single bird produce? Few studies of wild birds have been made, but in one ovary of a domestic hen 1,906 ova have been counted with the naked eye and 12,000 more under a microscope. Each ovum or egg develops within a follicle of its own.

299. Does the presence of so many ova mean that a single hen may lay nearly 14,000 eggs? By no means do all of the ova produced by the ovaries grow into fully developed eggs. Wild birds appear to have some control over the number of eggs which develop. While many species of birds lay a certain number of eggs in a clutch, should the clutch be destroyed, a new one would be laid promptly.

300. Must copulation take place to fertilize each egg? The copulation to fertilize the first egg usually takes place but a few days before it is laid. This may be repeated several times. However, sperms can remain alive for a long time in the body of the female so a single mating may fertilize several eggs. Domestic hens have laid fertile eggs as much as a month after the cock has been removed from the chicken yard.

301. What do the male reproductive organs consist of? The chief reproductive organs of the male bird are two oval (or ellipsoid) whitish organs lying near the front end of the kidneys. These are called testes. From them extend coiled tubes which take the sperm produced by the testes to the cloaca. In many birds the enlarged end of these tubes forms a temporary storage place for sperm before breeding.

302. Do birds have a penis? Some species of birds have a protuberance resembling a penis. Ducks, which frequently mate under water, have this, as do kiwis, ostriches and their relatives, and members of the order of cassowaries. A trace of the structure is found in herons and flamingos.

303. How do birds without a penislike structure fertilize the eggs? By direct contact between the cloacae of the two sexes.

304. Is there a seasonal change in the reproductive organs of the male?   The testes of the male enlarge several hundred times during the breeding season and then shrink or regress to such an extent that they are scarcely the size of a pinhead. Because of this regression of the sex organs of both male and female after the breeding season, it is almost impossible to detect the sex of such birds in autumn and winter if they have similar plumage.

305. What causes the spectacular enlargement of the sex organs of birds for the breeding season?   It is believed by many scientists that the factors which bring both male and female birds to a synchronized sexual cycle at the time of year when their reproductive efforts are most likely to be successful involves a number of factors. Of these factors, at present it is believed that light, temperature and food are the most important. As the length of days grows, temperature rises and food becomes more abundant, there appears to be a corresponding growth in the gonads of birds. But before any satisfactory answer can be given a great deal of research is required.

306. Why are some scientists hesitant about accepting light, temperature and food as the chief factors causing the annual growth of the gonads of birds?   Emperor penguins begin breeding in the darkness of midwinter in the antarctic. Many species of birds in the tropics breed irregularly through the year. Some species apparently are influenced by the end of the rainy season. In Florida, brown pelicans have nested almost every month of the year. In the northern United States and Canada, evidence of breeding by red crossbills has been noted every month of the year except November and December. Other exceptions also to the rule of gonad growth which links it to the growing heat, light and increased food supply of advancing spring cause scientists to use caution in attributing the physical changes in the sexual organs of birds to these factors.

VI. THE EXTERIOR OF BIRDS

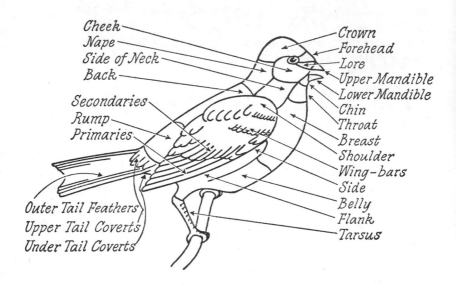

Cheek
Nape
Side of Neck
Back
Secondaries
Rump
Primaries
Outer Tail Feathers
Upper Tail Coverts
Under Tail Coverts

Crown
Forehead
Lore
Upper Mandible
Lower Mandible
Chin
Throat
Breast
Shoulder
Wing-bars
Side
Belly
Flank
Tarsus

FEATHERS

307. In what way are birds unlike any other member of the animal kingdom? Of all forms of animal life on this earth, birds and only birds have feathers. All birds possess them.

308. What is the evolutionary story behind the development of feathers? It is believed that the feathers of birds evolved from reptilian scales during the Mesozoic era. This may have occurred when the scales, which in some species of reptiles were long and fairly loose, frayed. The scales on the legs of birds and their feathers are both formed from similar germ buds. The same germ buds that develop into scales on the legs of a Leghorn chicken, on a ptarmigan develop as feathers.

309. What organ of a bird produces the feathers? The skin of a bird produces the feathers.

310. How are the feathers formed? A dermal papilla is pushed up by the epidermis. Its outer layer forms the feather's sheath. The inside cells form the feather itself. The base of the feather is imbedded in a feather follicle from which a new feather will grow when the old one is molted.

311. From an engineering standpoint, what are the chief characteristics of a feather? A feather is the most complex growth of the skin known to be formed by any animal. It is one of the lightest and at the same time one of the strongest materials formed by any creature. It is durable, complex and flexible, a superb functional structure for both flight and heat retention.

312. How many feathers does a bird have? The number of feathers a bird has usually increases with its size. Summer counts on a hummingbird indicate that it has about 1,500 feathers at that period. A robin has almost 3,000 feathers while a whistling swan has more than 25,000.

313. Do birds wear about the same number of feathers both summer and winter? Counts of feathers have shown that birds have the fewest feathers just before their molt, which follows the breeding season. Their plumage is most dense during the winter. An American goldfinch has about a thousand more feathers in winter than in summer just before its postnuptial molt.

314. Are feathers evenly spaced on a bird? If the feathers of most birds are parted, bare areas will be discovered beneath. The feathers grow in particular areas called feather tracts.

315. Where are the feather tracts located? These may be seen most easily on newly hatched birds. Where the natal down grows, feathers will eventually appear. There are eight feather tracts and usually an equal number of bare skin areas. The following diagram indicates the position and name of the feather tracts.

316. Is a knowledge of the feather tracts of value to the student? If a student knows the position of the feather tracts, he can make

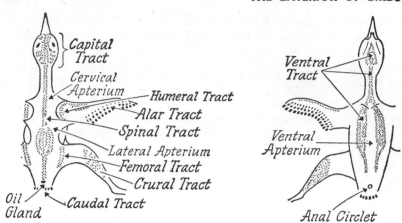

Diagram of Feather Tracts

better study skins than would otherwise be possible. Knowing the location of the bare areas, or apteria, he can make his incisions without disturbing the feathers.

317. Do all birds have feather tracts and bare skin areas? Some primitive birds such as penguins and kiwis do not have feather tracts but are covered with a fairly uniform growth of feathers. Among some of the ducks, particularly the northern sea ducks such as eiders, the skin is completely covered with down.

318. What are the parts of a feather? Note the diagram on the facing page.

319. How many individual parts does a feather have? The parts of a single feather add up to more than a million individual units, many of them so small they can only be seen with the help of a microscope. These parts interlock to form an extremely strong, light plane of great flexibility.

320. What happens if the parts of a feather separate? It is easy to separate the barbs on a feather with the fingers and of course this happens in nature. When a feather needs attention, the bird repairs the separation by drawing the feather through its bill. This repair work is part of the preening process.

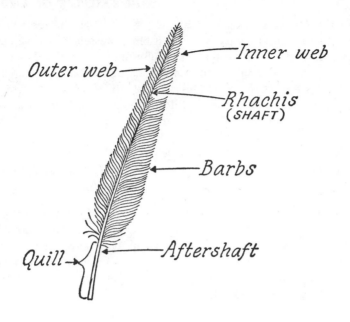

Inner web

Outer web

Rhachis
(SHAFT)

Barbs

Quill

Aftershaft

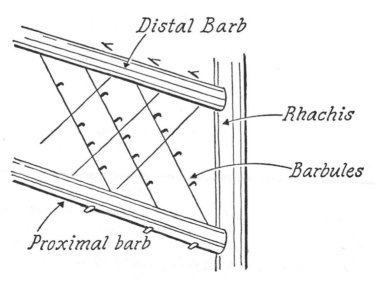

Distal Barb

Rhachis

Barbules

Proximal barb

Nomenclature of a Feather

321. Are the feathers on a bird alive? As long as the feather is growing, its soft central cavity is fed with blood vessels which supply pigments and food. Once the feather is fully mature, that is, has lost all of its sheath and is fully expanded, it hardens, the food supply is cut off, and the whole structure is made up of dead epidermis. The feather may then be considered dead, though it continues to be firmly clasped by the feather follicle until the next molt.

322. What are pinfeathers? When a new feather, completely encased in its sheath, pushes its way above the follicle, it is called a pinfeather.

323. What are the most important feathers? The most important and also the most numerous feathers are called *contour* feathers. These feathers cover the body, wings and tail. They have a stiff shaft and vane. They are divided into three groups: the general body feathers; the wing or flight feathers called remiges, which in turn are divided into primaries, secondaries and tertials; and finally the tail feathers or rectrices.

324. What are the chief functions of the contour feathers? The contour feathers protect the birds from cold and help to keep them cool on hot days. They act as padding for the tender skin. The remiges and rectrices are the chief instruments of bird flight. Many contour feathers have become modified for decoration. Among these are the topknot feathers of such birds as cedar waxwings and blue jays, the bobbing plumes on the heads of Gambel's quail, the bright flash patches on the crowns of ruby-crowned and golden-crowned kinglets and eastern kingbirds, the spectacular feathers used in display by the male European ruffs, and the delicate crests on the heads of the crowned cranes of Africa.

325. How can the contour feathers both warm and cool birds? Feathers are one of the best insulation materials in the world. By fluffing their feathers, birds can trap air, thus keeping out the cold. When heat is intense, birds hold their feathers tight against the body, squeezing out the air usually trapped there and in this way permit the escape of body heat.

326. Are such spectacular feathers as the tail coverts of a peacock and the dainty plumes of a snowy egret considered part of the

contour feathers? It is believed that both the tail coverts of the peacock and the plumes of snowy Egrets are modified contour feathers. However, certain spectacular breeding-time decorations may be modified filoplumes. The decorations of birds of paradise may be the latter type of feather.

327. What are filoplumes? Filoplumes are small, very slender, hairlike feathers usually scattered sparsely over a bird's body. Most of these have a slender shaft without barbs though there is a tiny tuft of delicate barbs and barbules at the tip. In some birds such as goatsuckers and flycatchers, these are believed to have developed into the strong, stiff bristles about the bill, where they are called rictal bristles. The bearded barbet of West Africa has particularly long, numerous rictal bristles. The hairlike growths which the housewife singes from a chicken are filoplumes. They are the closest thing a bird has to hairs.

328. What are down feathers? These are soft feathers without a shaft and having barbs that are but soft fluffy tufts. They are extremely strong and resilient. They provide the covering of many newly-hatched birds, particularly those of the precocial group. Some species of birds as adults have a down undercoating beneath their contour feathers. Ducks and geese have such an undercoating.

329. What are powder-down feathers? These scarcely seem like feathers at all. They form a powdery substance on some areas of the skin of such birds as herons and bitterns. These birds rub their bills in the powder-down feathers and spread the resulting powder over their plumage, giving it a "bloom" which rubs off when the bird is handled.

330. What are the various stages of plumage in a bird? The first stage of the plumage is natal down which appears on a bird upon hatching. In precocial birds this forms a dense covering, while in altricial birds it is sparse and grows only on the feather tracts. This is lost by the postnatal molt.

Juvenile plumage develops next and is lost by the postjuvenile molt.

The first winter plumage follows the juvenile plumage and is lost in the first prenuptial molt.

The first nuptial plumage appears at different stages with the various species. Most passerine birds develop nuptial plumage during the spring following their hatching. Gulls require three and sometimes four years to develop full nuptial plumage. Once a bird has developed nuptial or breeding plumage, it is repeated annually. The first nuptial plumage is lost in the first postnuptial molt. Thereafter, these form an annual sequence.

331. What is meant by the molt?   All birds periodically shed their old plumage and replace it with new. This periodic shedding is known as the molt.

332. How often do birds molt their feathers?   This varies with different orders and families. The typical molts of passerine birds are given above. Usually four plumages and molts occur in the first year. When birds do not arrive at full nuptial plumage at the end of their first year, second, third, fourth and even fifth winter plumages may reveal the age of a bird to the scientist. A bald eagle may take from three to five years to assume the pure white head of a fully mature bird.

333. Among nonbreeding birds, what is the spring plumage called?   The spring plumage of a bird is called the nuptial plumage, whether the bird is breeding or not.

334. Do any birds lack natal down when they hatch?   Kingfishers, hummingbirds and woodpeckers are among the birds which are completely naked when they hatch. Usually they skip the down stage altogether and go directly into the juvenile plumage.

Cormorants, gannets and boobies are among the species that offer a decided contrast to the above-mentioned birds. They are born completely naked but soon become covered with a dense coat of down.

335. Do any species of birds skip both a naked and a downy stage?   Some of the megapodes of the Australasian area pass through the

down stage within the egg and when they break out of the shell they
are covered with juvenile plumage.

336. Do all birds molt annually?   Almost all birds have at least
one molt annually. This usually takes place soon after the nesting
season has ended. At this time, some water birds such as ducks, coots
and rails lose so many feathers at one time that they cannot fly and
must escape enemies by rapid swimming, diving or hiding. Other
species such as gulls and crows lose but a feather or two on each
wing and on each side of the tail at once and thus retain their powers
of flight. However, their flight may not be as powerful and expert as
is normal with the species. Hawks, flycatchers and other species of
birds that secure their food by pursuit on the wing all lose but one
feather at a time from each side and thus are able to maintain powerful flight during the molt.

Some birds have a second molt that may be quite complete or
only partial. This comes in the spring just before the breeding season.
Among the birds that have a partial spring molt are bobolinks, goldfinches, scarlet tanagers and indigo buntings.

**337. If brightly colored songbirds which have dull winter coats do
not have complete feather replacement during the prenuptial molt,
how do they obtain their vivid colors?**   Strangely enough, many
species of these birds have their brilliant nuptial colors long before
they are visible to the eye. Neutral gray or brown tips may break
off or wear away, thus revealing the bright nuptial colors. Because
of this, though a prenuptial molt may be partial, the entire plumage
of the bird appears bright and new.

**338. Do any mature birds regularly have more than two annual
molts?**   A few species of birds have a third or triple molt annually.
Ptarmigan shed their feathers in the usual postnuptial molt, then have
another molt in late autumn when they assume their white winter
dress. In spring they molt completely when they acquire their nuptial
plumage.

339. How long do birds keep their juvenile plumage?   Few
passerine birds keep their juvenile plumage longer than two months,
though young swallows retain it during their migration. Hawks and

herons keep their juvenile plumage for a whole year. Because the new plumage develops very slowly and the final colors appear gradually, it is sometimes difficult to decide whether these birds are in their second or third plumage.

340. Does the molt affect birds except in their flight and color? To replace the great number of contour feathers, a bird requires far more energy than is generally realized. So much energy is required for this body activity that a bird must devote most of its life processes toward the replacement of its molted plumage. Song and fighting stop. Display is forgotten during this period following the nesting activities. Often the sexes separate. Birds are seldom seen because they are so quiet. Because they are neither vocal nor active physically, we overlook them. They skulk and hide. Once the molted plumage has been replaced, there is often a resurgence of vitality and some birds sing with almost springlike energy.

341. How long does molting take?   The molting period varies with each species. August is the month when most North American birds molt. With most species this is gradual, with the feathers molted in an orderly manner. It usually begins with the innermost primary feather and proceeds in a regular sequence until every feather on the entire body has been replaced. This usually takes several weeks or more. A coot requires about four weeks to molt and replace its flight feathers. During that period it cannot fly. Few studies of molting have been made so it is not known how long it takes birds to complete the molt.

342. What is meant by eclipse plumage?   This plumage is peculiar to the drakes of Northern Hemisphere ducks. They have a postnuptial molt in May or June, at which time they develop their fall or winter plumage. This is called the eclipse plumage. It is replaced in the autumn or early winter by the nuptial plumage. Thus most northern ducks spend but a short period of time wearing the eclipse or winter plumage, for they acquire their breeding plumage long before the season for nesting arrives. Though female ducks retain the same plumage pattern throughout the year, they molt their flight feathers all at once, so, like the drakes going into eclipse plumage, they are unable to fly until new primaries replace the fallen ones.

343. If a bird accidentally loses some of its feathers soon after new ones have grown, must it wait for the rejuvenation following the next molt? If feathers are pulled out, they are replaced quite soon. Sometimes the primaries of captured birds are pulled to prevent them from flying. Within a few weeks, those primaries are replaced and the birds can then fly in a normal manner. However, if a feather is broken with the base left in the follicle, it usually is not replaced until the next molt.

344. What proportion of the body weight of a bird is made up of feathers? This varies widely. The heavier the frame of the bird, the smaller is the proportion of feather weight to the total mass. Feathers make up almost a quarter of the total weight of frigate-birds, which have the lightest skeleton in proportion to wing expanse of any birds in the world. (See Question 182.)

345. Do big birds or small ones have more feathers in relation to their size? Small birds have more feathers in proportion to their body weight than do big birds. A whistling swan weighs about 2,000 times as much as a hummingbird, yet it has but about 25 times as many feathers as the smaller bird.

346. What causes the varied colors found in feathers? The riot of color found in birds is due to two different factors. Some are made by pigments of actual color but these are relatively few in number.

A greater proportion of color and pattern result from the reflection and diffraction of light due to the structure of the feathers. This type of color is influenced, of course, by the underlying pigments.

347. What are the pigments found in the plumage of birds? These are of two types. Carotenoids are oil pigments which produce animal red and animal yellow.

The second type of pigment is called melanin and appears in black, dull browns of all shades from reddish brown to dull yellow, and the almost colorless tones. These colors are granular and are soluble in acid. Combinations of these pigments not only produce different colors but a single pigment such as animal red may appear as the vivid color of a scarlet tanager or be diluted almost to the point of disappearance as in the chest and rump of a hoary redpoll.

348. What pigment colors are rare among birds?   There is no known blue caused by pigment in feathers. Green and violet caused by pigmentation are very rare.

349. Blue is a common color among birds and green is not rare. How is the presence of these colors explained?   To understand the presence of these colors in birds it must be remembered that apparently colorless light falling on a prism is broken into rainbow colors.

When light falls on the plumage of birds, the feather structure causes it to break apart. Some of the colors are absorbed while others are reflected. Absorption or reflection depends on the structure of the cells on which the light falls. The reflected color is also affected by the pigmentation of the feathers.

350. What is meant by "foxing," a term often used in reference to museum bird skins?   Museum bird skins are kept in dustproof and lightproof metal cases so it is clear that change in the colors of the feathers is not caused by light. Scientists believe that as the museum bird skins age, the pigment changes. Perhaps this is a form of oxidation. Because there are so many brown or brownish birds and most of these change to a fox or russet color, the change is called foxing. However, a color change not due to fading by light occurs not just in the brownish birds. Greenish birds tend to become more olive; yellows, salmons and cinnamons become whitish. The older a skin is, the less its colors agree with those of the living bird.

351. Have the colors of their feathers any value to birds?   The colors must have a survival value to birds, not only in regard to the individual but for the race as well. Many birds are colored so they match their surroundings. This is particularly true of birds that nest in the open. If both sexes incubate the eggs, they usually look alike if their nest is in the open and on the ground. Often if the sexes differ radically yet both incubate the eggs, as in the rose-breasted grosbeak, the nest is usually well concealed. Frequently among species where the male is gorgeously colored, he takes no part in incubation and perhaps does not even help care for the young.

352. Are any female birds more brightly colored than the male?
Female belted kingfishers and the females of all species of phalaropes are more brightly colored than the males.

353. Does the reversal of bright plumage in the sexes affect their behavior? If the female is more brightly colored than the male she is likely to take the initiative in courtship. The male may build the nest, incubate the eggs and care for the young with little or no help from the female. This is particularly true among phalaropes. The kingfisher male may do most of the digging for the nest burrow but the female apparently does most of the incubating.

354. Occasionally a robin or other bird normally brightly colored is either all white or shows many white feathers. What causes this?
White feathers lack pigment. When light falls on them it is reflected back as white light. A bird of a species normally colored which lacks pigment is called an albino. If the lack of pigment extends over the entire bird it will have red or pink eyes as well as completely white plumage. Often pigmentation is missing in but part of the feathers and white areas appear which are not part of the normal pattern for the species.

355. Are all white birds albinos? By no means are all white birds albinos. Proof of this may be found in the colored eyes of many white birds. Gulls, terns, egrets, white pelicans, swans, snow geese and whooping cranes are among the white or nearly white birds of North America. They are not albinistic though they lack pigment in some or all of their feathers.

356. What is melanism? Melanism is the opposite of albinism. Melanistic birds are darker than is normal for a given species. Thus we find individuals of a dark phase among jaegers, gyrfalcons, rough-legged hawks, red-tailed hawks and so on. Melanism is caused by an excessive amount of dark pigment.

357. What causes the iridescence on the feathers of many birds?
In some birds special feather structures cause an uneven dispersion

of light which results in the moving, changing colors. In others the iridescent effect is caused by the fact that the feathers are unevenly colored. Iridescent colors are conspicuous on the nuptial plumage of starlings, grackles, hummingbirds and male barn swallows.

358. Does the food a bird eats have any effect on its color? How far the effects of food on the colors of bird plumage go is not known. Zoo keepers discovered that their captive spoonbills, flamingoes and other pink or reddish water birds often lost their delicate colors and became white or almost white. By being fed shrimp these birds were restored to their normal glowing color.

359. Can the sex of a bird be determined by its color and pattern? This varies with the species. Among the gulls, terns, alcids and many other water birds both sexes look alike. It is impossible to determine their sex by feather color or pattern. The same is true of many land birds. Owls, crows, jays and chickadees are among the species with similar plumage in both sexes.

On the other hand, the sexes of many species look so unlike that it is difficult to believe they are related. The sexes of warblers, tanagers, grouse and some swallows may be distinguished easily, at least in the nuptial plumage.

360. Is it possible to determine the sex of any young birds by their plumage? Among many species of land birds where the sexes look alike, the young birds in juvenile plumage look very much like their parents. The sexes cannot be distinguished by their plumage.

In some land birds where the sexes are unlike, the young birds in juvenile plumage resemble the female. This is true for redwings, bobolinks and cardinals. The sexes of these birds in juvenile plumage cannot be distinguished.

Certain juvenile birds have a plumage unlike either the male or female, as in robins and bluebirds. Again, the sexes cannot be distinguished by means of the plumage.

The sexes of belted kingfishers and many woodpeckers can be distinguished in juvenile plumage, for the male and female patterns are evident.

361. Some mammals turn white to match the snowy winter habitat in which they live. Do any birds do this? Ptarmigan become white in winter. Many arctic birds are partially or entirely white (some gulls, terns, owls, etc., while the antarctic snow petrel is white). Some gyrfalcons are white. Usually arctic peregrine falcons are lighter in color than their more southern relatives. However, except for the ptarmigan, the colors of the birds mentioned above are not seasonal, for in adult birds they remain practically the same throughout the year.

Of all the passerine birds nesting in the far North, snow buntings show the most white. Strangely enough, the white of these birds is more pronounced in summer than in winter.

362. Is there any noteworthy difference between the behavior of birds in which the sexes look alike and those that are different? Usually when the sexes look alike, both male and female share equally in nest building, incubation and care of the young. When the sexes do not look alike, there is usually a division of labor. Among passerine birds a gayly colored male may sing from various perches to indicate territorial defense, escort the female as she searches for nesting material and bring her food when she incubates. Among other birds with different sex plumages, such as the turkeys and other gallinaceous birds and hummingbirds, the males court the females but have nothing to do with the nest or care of the young.

Perhaps the most dramatic instance of labor division occurs in the hornbill family. In some species of these African and Asian birds the female is sealed within a cavity with an opening only large enough for her to thrust out the tip of her bill. Within this prison she lays the eggs, incubates them and hatches the young. In the meantime the male assiduously feeds her and later also supplies the young. It is said that occasionally he becomes so wearied with his labors that he dies from exhaustion at the end of the nesting season. Nest sanitation is maintained by throwing excrement through the tiny opening. (See Question 260.)

363. How do birds maintain the waterproof quality of their feathers? While it is often disputed, some scientists say that oil from the oil gland helps certain species to keep their feathers waterproof. Perhaps much more important is the formation of the feathers themselves. Birds appear to become wet voluntarily when they bathe, but water merely rolls off when it is poured over a bird that does not want a bath. Certain birds such as jays seem to have imperfect water-proofing, for their feathers become very wet and bedraggled during heavy rains.

364. Why do such birds as cormorants, anhingas and vultures spend so much time perched with their wings spread wide? It is often said that these birds spread their wings to dry them. However, they have been observed with their wings extended during rains so the theory appears weak. At present the reason for the extended wings remains unsolved.

365. Is it true that some birds produce musical sounds with their wing feathers? Goldeneye ducks are often called whistlers by hunters because of the whistling sounds produced by their wing feathers as they fly. Similar sounds are produced by the wing feathers of other birds, among them mourning doves, as they fly.

Many birds produce sounds deliberately with their wing feathers. Among such birds are the ruffed grouse, which makes booming sounds, turkeys that make clicking sounds, and woodcock which, with wing feathers having special development, plunge downward through the night, causing the air to whistle through them.

366. Does the sound made by the wing feathers serve any purpose? The sounds produced by the wing feathers of grouse, turkeys and woodcock all play a part in courtship activities. (See Questions 601, 603.)

367. Some screech owls are red and some are gray. Is this a matter of sex or age? Sometimes in a single brood of young screech owls, both red and gray phases are present. The color has nothing to do with age or sex. Gray is probably the normal color, while the red is caused by an excess of red pigment. This is known as erythrism.

368. In the past, man's desire for beautiful plumes resulted in much destruction to American bird life. May feathers still be possessed legally? It is illegal to possess or wear any wild-bird feathers, with a single exception: they may be used to make flies for fishing.

369. Is this true throughout the world? Unfortunately the wise laws of the United States in regard to wild-bird plumage are not subscribed to throughout the world. Many rare and beautiful species are threatened with extinction because of a demand for their plumage.

370. Feathers are used in many ways in the United States. How does this take place legally? The feathers of domestic birds (chickens, ducks, pheasants, ostrichs and so on) may be used legally. Many are dyed and perhaps clipped into attractive shapes. The use of these feathers results in utilization of a waste product of food production.

371. Is the use of down restricted by the same laws that apply to feathers? The down of comparatively few wild birds is used commercially. The one exception is the down of eider ducks. These large sea ducks were once brought to the verge of extinction through over-exploitation. Their nests were robbed of down, so the eggs did not hatch, and the ducks were shot and stripped of their down.

Now the collection of eider down is strictly regulated. The nuptial down grown by the female eider and plucked to line the nest and cover the eggs in her absence is one of the lightest, strongest, and most resilient and also one of the warmest animal materials known. Part of this down may be removed from the nest without injury to the eggs. When the young have hatched, the entire nest may be taken and cleaned by a special process. In Iceland the eider ducks have become virtually domesticated.

372. How are ostrich feathers obtained? The plumes are cut or plucked twice annually. Each wing has 42 quills. These birds are bred on farms throughout much of the world. A pair of ostriches is worth almost $1,000.

THE SKIN OF BIRDS

373. What are the functions of birds' skin? A bird's skin has many functions and even a partial list of them makes clear the complicated organ it is. One of its primary functions is that of supplying a complete unbroken covering for the body. The skin is the organ which produces the feathers of infinite variety that cover and decorate birds. It forms the scales on the legs of birds and a sheath on the bill. Special textures of the skin, such as sacs that can be inflated, combs, wattles, pouches, gular sacs, horny growths and tarsal spurs are all produced by the skin organ and form conspicuous features of certain birds.

374. Does the skin of a bird contain glands as does that of man? Glands are nearly absent from the skin of a bird. There are no sweat glands, excessive moisture being discharged by the respiratory system. The oil or preen glands are the only external glands most birds have. The oil gland is two-lobed or heart-shaped and is saddled at the base of the tail feathers. Usually there is a small nipplelike elevation opening from this gland.

375. Of what use is this gland? This is a matter requiring further study. For generations it was believed that the birds pressed oil from this gland with the bill and then spread the oil over their plumage. The apparent pressing of this gland by the bill, which is followed by preening of the plumage, gave weight to this belief. However, long ago scientific experiments indicated that no oil from the gland appeared on the feathers of birds. Also, it is contended that application of oil would break delicate down feathers. In spite of the evidence produced against the use of oil on the feathers, some investigators insist the oil does waterproof the feathers and others say that the oil spread over the feathers is acted upon by sunrays and in a complicated manner helps to prevent rickets. Most agree that the oil aids in keeping the bill in good condition.

376. Is the oil gland of comparable size in all birds? The oil gland is large in aquatic birds. It is smaller in land birds and in some is entirely absent. None of the ostriches have an oil gland. Many parrots and pigeons also lack this gland. Magnificent frigate-birds which never stray far from the vicinity of the ocean have an oil gland scarcely as big as a pea. It is not surprising to learn that this species does not swim, and if placed in the water, its plumage quickly becomes water-soaked.

377. How does the skin control the feathers? Birds have enormous numbers of muscles in the skin. Canada geese have at least 12,000 skin or cutaneous muscles for feather control alone. These control ever-necessary motion of the feathers, from fluffing or ruffling to pulling them tight against the body or adjusting the position of wing and tail feathers for the complicated positions of flight. The muscles expose the brood patch of birds about to incubate, erect crests or plumes, and shake water from the feathers after a bath and the dust from them after a dust bath.

378. Does the skin of a bird ever produce seasonal growths aside from feathers? The Atlantic puffin has a "horn" above the eye during the breeding season while the rhinoceros auklet has one near the base of the bill. White pelicans grow a knoblike projection on the upper mandible. Many other species grow temporary adornments of the skin which, like those mentioned above, are lost when the breeding season ends.

379. What is a caruncle? This is any naked, fleshy growth on a bird such as a comb or wattle. These are often highly colored, at least during periods of high emotion in fights or courtship.

380. What is a comb? A comb is a fleshy caruncle which appears on the top of the head. Many domestic roosters display large and colorful combs, some of them serrated on the top. They may stand erect or droop, according to the species. Some species of grouse have a comb over their eyes.

381. What are wattles? Like combs these are usually highly colored. Wattles hang beneath the chin or from the throat of a bird. They are conspicuous on domestic cocks. Wild turkeys which have caruncles above the bill (which expand and brighten in color during display) also have wattles under the chin.

382. What native North American birds have conspicuous pouches? Two kinds of pouches appear among the birds native in this area. Some, like those of the gannet, cormorant and pelican, are hung from the base of the bill or along the lower mandible. The brown pelican has the largest pouch of any bird in the world.

The second type of pouch is used particularly in connection with courtship and can be inflated or deflated at will. Often this type of

pouch is brightly colored. The frigate bird has a pouch at the base
of the throat which is bright orange-red when inflated. The sage
grouse has two orange-yellow sacs on its chest which are inflated
during a courtship dance. At the same time bright red caruncles are
inflated above the eyes. Dusky grouse can inflate a deep red sac on
each side of the lower neck when performing. It is believed these
pouches or sacs are inflated by means of indirect connection with the
lungs.

383. What are the lores often mentioned in descriptions of birds?
The lore is the area between the eye and the bill. This area is bare
in some species, among them the herons, ibises and spoonbills. Herons
as well as many other species with naked lores take on a bright color
in this area for a few days during the mating season.

384. What is the cere?   The cere is an area of naked skin at the
base of the bill in certain species. The cere is conspicuous in most
species of parrots and hawks.

385. Why do some birds have bare areas on their heads?   No
doubt this had a survival value or has contributed to the successful
propagation of the race. The pebbled skin on the forehead of sand-
hill and whooping cranes is brighter red during the breeding season
than at other times of year. The same is true of the rough, naked
heads of turkey and black vultures. The warty skin of wild turkeys
becomes flushed with bright color during the excitement of a courtship dance, then fades again when the dance is finished.

386. Is a bald eagle really bald?   The head of a mature bald eagle
is covered with white feathers. At a distance the white head looks
bald, thus deceiving careless observers.

387. Has the skin of birds any commercial value?   Except for the
ostrich, no bird has skin of commercial value at present. Ostrich
skin is tough and has an attractive texture. It is sometimes used for
wallets, handbags and coin purses. Ostriches are often raised as
domestic birds but their plumes, rather than skin, form their chief
value.

WINGS

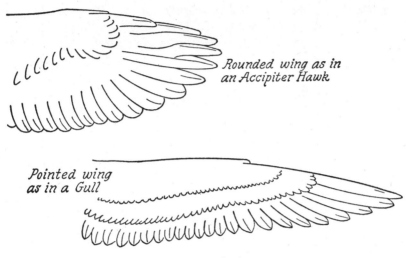

Rounded wing as in
an Accipiter Hawk

Pointed wing
as in a Gull

Two Types of Wing

388. Do all birds have wings?   The skeleton of a kiwi shows little
trace of a wing and none at all is visible on the outside of the bird.
Most birds, even those that are flightless, have visible wings.

389. Do flightless birds make any use of their wings?   Penguins
use their wings to "fly" under water. Ostriches sometimes lift their
wings as if they were sails when running with the wind. This increases
their speed.

390. How are the wings of birds adapted for flight?   A wing is
lightly made. The bones are usually hollow, which gives them additional strength without an increase in weight. The surface is curved
so that the concave side is below. The bones and feathers are arranged so the front edge is much thicker than the rear. This makes
for greater efficiency than if the wing were flat.

391. Can air pass through the wing feathers?   By means of micro-
scopic barbicels the wing can be controlled like a valve to permit

air to pass through or to prevent passage of air. Therefore it varies from being highly air-resistant to slightly so.

392. How does the wing sustain flight?   It acts somewhat like an oar and a carrier at the same time. The wing pushes back the air with its wide surface, then glides forward again with the least possible resistance.

393. What are the parts of a bird's wing?   The bones form the framework and lie at the front of the wing. The patagium or membrane stretches from the upper arm to the lower arm so the wing cannot be completely stretched. The primary feathers, attached to the "hand," and the secondary feathers, attached to the "forearm," are the parts directly connected with flight.

394. What are the bones of a wing?   See the following diagram:

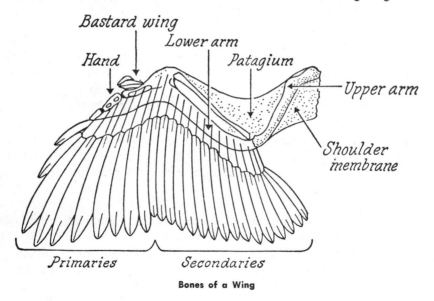

Bones of a Wing

395. What are the bones in the human arm?   See the following diagram:

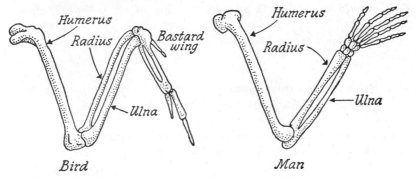

Bones of a Bird's Wing and Human Arm Compared

396. What part of the bird's wing differs most from the human arm? The hand, which in birds is long and narrow with many bones fused together. The fingers have fewer joints than human fingers. The index finger of a bird has two or more joints and the middle finger one or more joints, depending on the species. The thumb has only one joint and bears the bastard wing.

397. What is the bastard wing? The bastard wing on the thumb of birds consists of four small stiff feathers which can be separated and used to control the front edge of the wing.

398. Will the study of a bird's wing give any clue to its manner of flight? The shape and size of a wing can give the observant student a clear indication of the kind of flight typical of that species.

399. What is of first importance in the wing of a bird? The total surface of the wing in relation to the size and weight of a bird is of first importance. The larger the wing surface in relation to the weight of a bird, the more easily the bird is borne aloft.

400. Is there any relation between the breadth of a wing and the speed at which birds can fly? Air will not flow smoothly over a broad wing. Therefore a bird with broad wings cannot speed. The shape of the wings slows it down.

401. How does the length of a bird's wing affect its flight? Long wings cannot be moved as quickly as short wings. Therefore, we find that birds which spring suddenly into the air and turn quickly have short wings.

402. What are the chief types of wings? *Extremely long, narrow wings.* Albatrosses and frigate birds soar almost endlessly above the sea on this type of wing.

Broad wings, shorter than those above. Vultures, condors and other birds that soar above the land have this type of wing.

Moderately long, narrow, triangular wings. Swallows, shore birds, falcons and other small- or medium-sized birds with rapid flight have this type of wing.

Large, distinctly curved wings that are flapped slowly. Herons have this type of wing.

Short, broad wings with flexible tips which can be set at varied angles without twisting the whole wing. Gallinaceous birds which usually inhabit dense cover find this type advantageous.

403. Why should birds that soar above water have wings shaped differently from those that soar above land? This is a matter not completely understood. Albatrosses, shearwaters and other soaring birds of the ocean glide at a slight angle and maintain their height because of the endless series of rising air currents above the slopes of the waves.

Vultures, condors and other birds that soar above the land utilize, as do man-made gliders, the warm air currents which rise gently above the earth. For reasons not well understood, the breadth of wing and the arrangement of the primaries, usually with a space between them, is most efficient for land soaring.

404. When is a wing termed long? A wing is long when it exceeds the length of the body.

405. When is a wing called short? A short wing is less than the length of the body.

406. What are the primary wing feathers? The primary wing feathers are the flight feathers which grow on the hand of a bird.

407. How many primary feathers do birds have?   In most species there are about ten primary feathers.

408. What are the secondary feathers?   The secondary flight feathers grow from the forearm of the bird.

409. How many secondary flight feathers do birds have?   The number varies greatly with different species. Passerine birds have nine or ten secondaries but some species of grouse have as many as 20.

410. What are the tertiaries?   These are the flight feathers which grow on the upper arm. However, in many species these are not conspicuous and occasionally the feathers growing from the elbow, particularly if they differ in color from the other secondaries, are sometimes referred to as tertiaries. In some cases, if the scapulars are particularly long or conspicuous, they are referred to as tertiaries.

411. What are remiges?   This term is used to cover all the flight feathers. Remiges give the general wing character and mainly determine its size and shape. The bony and fleshy framework of the wing is insignificant in comparison to the remiges.

412. Do any birds have extra growths on their wings similar to the spur on the legs of gallinaceous birds?   Some birds have a spur of horny texture forming an offset on the side of the hand. It is precisely like the spur on the leg of a chicken. Spur-winged geese and screamers display wing spurs. The only good example of a spur-winged bird appearing in the United States is the jacana. It is believed the spurs are used in fighting.

413. In what ways do birds use their wings aside from flight?   As suggested above, some birds, such as jacanas and screamers, use their wings in fighting. Both geese and swans use their wings in defense of their nests. There are records of both having used their wings so effectively for this purpose that they have broken the arm of a man interfering with their nests.

414. What is meant by the term "wing-clipped bird"?   Zoos and other organizations or private individuals with Federal and local permits to keep captive wild birds often wing-clip these birds. The flight feathers, particularly the primaries, are cut off. The clipped feathers grow in again at the regular molting time, usually once a year.

415. What is a pinioned bird? If the hand is amputated a bird is said to be pinioned. If this is done the primaries can never grow in again.

416. What is a pulled wing? If the primary feathers are pulled out, the bird cannot fly until they grow in again. But unlike the wing-clipped bird which does not grow new feathers until the regular molt, pulled primaries are quickly replaced.

417. What is a brailed wing? The hand of the bird is bound to the forearm so the wing cannot be opened.

418. Are both wings clipped, pinioned or brailed? Usually but one wing is treated. Sometimes birds with very strong wings can still achieve labored flight after one of the above operations. Usually they find great difficulty in getting off the ground and if they succeed, flight is limited to low circles.

TAILS

419. Exactly what is the tail of a bird? As far as the measurements or descriptive ornithology are concerned, the tail feathers constitute the tail of a bird. But the student of anatomy ignores the feathers and calls the bony and muscular part of the bird's body at the rear the tail of the bird. To him, the feathers are merely an outgrowth of the tail.

420. Is the actual tail made up of separate parts comparable to those in the tail of a dog? The number of true tail bones is few, generally about nine. They are so short and stunted that they not only do not project beyond the plumage but scarcely beyond the border of the pelvis.

421. Is there much variation in the actual tail of birds? Except for the fact that the tail varies in accordance with the size of a bird, there is little difference in the development of the tail in various species. The variations occur, not in the tail but in the feathers growing from it.

422. Are the tails of birds today quite like those found in the earliest bird fossils? Early fossils of birds indicate that they had long lizardlike tails. In fact, if it were not for the feathers growing along the edge of the tails, scientists would say those early fossils were lizards, not birds.

423. What are the feathers growing on the tail called? Tail feathers or rectrices (singular form: rectrix).

424. What are tail coverts? The tail coverts are the feathers immediately above and below the tail. Those above are called the upper tail coverts. The feathers immediately beneath are called under tail coverts.

425. Is the number of rectrices constant within a species? Except when feathers are lost by accident or the normal molting processes, each species has a definite number of rectrices. They grow in pairs; thus there is an equal number of feathers on each side of the tail.

426. What is the average number of rectrices? Twelve rectrices is the typical number. However, there is great variation, for an ani has but eight rectrices while penguins have up to 32 or more, depending on the species.

427. What is the typical shape of a bird's tail? The typical shape is the fan. This varies from a square to a rounded end, deeply forked and wedge-shaped through all possible variations. The lyrebird of Australia has a lyre-shaped tail of extraordinary beauty.

428. In what ways does a bird use its tail? The tail is used for good balance and to give an extra lifting surface in flight. It serves as a rudder for steering and as a brake. Some birds make use of the tail in their courtship displays. It is believed that the tails of some birds are useful in perplexing enemies.

Frigate-Bird

Kiwi

Extremes of Tail Development: 1. The Kiwi appears tailless, and Frigate-Birds have long forked tails.

429. How is it possible for the tail to help a bird escape enemies?
Scientists believe that birds such as the magnolia warbler, with white spots on its tail, and juncoes, with white outer tail feathers, flash these white areas in such a way that predators are perplexed and thus the threatened bird escapes.

430. Do any birds lack tail feathers?   All birds have rectrices but in some species these are very short and soft. Grebes appear tailless. The strange kiwi also appears to have no tail.

431. What happens when an enemy damages the tail of a bird?
If the rectrices are merely broken, the bird usually has to endure the handicap of a poor tail until the arrival of the next molt period. However, if the rectrices are pulled out, new ones replace those lost fairly quickly.

Sage Grouse Cock

2. Sage Grouse have spectacular tails.

432. Which bird in the United States has the longest tail? Many birds have extremely long tail feathers, both in proportion to their bodies and in actual length. The ring-necked pheasant, brought to America from Europe and naturalized, has the longest tail feathers. Its relative, the golden pheasant, often raised by pheasant fanciers, has an even longer tail. Of the native birds, the wild turkey has the longest tail feathers while the scissor-tailed flycatcher has the longest in relation to its body length. In all these instances, it is the male bird of the species that shows the extreme length of the rectrices.

433. What are some foreign birds with unusually long rectrices? Among the long-tailed birds in other parts of the world, the long-tailed manakin of South America, the long-tailed bird of paradise found in New Guinea, the lyrebird of Australia, and the Indian paradise flycatcher show spectacular development, but there are many

Lyre Bird

3. The Lyre Bird displays an exotic tail.

others. The whidah finch of Africa is the size of a canary but it has rectrices a foot long.

434. Why is the peacock not included among the birds with spectacular tails?   Oddly enough the rectrices of a peacock are modest in length and color. It is the upper tail coverts of this species that exhibit the extreme elongation together with iridescent colors and dramatic ocellate spots.

The same is true of the national bird of Guatemala, the quetzal, once worshiped by the Mayan Indians. This species of trogon is sometimes called the American bird of paradise because of its beauty and color, dramatized by the very long upper tail coverts.

435. How do birds with extremely long tails such as the pheasant, or very broad tails like those of the turkey, control them? Among the multitude of skin muscles of a bird are many that control the tail, making instantaneous work of extreme adjustment whether tilting, fanning or contraction.

436. Aside from use in flight and courtship, what are some specialized uses of the tail? Brown creepers press their long, flexible tails against the trunk of a tree for support as they search the crevices of the bark for food. Woodpeckers have stiffened spinelike tail feathers which are very strong. These are pressed against the trunk of the tree for additional support when the bird digs for insects or hollows its nest. Chimney swifts also have spinelike tail feathers that are used as props when clinging to the chimney wall.

437. What type of tail is most suited to graceful, quick maneuverability? Probably long, forked tails are most efficient for graceful, swift movements. Scissor-tailed flycatchers, barn swallows, arctic terns, magnificent frigate-birds and swallow-tailed kites all have greatly elongated outer tail feathers. Each of these birds exhibits inimitable grace and dexterity in swift turns and sudden changes of direction.

438. Chimney swifts have extremely short tails, yet their flight speed is great and they swoop and swerve easily. How do they manage this? The tail of a swift is very short but this is counterbalanced by wings of extreme flexibility and wing feathers that may be controlled individually. Thus they are able to follow the erratic flight of insects. (See Question 96.)

439. Is the tail of a hummingbird used in its bulletlike flight? Hummingbirds make no unique use of their tails in direct flight, but when they hover before a flower, the tail is in constant motion. This motion is studied easily, for hummingbirds regularly visit the flowers in gardens and vials of sugar-water placed where they may be watched at close range while feeding.

440. It is said that handsome tails are a handicap to birds. Is this true? The handsome tails of many species of birds have undoubtedly played an important part in the success of the species. Nevertheless, the beauty of these feathers has often aroused the covetousness of man. Primitive men decorated themselves with feathers, and certain kinds indicated their rank and standing as warriors or hunters within the tribe. As man became "civilized," the use of feathers was no longer restricted to men. The wearing of feathers became a fashion. In recent centuries the use of feathers for decoration reached such a peak that the world was scoured for the most beautiful plumes. Late in the nineteenth century it seemed that human covetousness would wipe birds from the face of the earth. Now in the United States almost all traffic in wild bird feathers has been halted by law. This is not true in many parts of the world. Destruction of birds for the sake of fashion still threatens the extinction of many of the most beautiful species. Beautiful tail feathers can indeed be a handicap to birds when Homo sapiens desires them for himself.

441. Can a bird fly if it loses its rectrices? If a bird loses its rectrices through accident or by molting them, its flight may be labored and its balance uncertain. But as long as their wings remain in good condition, birds can fly, though they have lost all of their rectrices.

THE BILLS OF BIRDS

442. Do all birds have bills? One of the characteristics of Aves, the class of birds, is the toothless, horny bill or beak. Some species of birds which catch their food in their open mouths as they fly about (swifts, swallows, nighthawks) have extremely short, weak bills. No birds, even those that probably could survive with soft mouth parts, have lost the hard bill.

443. Is the bill a characteristic of birds only? The toothless, horny bill is by no means the exclusive possession of birds. Turtles, perhaps, are the most widespread of the animals which share this characteristic with birds.

444. What are the parts of a bird's bill? The bill consists of an upper and a lower jaw (upper and lower mandible). The space where the two mandibles come together is called the gape.

445. Is the bill a part of the skull bones or is it a growth of the skin? The mandibles are a bony modification of the skull. These are covered with a tough, durable, horny covering or sheath which is a product of the skin.

446. Why do the bills of birds vary so greatly? The evolutionary process, continued for more than 100 million years, has brought about great divergence in the size and shape of the bills of birds. The results which we see today are instruments perfectly developed to enable each species of bird to obtain its food in the most efficient manner. It should be remembered that just as wings are an adaptation for flying, the bills of birds are an adaptation of the mouth parts for feeding. Practically every form of life in the world offers food to some kind of bird.

447. Can family relationships be detected through a study of a bird's bill? In a limited way the bills of birds give an indication of family relationships. For instance, a careful study of their bills will aid in the separation of warblers and vireos, two families that beginning students often confuse. Study of the similar bills of gallinaceous birds will help a student see the relationship between the species in this family, which has wide variation in many of its characteristics.

448. What are some of the pitfalls in trying to determine family relationships through study of the bills? Certain species of birds, though in widely separated orders, feed on the same kind of food. Kingfishers and terns dive for fish. Herons spear fish. All of these species have similar bills, yet they are widely separated according to classification.

449. Do birds within a given family ever show great bill variation? Perhaps no single family displays greater variation in bill formation than the fringillid or sparrow family. Within this family of 426

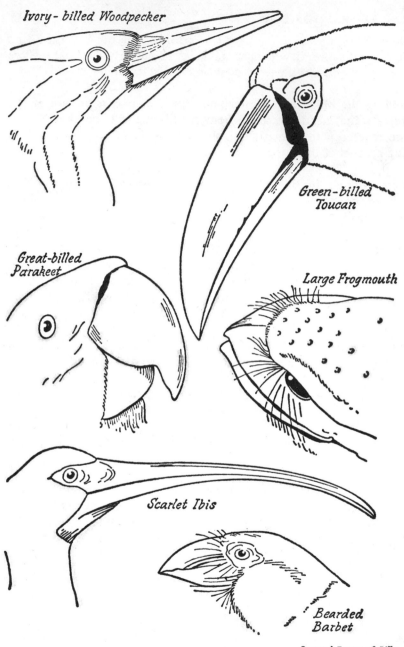

Ivory-billed Woodpecker

Green-billed Toucan

Great-billed Parakeet

Large Frogmouth

Scarlet Ibis

Bearded Barbet

Several Types of Bills

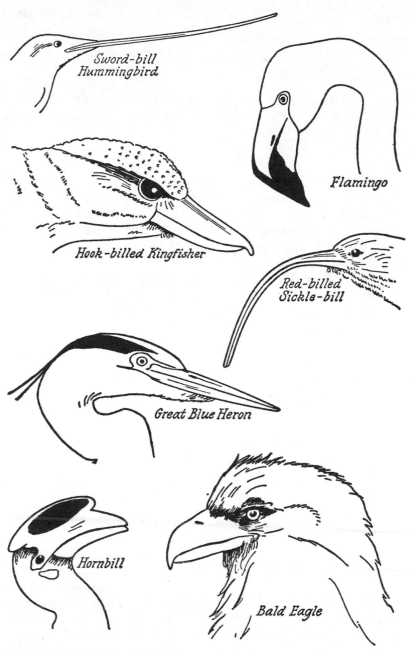

Sword-bill Hummingbird

Flamingo

Hook-billed Kingfisher

Red-billed Sickle-bill

Great Blue Heron

Hornbill

Bald Eagle

(Not drawn to the same scale)

species are the grosbeaks with thick, long, triangular bills, crossbills with the tips of their bills crossed, and redpolls with extremely short sharply pointed bills.

450. Are there blood vessels and nerves in the bill? There are some blood vessels and nerves present in the bills of birds. The abundance of nerves varies greatly with the species. (See Question 538.)

451. Can birds use the bill as an organ of touch? It is believed that woodcocks and many other shore birds which probe in mud for their food discover it by means of the sense of touch, since they cannot see it. The same is true of ducks, which extract their food from the debris at the bottom of ponds and streams.

452. Does the color of adult birds' bills ever change? The bills of many adult birds change in color for the breeding season. During the winter the bill of a starling is black, but with the approach of the breeding season it turns yellow. Black skimmers, laughing gulls and common terns are among the birds that have brighter-colored bills during the breeding season than at other times of year. These changes are due to additional hormones. Usually the change in the color of the bill is most pronounced among birds which retain the same plumage color and pattern throughout the year.

453. Does the shape of a bird's bill remain constant? Most frequently the shape of a bird's bill is well developed before the young bird breaks out of the shell, but there are many striking exceptions to this generality. For instance, young crossbills have perfectly parallel mandibles when they hatch, while those of young flamingoes are straight, without a trace of the bend which makes the bill of an adult so distinctive.

Some birds display a change in the shape of their bills at breeding time. This is readily observed in the white pelican, which develops, when ready to breed, a horny projection on the upper mandible. Usually this is shed by the time the eggs hatch. Early in the breeding season rhinoceros auklets develop "horns" on their bills which are shed by the time that season terminates. Atlantic puffins develop a huge brightly colored sheath over the entire bill for the breeding season. Scientists report that this is shed in nine pieces after the breeding time is past. During the remainder of the year the puffin has a fairly conservative stocky black bill.

454. What are some extreme adaptations of bills among North American birds?   The bills of woodpeckers are capable of excavating solid wood and acting as drumsticks on metal or wood. Among the birds of prey, the bald eagle has the largest, most powerful beak for tearing flesh. The bills of mergansers are saw-toothed on the margins for holding slippery fish. A black skimmer's bill is broad and flattened vertically, with the upper mandible much shorter than the lower. Frequently these birds, flying close above the surface, may be seen "skimming" with the lower mandible cutting water like a knife as they feed. The upper mandible of a woodcock's long bill is flexible, which is of service as the bird probes in the mud for food. The very long, needlelike bill of a hummingbird is a perfect instrument for obtaining nectar from the bottom of long, slim flower tubes. Swifts, which catch their insects while on the wing, have a widely gaping mouth. Their bills have become small and weak. No doubt swifts would survive as well with soft mouth parts.

455. Among the birds of other continents, what are some bills that show extreme adaptations?   The sword-billed hummingbird of northern South America has a rapierlike bill almost as long as its entire body, including the tail. The bill of the large frogmouth of Malayasia is so reduced that it is little more than a horny rim.

The hornbills of Africa have very large bills and above these in some species is an enormous casque. This is particularly large in the Malabar pied hornbill.

The huge spongy bills of toucans not only have reached spectacular proportions, but their color is often vivid. The green-billed toucan of Brazil has one of the most vividly colored bills of these exotic fruit-eating tropical birds.

One of the strangest bill adaptations was that of the now extinct huia of New Zealand. The male had a sharp, straight bill for tunneling in dead wood for grubs. When one was located, the female took over. With her thin, decurved bill she pulled forth the grub which the male could not reach.

456. How do the various kinds of birds use their bills? In many instances the bird student can answer this for himself. Some birds use their bills as if they were tweezers for picking up insects or seeds. Woodpeckers drill into trees to reach the insects secreted in them. Brown pelicans, kingfishers and terns are among the birds that dive for fish beneath the surface and catch them in their bills. Loons, cormorants and diving ducks pursue fish and catch them in their bills. Herons spear their food. Geese often graze like cattle. Swallows dart about and with open bills scoop up insects. Flycatchers perch on a favorite twig until an insect appears; then they dart out, catch the insect with a distinct snap of the bill and return to the perch to await another insect.

The secretary-bird of Africa kills its prey with hammerlike blows of its bill. Both flamingoes and spoonbills move their bills from side to side along the bottom ooze, but the flamingoes turn their bills backward as they do this. Study of a bird's bill helps the ecologist understand the food demands of birds.

457. Aside from acquiring food, how do birds use their bills? Many birds, among them herons, gannets, cormorants and gulls, use their bills in fighting and in the defense of their territories. Many species of birds use their bills in courtship and also in greeting ceremonies at the nest. They use the bill in grooming the feathers, for, because of the very flexible neck, birds can reach every part of the body with the bill except the head. Herons use the bill to break up the powder-down feathers and spread the powder over their plumage. Except for birds of prey, almost all birds use the bill in gathering and carrying nesting materials. A few (the Baltimore oriole is especially dexterous) use the bill with great skill when weaving the nest. Swifts break off suitable twigs as they fly, and white ibises have been seen to jump repeatedly toward low twigs of shrubs and try to break them off with the bill.

458. What is the egg tooth? The egg tooth is a sharp, rough, hard projection on the tip of the upper mandible at hatching time. The movements of the young bird within the shell cause this rough area to scratch or file the inside of the shell, weakening it and helping the bird to break forth. The egg tooth disappears soon after the bird hatches.

459. Why do so many species of gulls have a bright spot on the lower mandible? Ornithologists have discovered through experiments that the spot of color on the lower mandible plays an important part in the feeding rhythm of the gulls that possess it. The young birds pick at the spot and thus stimulate the parent birds to regurgitate food for them.

460. Are the bills of both male and female birds always alike? When the plumage of both sexes is alike, the bills usually are alike, too. But if the plumage of the sexes shows a difference, the bills of the male and female bird may be different. The bill of a female cardinal is less brilliant than that of the male. The male English sparrow has a blackish-blue bill during the breeding season, while that of the female remains horn-color.

Probably the species showing the greatest sexual variation was the huia. (See Question 455.)

461. Many birds have an enormous bill. How does the scientist explain this development in a group of animals where lightness is essential to flight? Lightness is vital to the easy flight of birds. Their skulls are thinner than in most creatures. They have no teeth to add weight to the fore part of the body. But it is true that some birds have bills that appear to have developed beyond all apparent reason.

However, enormous bills, such as those of the toucan and hornbill, are made of extremely light, spongy material. The bills of eagles, owls, parrots and woodpeckers are large and strong, but they are also very light in weight.

THE LEGS AND FEET OF BIRDS

462. Why do not all birds stand upright on their two legs as man does? Though the hip joint of a bird is at the end of its body, the thighbone does not descend from this point, but runs horizontally forward and is embedded in muscles. The leg becomes free only at the knee. The kind of life led by a bird determines the position of its center of gravity. Among passerine birds, the center of gravity is near the center of their bodies. The feet are placed in a forward position under the body, which is held obliquely and balanced between the knees.

463. Do any birds as a group differ from this oblique posture?
The center of gravity of water birds is very far back. Therefore the legs also are placed far back, usually so far that they extend beyond the tail in flight. Because of the placement of the center of gravity, water birds stand upright if they walk. Nevertheless, the thighbone of these birds, as in passerine birds, is embedded in muscles and held in a forward position.

464. How can birds possibly walk or hop with their thighbones embedded in muscles? The thighbone of a bird is proportionately much shorter than that of man. Its loss as an instrument for walking is compensated for by an extremely long bone called the tarsus.

465. Does the knee of a bird bend the opposite way to that of man?
The knee of a bird bends the same way as the human knee does. Many people mistakenly believe the heel of a bird is its knee. This is not surprising, because the forward-bending thighbone is concealed in the muscles, and the leg becomes free only at the knee. From the heel to the toes of a bird is often a long distance. The area between the heel and toes is called the shank or tarsus.

466. Is the part of a bird called its foot really just its toes? In speaking of the feet of birds, only the toes are considered. The heel is lifted high in the air so that the bird walks only on its toes. Men walk with their heels on the ground.

467. Do birds ever rest the whole foot from heel to toes on the ground? Nestlings frequently rest the tarsus on the nest platform. Many birds when incubating fold their legs so the tarsus assumes a horizontal position. Many species of birds sleep or rest on level surfaces and may crouch with the tarsus flattened.

468. How many toes do birds have? Birds have but four toes instead of five. One toe (sometimes two) projects backward. This corresponds to the first or big toe of man and is called the hallux. There is no toe corresponding to the little toe. It must be kept in

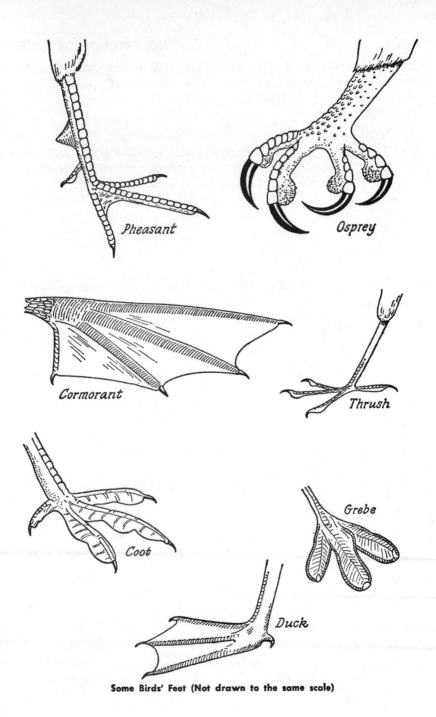

Pheasant

Osprey

Cormorant

Thrush

Coot

Grebe

Duck

Some Birds' Feet (Not drawn to the same scale)

mind that while four toes is the general rule among birds, in some species the toes have been reduced to three as in the three-toed woodpeckers or to two as in the ostriches.

469. Is the leg of a bird an efficient mechanism? The leg of a bird, made up of three single, rigid bones joined together and with toes at the end, is a beautifully designed instrument for perching, running, catching food, and taking the strain of landing. Because the knee and ankle joints of a bird are a considerable distance from the hip and toe joints, which work in opposite directions, they constitute what is probably the most effective shock-absorbing instrument in the animal kingdom.

470. Why have so many kinds of feet evolved among birds? Birds having wings instead of forelegs employ their feet for many activities beside walking. It is these varied activities which determined the development of the different types of feet. In each species, the feet have been molded to form the most efficient tools for the kind of life lived by the bird.

471. Besides locomotion, what are some of the things birds demand of their feet? Many birds use their feet to carry nest materials. Those birds are likely to use their feet to obtain and carry their food. Some birds, such as the ostrich, run to catch their food and to escape enemies; other birds, such as hawks and owls, use their feet to kill their prey, while woodpeckers, nuthatches and creepers are a few of the birds that have feet adapted for clinging to vertical surfaces as they search for food.

Coots and gallinules use their large feet to push enemies in fighting, while an ostrich is able to use its feet as weapons powerful enough to disembowel a man. Birds such as falcons, which kill their prey by striking it with closed fists, and hawks and owls that sink their talons into their prey, also use their claws in fighting or self-defense.

Many birds use their feet both in the air and in the water as rudders. Water birds use their feet to propel themselves through the water. In flight, birds use their feet as a spring in the take-off and as shock absorbers when landing.

Birds use their feet when they groom the feathers on their heads.

Herons have a "comb" on the middle claw with which they comb powder down over their plumage.

472. Are the feet alike among birds that habitually swim? The webbed toes of loons, ducks, cormorants and gannets might be called typical of water birds. However, many water birds either do not have fully webbed toes or any webs at all. The webs between the three front toes of sooty and bridled terns are deeply incised. Grebes have wide skin flanges on each front toe. Coots and phalaropes have lobes on their toes.

473. How are the feet of walking birds adapted for that purpose? The feet of walking birds vary from the two-toed members of the ostrich family to the tremendously long toes of the four-toed jacanas. In spite of the variations, the foot of the domestic chicken is fairly typical of walking birds. There are generally four toes, three in front and one turned backward. Ostriches usually live in open prairielike country and depend on their fleetness of foot to escape enemies. The jacanas with toes (including the claws) as long as the tarsus, also herons and rails which move on unstable ground or over marsh vegetation find the wide spread of their toes of great advantage. Walking birds that live in sandy areas, such as sand grouse, generally have short, thick toes, sometimes joined together. Shorebirds such as sanderlings and knots which feed at the edge of waves have slim toes, but some, such as the semipalmated sandpiper, have partially webbed toes.

474. What adaptations make a perfect foot for a bird of prey? The gripping foot is fairly characteristic of birds. Among birds of prey, the tarsus and toes are exceptionally powerful, while the claws are long, curved and strong as steel.

475. Do robber birds which steal from other species have feet like the birds of prey? Eagles, which are birds of prey, frequently pursue ospreys and force them to drop their fish, whereupon the eagle seizes it before it drops to earth. Frigate-birds consistently prey upon terns, forcing them to drop the fish they catch. These aggressive robbers have powerful claws at the tips of their slightly webbed toes. Jaegers have large strong claws on their fully webbed feet.

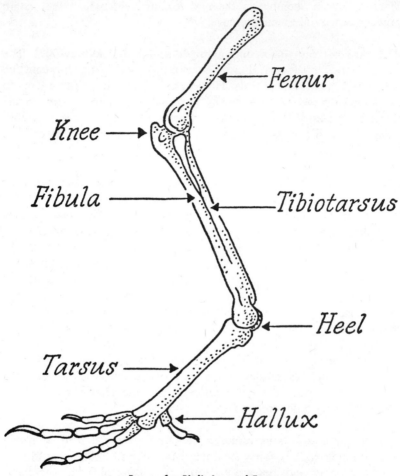

Femur

Knee

Fibula

Tibiotarsus

Heel

Tarsus

Hallux

Bones of a Bird's Leg and Foot

476. Do birds that chase insects through the air have distinctive feet?   Birds that spend their feeding time skimming through the air, scooping insects into their open mouths, have no need for strong feet. It is characteristic of such birds to have small weak feet, useful only for perching or clinging. Swallows, swifts, nighthawks and whippoorwills are among the birds which feed in this manner and have weak, small feet. Not all birds that catch insects share this characteristic, however. The swallow-tailed kite pursues and catches insects on the wing but instead of scooping them up in the open mouth they catch them in their claws.

477. Are there any birds that cannot walk? A common loon really cannot walk. It progresses on land chiefly by pushing itself along with its breast on the ground. Grebes walk poorly. The small, weak feet of swifts and hummingbirds make walking very difficult or impossible, but even these birds can push themselves across a level surface.

478. Can any birds walk easily on snow? When autumn comes, ptarmigan and some other species of grouse grow appendages on their toes which act as snowshoes in winter.

479. Are the feet of any birds feathered? While the tarsus and toes of a bird are usually covered with scales, some birds are feathered on the tarsus, and a few species even have feathered toes. Many owls are feathered to the claws. Ptarmigan have feathered feet. Some hawks, particularly the rough-legged hawk, and some eagles, particularly the golden eagle, have a feathered tarsus.

480. Is the tibia of a bird always feathered? Many species of birds lack feathers on the lower part of the tibia. This is particularly true of shore birds, marsh birds and wading birds. Herons, ibises, rails, gallinules, cranes, flamingoes, plovers and sandpipers all display considerable bare areas above the heel.

481. Do the tarsus and toes of birds always remain the same color? The fleshy parts of a bird assume different colors at the various stages of development. Once a bird has become an adult, the amount of color change in the fleshy areas varies least among species that have seasonal changes in plumage color and pattern. Even among these species there is often a detectable color change correlated with the arrival and conclusion of the breeding season. However, the changes are most conspicuous among the species which retain the same plumage colors throughout the year. Black-crowned night heron legs and yellow-crowned night heron feet become pink at breeding time. The leg color of ibises and spoonbills becomes brighter and richer. Snowy egrets, the black-legged herons with the golden toes, assume a more glossy black on the tarsus, while for a few days at the height of breeding fervor the feet become tinged with cherry red.

482. Do all birds let their feet trail behind when they fly? Passerine birds fly with their toes brought forward.

483. Vultures belong to the hawk family yet they have relatively weak feet. How did this develop? Vultures and other members of the hawk family that live chiefly on carrion do not need powerful claws for they do not normally strike down living creatures.

484. Ospreys dive for fish. How do they catch them? Ospreys or fish hawks locate fish swimming near the surface, then plunge, sometimes from a considerable height, feet first and catch the fish in their claws.

485. Fish are very slippery. How do the ospreys manage to hold them? Ospreys have strange, rough, horny growths on the inside of their toes that help them to grip the fish firmly. Moreover, the outer toe is reversed so two toes point forward and two backward, insuring a firm grip on the fish.

486. Do other bird fishers such as terns, kingfishers and gannets catch fish in their feet as ospreys do? All of the species mentioned above dive head first into the water and catch their prey in their strong bills. Terns and gannets both have relatively weak, webbed feet, while the toes of a kingfisher are not only small and weak but so stubby they look as if they had been chopped off. It is doubtful that a kingfisher can walk; probably it has to push itself as a loon does.

487. How fast can an ostrich run? It is said that an ostrich can maintain a speed of 50 miles an hour for some distance.

488. Why don't birds fall from their perches when asleep? The grip of a bird is tightened by an arrangement of tendons so that the foot is not relaxed in sleep. As the bird sinks into a resting position, the large flexor tendons in the toes are stretched in such a way that the toes are automatically pulled inward, making the grip ever tighter.

When a bird is in sleeping position, it lays its head on its back so it is supported without muscular effort. Perfectly balanced and with the tendons pulling the tips of the toes inward, a bird sleeps safely, even though a high wind shakes its perch. Anyone still puzzled by the tightening of a bird's toes as it relaxes in sleep may demonstrate this apparent contradiction by asking his butcher for the entire foot of a chicken. An examination of the severed heel area will reveal two threadlike tendons. Pull these forward as they would be pulled as a bird crouched in a relaxed position of sleep. As the tendons are pulled, the toes will fold inward as they would around a perch. This simple demonstration clearly shows why the toes of a bird clutch the perch so firmly as the bird relaxes in sleep.

489. Often a flamingo, duck or shorebird will stand for hours on one leg. How is this possible? These birds all hold the body in an oblique position. The body is held this way by strong muscles and is balanced between the knees. The rigid frame of a bird has already been mentioned. It is this rigid frame which makes the oblique position possible. The rigidity, oblique position and central balance make it possible for a bird to stand on one foot for long periods of time.

490. Accidents frequently happen to the delicate leg bones of birds. Can a bird survive if it loses a leg? When a leg is broken, it usually dries up and eventually falls off. Most species can survive such an accident. However, shorebirds often hop about on one leg with the other tucked in the body feathers, so all birds apparently one-legged may not actually be so.

491. How do birds use their feet when diving? Coots push their feet backward alternately. Other diving birds thrust their feet forward under the body, then up and outward, bringing them together in back.

492. How do water birds maintain a stationary position when sleeping? Sleeping water birds paddle with one foot, thus propelling themselves in a circle.

493. Do birds ever swim with one foot when awake? Swans frequently propel themselves with one foot. They swim in a straight line by tilting the body on one side, bringing the swimming leg under the back center of the body. The other foot is held above the water, tucked in the feathers.

494. What group of birds is most dexterous in the use of its feet? Undoubtedly the parrot family is the most dexterous in the use of its feet. Not only do these birds walk easily and climb skillfully but they use their claws as hands most expertly. The clinging power of birds that explore the trunks and branches of trees (woodpeckers, creepers, nuthatches, etc.) indicates dexterous use of their strong, flexible toes. Many species uncover a large part of their food by scratching. Most gallinaceous birds, including hens, scratch with one foot, while towhees, brown thrashers and catbirds scratch with both feet at once, using a hopping motion to do this.

VII. THE SENSES OF BIRDS

495. Do birds possess the same senses that humans have? Birds have the same senses that humans have but usually they are developed to a different degree. Some of the senses of birds are superior while others are inferior to those of humans.

496. Are the senses of all birds developed to the same degree? There is considerable difference in the development of the senses among the various species of birds. Range, habitat, manner of life and the way food is obtained all affect the development of the senses.

497. Usually the senses are limited to five. Do birds possess any other well developed senses? The sense of direction and of location is strongly developed in birds. Also, they have an extraordinary sense of balance. Since most birds move freely in the air and on land, while many others move as freely in the water, the sense of balance is essential to their way of life.

THE EYES OF BIRDS

498. Can birds see as well as humans? Birds which have conquered that most difficult medium, air, have developed powers of sight to a remarkable degree. Probably they surpass all other creatures in their excellence of vision.

Not only can the focus of their eyes change with amazing rapidity, but most birds see clearly both at shorter and longer distances than man. It is as if the eyes of birds combined the properties of a microscope and a telescope in a single instrument. The acuteness with which a sparrow hawk can see is rated by some scientists as eight times that of man. An owl is said to see in dim light ten times better than man.

499. The eyes of birds, being fixed in their sockets, cannot move. How, then, can they see so quickly what is going on around them? The flexibility of a bird's neck compensates for the fixed eyesocket.

In birds the number of neck or cervicle vertebrae varies from 8 to 25, while 14 is an average number. Because of its flexible neck an owl can turn its head with lightning speed through at least three fourths of a circle. Man, like all mammals, has seven cervical vertebrae.

500. In what outward ways do the eyes of birds differ from those of man? The eyes are placed at the side, not the front, of the face in most birds. Usually they are placed higher on the head of a bird than is true in man.

Only the pupil, black as in man, and the round iris, often brightly colored, are visible in birds. The rest of the eye is concealed behind movable eyelids. Birds alone of living creatures close their eyes in death.

501. Is it true that birds have three eyelids? The third eyelid (of which a vestige remains in the inner corner of man's eyes) is known as the nictitating membrane. This is a semitransparent membrane that in birds closes obliquely across the eye from the bill toward the ear. The nictitating membrane undoubtedly aids in cleansing the eyes and also protects them. It may be called a bird's built-in sunglasses, windshield or aqua-mask, for it cuts down on glare whether from sun or water, protects the eyes when a bird faces into the wind, and it is believed that diving birds use it as a protective device when they swim under water.

502. Do birds blink? Most birds blink chiefly with the nictitating membrane. This is particularly conspicuous in large-eyed birds such as owls. Pigeons and a few other species of birds blink with all three eyelids.

503. Chickens and robins habitually appear to examine food and other objects with one eye. Do they actually do this? Most birds, including chickens and robins, have what is called monocular vision. That is, each eye may be used independently of the other. This is understandable since the eyes of most birds are placed high on the sides of their faces. In order to see an object clearly they must cock the head, thus focusing one eye directly upon it.

504. Are there disadvantages to monocular vision? When a single eye is focused on an object it is quite difficult to judge distance and size. This flaw in its monocular vision may be put to use when one stalks a bird. By moving directly toward the bird with no sudden jerks it is sometimes possible to approach fairly close.

Coots, gallinules and shorebirds, among others, compensate for their monocular vision by jerking their heads as they move, thus giving themselves a series of rapidly changing views of their surroundings.

505. What is binocular vision? When both eyes focus on a single object, it is called binocular vision. Man, owls and falcons with their eyes directed forward, see through both eyes as through binoculars. It is believed that owls have only binocular vision but most species of birds have not only monocular vision but to a lesser degree, binocular vision. Songbirds and waterfowl have a wide range of monocular vision with but a narrow range of binocular vision in the center. Most hawks have but a narrow monocular range at the side while their field of binocular vision ranges from 35 to 50 degrees.

Woodcock, with their eyes placed far on top of the head, have binocular vision both forward and backward or upward and downward, depending on the angle at which the head is held, as well as monocular vision for almost half of a circle on both sides. Bitterns have their eyes placed so low on their heads that if they point the bill upward, they have binocular vision straight forward.

506. Do birds see color or are they like certain animals that see only in terms of black, white and gray? Most birds appear to have a well-developed color sense. Recent experiments indicate that birds are sensitive to all colors, though some scientists believe they are less receptive to the blue end of the spectrum. The fact that birds see colors should be no surprise, for of all forms of animal life, birds are among the most colorful.

507. Is the color discrimination of birds of any value to them? The bright colors of their plumage and also of their fleshy parts appear to play a part in the courtship of many species. People who wish to attract hummingbirds find that these birds respond most quickly to vials of red or yellow. It is believed the red of many berries and fruits is a factor in attracting birds that disseminate seeds. Bright red flowers predominate in the tropics where nectar-eating birds distribute pollen. Experiments with dyed food indicate that color plays an important part in the birds' choice of food.

508. How does the size of a bird's eye compare with that of man or other animals?   The eyes of birds are the largest structures in their heads and often weigh more than their brains. Of all land animals in the world, the ostrich has the biggest eye. Large hawks and owls, though most of their eyes are concealed by the lids, have eyes almost the same size as the eyes of man.

509. How does the eye of a bird make its dramatic shifts of focus?   The curvature of the cornea is controlled by special muscles and the ciliary body, made up of more muscles, can quickly change the shape of the fairly soft lens. Thus instantaneous shifts of focus from far to near are possible. This rapid change of focus is vital in birds that pursue their prey at great speeds. Among these birds are the falcons, flycatchers, nighthawks and swallows.

510. What is the pectem?   This is a comblike or folded structure within the eye which helps to increase the blood supply of the organ. Similar structures are found in the eyes of a few reptiles, but they are not present in the eyes of mammals.

511. How does the retina of a bird differ from that of man?   This image-forming tissue is amazingly developed and is almost twice as thick in birds as in humans. The retina is packed with rods that are sensitive to even low intensity of light, and cones that function in bright light, enabling birds to discriminate in the matter of colors and also to form sharp images.

512. Are all birds equally supplied with rods and cones?   Diurnal birds have many cones (for seeing colors) and comparatively few rods for use in low light. Nocturnal birds have many more rods, which is one reason for their ability to see in dim light, but the absence of cones leads to the belief that they see little color.

513. Are the rods and cones evenly scattered over the retina?   In both nocturnal and diurnal birds the cones are scattered sparsely over the retina except for concentrations called fovea. At these points of concentration the sharpest vision occurs. Most mammals, including man, have but one fovea.

Most birds have a central fovea for sharp side or monocular vision. Certain species have an additional fovea called the temporal fovea for sharp forward or binocular vision. Hawks have central foveae for seeing on either side and temporal foveae for forward binocular vision. Thus they have three views at once; one on each side and one forward. The central fovea is called the search fovea while the temporal fovea is for pursuit.

514. Are the foveae in human eyes as effective as those of birds?
Canada geese have been observed to cock their heads and apparently locate groups of geese too high for human eyes to see. Upon inspecting an apparently empty sky, geese have been observed to call, and soon thereafter another flock has appeared and joined the first. Tame hawks have located birds in the sky that are invisible to man without the aid of binoculars. The eyes of Buteo hawks are four to five times better than those of humans. Buteos can discover, watch and follow a mouse at a height so great the human eye could not possibly distinguish so small a mammal. Moreover, the rapid changes essential in the eye of a peregrine falcon as it plunges from the sky to strike its prey is impossible of imitation by the human eye.

When the human eye is studied, scientists find about 200,000 visual cells per square millimeter in the fovea, while English sparrows have about twice as many. Some hawks have as many as 1,000,000 visual cells in a square millimeter. Undoubtedly the abundance of visual cells in the foveae of birds' eyes has much to do with their remarkable powers of sight.

515. Can owls see in the daytime?   Owls can see in the daytime as well as people do. Large numbers of rods in their visual cells permit them to see in ordinary light and in addition, see well in light of very low intensity.

516. Legend says that eagles are the only birds that can look directly at the sun. Is this a fact?   Members of the hawk family, which includes eagles, frequently look upward, no doubt because they have discovered something too far away for man to see. Should they wish to do so, they can look at the sun because they can cut off some of the light by closing the nictitating membrane. Any bird that wishes to look at the sun can do the same thing.

517. Are there any exceptions to the excellent vision so prevalent in the bird world? The strange little kiwi of New Zealand is nocturnal in habits and appears to have poor vision. (See Question 522.)

518. Many species of birds have brightly colored eyes. Is this color constant? Most birds have dark eyes when they hatch. The dark color remains throughout life in many species, particularly among passerine birds. In other species, the color of the eyes may go through several stages until the color of the mature adult is attained. This is noted easily in the herring gull, for the species is widely distributed and the eyes are large enough to be conspicuous. As fledglings and first-year birds, these gulls have dark eyes. During the second year and well into the third year the eyes become lighter and more yellow. In the third year or early in the fourth year the eyes become clear bright yellow and remain so for the remainder of life.

Among birds of the South, the brown pelican is observed easily. The dark eyes of youth gradually become lighter until a fully mature bird has yellowish gray eyes.

Among many species of birds including pelicans, herons, and anhingas, the flesh around the eyes takes on new and brighter colors at breeding time. Though the color of the eyes themselves remains the same throughout adult life, the change in the fleshy skin about the eyes makes them appear to change color for the breeding season.

THE SENSE OF SMELL

519. Do birds have noses? The nostrils or external nares of birds are usually located near the base of the bill on the upper mandible.

520. What do the nostrils of a bird look like? In many species the nostrils are mere slits or oval openings in the horny bill. The nostrils of hawks are surrounded by soft membranes known as the cere. Those of pigeons are surrounded by a spongy, sensitive and swollen area called the operculum. The order of tube-nosed swimmers is made up of 105 species that vary greatly in size, appearance and habits, but all have tubelike nostrils.

521. Do birds have a keen sense of smell? There has been much conflicting testimony concerning the sense of smell in birds. Scientists, generally, believe that birds have a relatively poor sense of smell. This belief is based largely on the fact that the nostrils of a bird open into a dry, horny beak. Mammals that have the keenest sense of smell have nostrils that are large and moist and that open on a large, moist muzzle. Nevertheless, the organ of smell is well developed in some birds. This organ consists of two lobes at the anterior part of the brain. From these extend the olfactory nerves, which lead to three small projections called the turbinal bones, located on the bony wall within the bill.

522. Is the sense of smell important to any species of bird? It is generally believed that the nocturnal kiwis of New Zealand, which have poor eyesight, find their food chiefly through their well-developed sense of smell. Unlike the nostrils of most birds, those of the kiwi are located at the tip of the bill and actually open on its under side.

523. Vultures eat chiefly carrion that smells so highly humans avoid its vicinity. Do these birds locate their food through the sense of smell? Vultures depend on their extraordinary eyesight to locate most of their food rather than on the sense of smell.

524. Do scientists believe the olfactory sense in birds is declining or improving? Birds have the best vision of any kind of animal in the world. It is almost an axiom that as one sense develops extraordinary powers, others tend to atrophy. Probably the sense of smell in birds has declined through the ages. It may well be that long ago birds had a much better sense of smell than they now possess. Birds belonging to the more primitive orders have a better sense of smell than do the highly developed passerine birds.

525. Since birds cannot talk, how do scientists decide whether a bird has a good or poor sense of smell? Scientists are most imaginative In devising tests that reveal the secrets of animal reactions. Many methods have been used to determine the keenness of a bird's sense of smell. Carrion has been hidden from vultures to discover whether they are attracted by the smell of food. Most of the experiments of this type are inconclusive because the conditions were not properly controlled.

Kiwis were offered several identical buckets filled with sand except that one contained worms desired as food by the birds. The kiwis ignored all the buckets except the one containing the food they preferred.

In another type of test, a favorite food is impregnated with a colorless but strongly scented solution distasteful to the bird. Then trays of both scented and unscented food are presented to the bird. If the bird turns away from the scented trays without tasting the food but eats freely from the unscented trays, it is assumed that the sense of smell determined the choice.

THE HEARING OF BIRDS

526. If birds have ears, where are they?   Of course birds have ears. They are on the side of the head in much the same position as human ears.

527. Are the ears of birds ever visible?   While the ear is inconspicuous in many species, they may be seen readily on birds with naked heads such as chickens, vultures, wood ibises and spoonbills. The ears of some young birds, such as the gannet and white ibis, are covered with round pads of longer down that look like ear muffs.

528. How do the ears of birds differ from those of mammals?
Birds lack the external pinna which all mammals have for collecting sounds. Birds with feathered heads have special feathers over the ears. These are delicate and loose and may actually be erected slightly when the bird listens intently. These feathers are known as auricular feathers.

Birds have an eardrum not unlike that of humans. Sound is carried to the inner ear by a single bone called the columella, whereas three bones do this in human ears.

529. How does the hearing of a bird compare with that of a human? The human ear has a hearing range from about 20 to about 17,000 cycles per second, or about nine octaves. It must be remembered that not all people with normal hearing ability have quite as great a range as this, while some individuals have a greater range. Comparatively few species of birds have been thoroughly tested for hearing range. Those tested showed a range considerably narrower than that of a person with normal hearing. Among the birds tested is the English sparrow, with a hearing range from about 675 to 11,500 cycles per second. Pigeons ranged from about 200 to 7,500 cycles per second and starlings from about 700 to 15,000 cycles per second.

Most passerine birds have a singing range from 1,100 to 10,000 cycles per second. There is little doubt that they hear sounds within those frequencies. However, it should not be assumed that their hearing ability is limited to the range within which they sing, for no human voice can begin to reach as high or as low as the limits of human hearing.

530. Can birds hear sounds from as great a distance as man? Birds appear to hear airplanes before the most alert sky-watcher detects them. It is said that birds in French aviaries during the First World War were disturbed by battles as much as 200 miles distant, which were completely inaudible to humans.

531. Can birds hear sounds close by that are inaudible to man? Many people believe robins running on the lawn stop and cock their heads to listen for worms in the earth. Woodpeckers apparently detect sounds of insects within the trees, for they dig holes straight into the heart of ant colonies and to the place where wood-boring beetles are working.

532. Do birds hear the songs of all other birds? Birds can hear only the songs within the frequency range of their own ears. It has been stated that birds such as the great horned owl, with a very low range of hearing, cannot hear any of the high pitched songs of birds such as the Blackburnian warbler and golden-crowned kinglet. In spite of this assumption, which is based largely on the low-frequency voice of the great horned owl, this species apparently hears the high-pitched squeak of mice, flying squirrels and other small mammals.

533. Are there any birds to whom the sense of hearing of a particular importance?   One of the strangest birds in the world is the oilbird or cave bird of northern South America. These birds nest in the complete darkness of caves and appear to avoid obstacles in the same way bats do by uttering high-pitched notes that are echoed, the time between cry and echo giving the location of the obstacle. The cry used by oilbirds to locate obstacles is not supersonic; that is, it is audible to human ears.

Owls have exceptionally large ear openings as well as unusually long auricular feathers, leading to the belief that a discriminating and acute sense of hearing helps them locate their prey. Barred owls, barn owls and the brown owls of Europe all have a curious flap of skin in front of the large ear opening. When this is raised, it undoubtedly helps to catch sounds.

534. Do the "horns" on some species of owls and on horned larks have any bearing on the hearing of these species?   It is doubtful that the clusters of feathers resembling horns on the heads of certain species have any bearing on their ability to hear.

535. Is the absence of an ear trumpet or pinna, present in most mammals, a handicap to the hearing of birds?   The absence of a pinna or ear trumpet in birds adds to the streamlining of their heads, of great value to them in flight. No doubt the extremely mobile neck compensates for a lack of this ear flap by permitting a bird to focus its ears on a sound.

536. Has the acute hearing of birds ever been turned to the advantage of man?   The best-known episode in history involving the hearing of birds is the reputed saving of Rome by geese. These domestic birds, hearing the approach of invading Goths, gabbled so loudly they awakened the Roman soldiers in time for them to make an effective defense of their city, then the greatest in the world.

During the First World War parrots were kept in French forts and on the Eiffel Tower. The parrots gave warning of approaching airplanes long before they could be discovered by human ears. Thus, in the primitive days of aerial warfare, the acute hearing of birds played a part.

THE SENSE OF TOUCH

537. Do birds have a keen sense of touch? Scientists are not in accord in this matter, but the weight of opinions appears to be on the side of a well-developed sense of touch.

538. What part of a bird is most sensitive in this respect? This undoubtedly varies with the species. Ducks, geese and swans, particularly those species that feed at night or probe for food in debris where they cannot see, have particularly sensitive bill tips. Almost 2,000 tactile corpuscles connected to nerve endings were counted in the tip of a goose's bill. It is believed the swollen operculum of pigeons is a sensitive tactile area and may have an important part in stimulating courtship ardor.

Birds which explore for food with their bills or tongues, as many shorebirds and woodpeckers do, must have sensitive nerve endings in these parts to guide them to edible morsels.

539. Some birds have bristles around their bills. Do these serve a bird as its whiskers do a cat or a mouse? Undoubtedly these structures, known as rictal bristles, which have sensory nerve cells at the base, act as organs of touch.

540. Which birds have conspicuous rictal bristles? Species that catch insects on the wing have particularly long rictal bristles. Swallows, flycatchers and goatsuckers all have long rictal bristles. The bearded barbet of West Africa and the large frogmouth of Malayasia have exceptionally long rictal bristles.

541. Are ordinary feathers able to conduct touch sensations? While a fully developed feather, like human hair, is made up of hardened, dead material formed by the skin, its base is clasped by a follicle in which there are sensory nerves. Therefore if a feather comes in contact with another object or is moved ever so slightly by an air current, it is sensed by the bird.

542. Is the brood patch of a bird an area sensitive to touch?
Some scientists believe that the brood patch supplies a kind of touch
picture to the bird, indicating when the correct number of eggs has
been laid, and that in some unknown way it stops the formation of
more eggs. If this is true, the sense of touch automatically controls
egg production.

TASTE

**543. Most birds are highly selective in the matter of food they
will eat. Does this indicate a well developed sense of taste?**
Since the senses of taste and smell are closely related, it should
come as no surprise that birds are believed to possess a poorly
developed sense of taste.

**544. Is there any physical basis for the belief that birds have a
limited sense of taste?**   The sense of taste is centered in taste buds, a
specialized type of cell. Birds have relatively few taste buds. Moreover, birds bolt their food. In the case of young birds, the adults
usually place the food so far back in the throat that taste buds, even
if they were present in the mouth in abundance, could not be brought
into play.

**545. Is there any difference between the taste discrimination of
insect-eating birds and seed-eating birds?**   It is thought that in
general insect-eaters have a better sense of taste discrimination than
seed-eaters. However, this varies greatly in different species. So many
insects have an unpleasant taste and may even be actively poisonous
to birds that a developed sense of taste would appear to be a safeguard.

**546. How do birds avoid poisonous insects if they cannot do so
through their sense of taste?**   This seems to be a matter of learning.
Young birds sometimes eat (and even die from) poisonous insects
that adult birds will not touch. Color and shape as well as taste may
enter into the choice of the insects.

547. Birds have been known to develop new food habits. How does this happen? Birds at feeding shelves are often observed sampling new foods cautiously before deciding to swallow them. In the wild, birds probably are governed by accident. For example, settlers in New Zealand imported vast flocks of sheep. The kea parrot developed the habit of pecking through the hide of living sheep to get the fat around the kidney, and thereby turned man's hand against this species. Undoubtedly the kea developed a taste for kidney fat through first sampling that of an injured sheep. The kea simply took advantage of an abundant supply of a new kind of food.

548. Do carrion eaters such as vultures taste the food they eat? It is generally believed that vultures have a very rudimentary sense of taste. Nevertheless, it would be unsafe to say vultures lack any sense of taste because they eat food that is unacceptable to man. Choice of food is the result of custom, habit and a supply of the materials dictated by these. Within certain limits, the food of birds varies in different areas or at different seasons, even as the food of man varies according to the part of the world he lives in and the seasons.

549. Hummingbirds feed at certain flowers and not at others. Does this indicate a taste choice? The apparent preference of hummingbirds for flowers with bright colors and long tubes may result more from ease of locating vivid flowers and the concentration of nectar often found in the bottom of tubed flowers than from taste discrimination.

However, many people who attract hummingbirds by placing sugar water in colored vials have found that the favorite red color is not sufficient inducement. The sugar solution must reach a certain standard. A solution of four parts of water to one of sugar is usually acceptable.

VIII. THE ANNUAL CYCLE

BIRD SONG

550. What is meant by a songbird? The systematist classifies as oscines or true songbirds all those species which have the "syrinx with four or five distinct pairs of intrinsic muscles, inserted at ends of three upper bronchial half-rings and thus constituting a highly complex and effective musical apparatus." These species form a suborder of the Passeriformes or perching birds. This may be an acceptable term for a systematist but it is difficult for a field student to confine his use of the term *songbird* to this group, thus eliminating such gifted singers as many shorebirds, goatsuckers, flycatchers and others.

551. What is considered a bird song? A bird song may consist of from one to a long series of sounds consistently given in a more or less uninterrupted manner and in a definite pattern. In some species it is confined entirely to the breeding season and in all it is loudest and most frequent at that time. Though most often vocal, it may be mechanical, as in the tapping of woodpeckers, the drumming of grouse, and the booming of nighthawks.

552. Why do birds sing? The chief function of song in most species is to proclaim territory. It warns males of the same species to keep away. But song also serves as a mating invitation to the opposite sex, and subsequently helps maintain and strengthen the bond between the pair. There are also many types of social songs such as the canary-like one used by American goldfinches in flock formation. At times song apparently serves as an escape valve for excess energy, as a manifestation of the peak vitality reached by a bird during the period of reproduction, or is given simply because a bird is bubbling over with the joy of living.

553. How does a bird know which song to sing? Voice characteristics are greatly influenced by the construction of the syrinx inherited by the bird. The melodies produced are possible only because of the anatomy of the vocal apparatus. Undoubtedly a barred owl will hoot and a limpkin will wail even if it has never heard one of its relatives. So one might say a bird inherits its ability to sing.

On the other hand, the perfected song characteristic of the species is probably learned. This is particularly true of birds with elaborate songs. If a bird is reared in captivity and out of hearing of its own species, the song may have the quality of its relatives, but be quite different in pattern. As soon as the bird hears a member of its own species, however, it tends to fall into the typical phrasing and rhythm of the species. Thus through imitation, stimulation and practice it perfects its performance. This is well known by those who raise and train canaries to sing, as the young are raised where they hear only exceptionally expert singers.

554. Does each species have only one definite song? Each species ordinarily has two or more very distinct types of song, with variations for each type. Thus one may recognize a common yellowthroat or blue jay song whether he hears it in Maine, Michigan or Florida. It is true that widely distributed species often have pronounced local variations or accents, and in a few geographical races the songs may be quite different.

A cardinal may have two dozen or more song variations but they are all typically cardinal in quality. Something in the quality of the voice and general phraseology leaves no doubt as to the performer's identity. Research workers have found that many birds have very specialized songs reserved for distinct occasions. In the American goldfinch, for instance, one song may have to do with off-territory courtship, the next with on-territory courtship, and still another only with flock formation. Aretas Saunders, after decades of extensive study, has noted as many as 884 variations in song sparrow songs.

555. Can a bird be taught to sing a song other than its own? Yes, but songs so acquired are seldom given with perfection. A young blue jay raised on an island by the authors was constantly exposed to a human imitation of a robin song, day after day and week after week, until the jay itself sang a song unquestionably based on the notes and phraseology of a robin. Visitors to the island would ask about the harsh queer-sounding robin song. Moreover, the authors have heard a parrot once owned by an opera star deliver recognizable soprano scales the singer had practiced regularly. Starlings and most members of the Mimidae family imitate the songs of other birds or sounds which they hear frequently. (See Question 575.)

556. How frequently does a bird sing in one day?   This varies considerably from species to species, and even from male to male in the same species. A male American redstart, for instance, if fairly isolated from other males of its species will give few songs in comparison with one that has several neighboring males disputing his ownership of territory. Thus, in areas where population pressure is heavy, the males must of necessity sing persistently to warn all would-be intruders to keep away. Naturally there are very few records to show exactly how many times a species normally sings in one day. One scientist kept records of a bobwhite that gave 1,403 songs in a day, and the patience of another scientist revealed that one song sparrow gave as many as 2,305 songs between dawn and dark.

557. Do birds sing at any time of day?   To begin with, some species are chiefly diurnal singers and some essentially nocturnal, while others are generally crepuscular. Whip-poor-wills and chuck-will's-widows seem to be most vociferous just as darkness sets in and again just before dawn. Common loons and great horned owls may sing throughout the night, particularly when the moon is full. Although diurnal birds may sing at any time during the daylight hours, especially when territories are being established and mates won, each species has its favorite hours. American robins regularly break into song at the first hint of dawn, give a minimum of music in the afternoon when the temperature is high, and then break forth in full song again toward evening. Red-eyed vireos which feed as they sing may be vociferous throughout the day, while the wood, hermit, Wilson's, Swainson's and gray-cheeked thrushes give their most superb performances around sunset.

558. Do diurnal passerine birds ever sing at night?   A few diurnal passerine birds such as the mockingbird, nightingale and long-billed marsh wren give magnificent vocal performances at night. Moreover, the authors believe any bird may occasionally sing at night. Over the years they have heard nocturnal songs given by such distantly related species as the olive-sided flycatcher, house wren, common yellowthroat, hooded oriole, cardinal and song sparrow.

559. Do birds sing at any time of the year? This varies considerably according to species. In the South permanent residents such as the mockingbird, cardinal and Carolina wren, though most ardent and vociferous during the breeding season, seem to sing all year round. With migrating birds, singing usually reaches a peak in spring and early summer when territories are being established and mates won. Some species apparently stop as soon as mating is accomplished; some sing throughout the incubation period; and others even sing while the young are being fed. As a rule, however, song diminishes considerably by midsummer, and many birds are not heard after that time.

In autumn, after the postnuptial molt, there seems to be a slight renewal of singing in some species, but at this season songs are generally short and weak compared to the full rich ones given in spring. Even in the North some species sing periodically during the winter, especially when exceptionally warm sunny spells occur. By late winter and early spring song begins to pick up, and even some winter visitants such as the slate-colored juncoes may be heard singing around New York City and house wrens become vociferous in Florida.

560. Do female birds sing? As might be expected, the singing ability of female birds varies considerably from species to species. In the majority of cases the females do not produce sounds that are entitled to be called songs. In some, such as the song sparrow, the female's song is shorter, softer and less impressive. The female black-capped chickadee gives the clear whistled *fee-bee* note, though less frequently than the male. On the other hand, in birds such as the cardinal, rose-breasted grosbeak and black-headed grosbeak the females may rival their mates in richness of musical performance. In a few species such as the phalaropes, the female's song is even more elaborate than that of her mate. In some tropical American wrens the females sing lovely stirring duets with their mates.

561. Do young birds sing? Careful research has revealed that some birds begin singing at a surprisingly early age. At first the performances tend to be decidedly poor, but by imitation and repetition the birds gradually develop and perfect their full characteristic song. Mrs. Margaret Morse Nice, a painstaking research ornithologist, brought together and published data naming 16 different species wherein the young commenced to sing at ages ranging from 13 to 24 days. She mentioned 15 additional species whose young sang when less than eight weeks old.

562. Does weather affect singing in birds? The amount of singing by birds may be influenced considerably by the weather. An unseasonal cold snap or the high temperatures of a late summer afternoon generally decreases the amount of singing. Wind, particularly a strong one, will diminish singing or even stop it altogether. Likewise, heavy rain generally stops most bird song. On the other hand, the periods of high humidity immediately preceding and following a storm often induce singing. At that time American cuckoos generally become vociferous and consequently are frequently referred to as "rain crows." The common loons grow noisy as a storm approaches, and northern woodsmen say they can foretell bad weather by the wild yodeling of the loons.

563. What is meant by a singing perch? In many species of birds, the males select several prominent perches in their territory from which to proclaim ownership of land, sing to a sex partner, or attract a potential mate. These few favored perches are generally used whenever the male sings and are known as singing perches. In recent years TV antennas have served as excellent prominent singing perches for many birds.

564. What are flight songs? In many species, particularly those inhabiting large fields, extensive prairies and other wide-open treeless country, the males, instead of selecting prominent perches from which to sing, regularly present their songs while performing aerial maneuvers. The skylark of Europe, which has inspired many a poet, is an excellent example of a bird having a flight song. The woodcock, common snipe, horned lark, water pipit, lark bunting, bobolink and American goldfinch render impressive flight songs. But such performances are not limited to species inhabiting wide-open areas. The purple finch and white-winged crossbill give elaborate flight songs as they flutter on vibrant wings above northern conifers.

565. What is meant by an ecstasy song? These are differentiated from the regular flight songs given chiefly by birds inhabiting prairies, fields and other treeless regions, because they are not typical songs

The Saw-whet Owl does not hoot, but emits a series of evenly-spaced mechanical repetitious whistles sounding like someone whetting a saw.

These magnificent frigate-birds represent the class Aves. Birds and birds alone have feathers. Therefore any animal that grows feathers must be a bird.

Gobbler turkeys engage in elaborate courtship displays before the females.

Loons are the most primitive birds now living in North America.

Two sooty terns taken from their nests on the Dry Tortugas, 60 miles west of Key West, Florida, were released at Cape Hatteras, North Carolina. They were back on their nests 1,000 sea-miles away in 5 days.

All mammals, even the giraffe, have only 7 neck vertebrae. Swans have 23 in their neck. Thus a bird's neck has great flexibility, even surpassing that of a snake in freedom of action.

The heart of a hummingbird often beats as fast as 615 times per minute.

Zoo keepers discovered that their captive spoonbills often lost their delicate pink coloration and became white or almost white. By feeding shrimps to the birds they restored their normal pink plumage.

Notice the aluminum band on the right leg of this ring-billed gull.

A lesser yellowlegs banded at Cape Cod, Mass., on August 28, 1935, was killed on the island of Martinique in the West Indies on September 3 of the same year.

The order of tube-nosed swimmers is made up of 105 species that vary greatly in size and appearance, but like this Leach's petrel all have tube-like nostrils.

In spite of popular belief to the contrary, black vultures depend on their extraordinary eyesight, not their sense of smell, to locate most of their food.

Diving ducks must run along the surface to gain momentum before taking flight, while dabbling ducks can rise immediately from the surface.

This American egret is nesting in safety in a sanctuary of the National Audubon Society.

Brown pelican adults are virtually mute.

Thousands of ducks winter on the refuges maintained by the U. S. Fish & Wildlife Service.

of the species giving them. Some birds that normally sing from a favorite singing perch may on widely scattered occasions excitedly rise on quivering wings and bubble forth with ecstasy. Such performances are irregular or unpredictable in occurrence, and the songs are usually quite different from the normal one given by the species. The bird appears to be releasing a superabundance of energy or expressing a high degree of emotion. The common yellowthroat, ovenbird and Louisiana waterthrush periodically perform in this manner.

566. Do birds ever sing on or above the nest? Most birds do not sing in the immediate vicinity of the nest. In fact, the nearest singing perch is ordinarily quite far off and the male tends to slip silently in and out of the nesting site. However, the authors once located a rose-breasted grosbeak nest because the male was singing softly while incubating, and others report this experience with black-headed grosbeaks. The authors, too, once found a warbling vireo's nest while searching for the singing bird, and if the male is indeed the only sex (the sexes of this species cannot be determined in the field) to give a rich warbling song, he was performing on the nest.

567. Is the larynx of a bird the same as that of man? Unlike humans, which have a complex larynx with its cartilage and vocal cords situated at the upper end of the trachea or windpipe, birds have a larynx which is little developed. Instead, the voice box of birds, called the syrinx, is situated at the lower end of the windpipe where the two bronchial tubes branch.

568. How can even the smallest birds give extremely long songs apparently without stopping to take a breath? In addition to lungs, birds have a complex and remarkable system of air sacs which virtually fill the body cavity. The degree of development of these air sacs varies considerably from species to species. It is believed that birds with extensive uninterrupted songs such as winter wrens, purple finches and highly trained canaries utilize the reserve air supply stored in these air sacs. (See Questions 222, 223, 225.)

569. How do birds such as the sand-hill crane, whooping crane and trumpeter swan achieve such resonance and volume of sound? In most birds the trachea or windpipe usually extends straight down through the neck to the lungs. In the species mentioned above, however, the windpipe forms large loops, some of which are situated inside the breastbone. Thus, in a whooping crane, the windpipe is actually four feet long. This length in conjunction with the peculiar construction of the vocal apparatus undoubtedly accounts for the impressive character of the sounds produced by these birds.

570. What is meant by a call note?   In its broadest sense the term *call note* applies to a great variety of bird utterances. Calls of alarm, anger, begging, summons, scolding, warning and location are but a few examples. The cheeps of warblers help these nocturnal migrants to stay together and more easily follow the main line of flight. The wild special caw of a crow given as it spots an owl quickly rallies all crows within hearing distance to join the mob and annoy the unfortunate owl. The clucking of a hen on finding food brings her chicks to the feast. Every blue jay in the neighborhood screams with anger if a cat is seen entering the woods.

571. What is a hoot owl?   People with little knowledge of birds and unable to identify one species from another usually refer to any owl that hoots as a hoot owl. In the eastern United States this term generally refers to either the barred owl or great horned owl. The former ordinarily gives eight hoots divided into two groups of four with a distinct drawl at the end. It is roughly baritone in quality and is easily imitated by the human voice.

In comparison the great horned owl hoots are bass and normally fit into the rhythm: *who who-who who who.*

572. Do all owls hoot?   Many owls have songs or calls which are not hoots. For instance, the most common and best-known song of the screech owl is a quavering series of plaintive whistles which usually descend the scale.

The barn owl has several explosive steamlike hisses, and at times gives a call which sounds as though the bird were slamming on rusty brakes.

The well-named saw-whet owl sings with a steady series of evenly spaced mechanical, repetitious whistles resembling the sound made by running a file over the teeth of a saw. (See Questions 979, 980, 981.)

573. Is a mute swan really mute? Though generally rather taciturn and soft-spoken when compared to such relatives as the whistling, trumpeter and whooping swans, the mute swan is by no means mute. Not only does it produce a loud hiss when angry or annoyed but its whining *whee-you* is one of the typical sounds on park ponds.

574. Is any bird mute? The adults of a few species such as the brown pelican and magnificent frigate-bird are virtually mute. Some others such as the double-crested cormorant and turkey vulture utter only the most rudimentary grunts. The young of all these birds, however, are quite noisy.

575. Do mockingbirds actually mimic other birds? While mockingbirds have very definite characteristic songs of their own, they frequently include parts of the songs or calls of other birds in their performances. There is great variation in this tendency from one mockingbird to the next. One individual may seldom mimic, while the next may regularly include phrases copied from another species. Some people question this, but there is no doubt that mockingbirds are mimics. On several occasions the authors have heard a mockingbird suddenly give scolding jay notes as a blue jay flew past, repeat unquestionably great crested flycatcher *wheeps* as that species appeared, and emit a distinct *pill-will-willet* as a willet circled over. Many scientists have analyzed the songs of mockingbirds and some have listed over three dozen fairly perfect imitations of other birds given by a single mockingbird.

576. Which bird has the most beautiful song? This is purely a matter of opinion, and the choice of the favorite song usually is influenced by the setting or by some special association with the bird. Many people in North America would choose the simple plaintive notes of the white-throated sparrow. Some have said that the hermit thrush's performance surpasses all others, but is it more beautiful than that of the Wilson's, wood or Swainson's thrush? And do any of these deserve to be ranked above the indescribable flow of delicate complex trills and warbles of the winter wren, or even above the wavering resonant laughter of a common loon on its spruce-rimmed lake?

577. Why do woodpeckers frequently drum on a metal roof, drainpipe or TV antenna support? Most birds sing to proclaim territories and warn other males to keep away. Since many woodpeckers have relatively poor voices they drum instead of sing to proclaim ownership of their nesting area. Ordinarily they select a hollow tree to obtain the maximum volume. Some individuals have discovered that they get the most volume from a metal roof, drainpipe, or antenna support and consequently use these objects as their favorite drumming posts.

578. Is it true that a woodcock sings with its wings? Many birds produce very musical sounds with their wings. A mourning dove generally leaves its perch with loudly whistling wings, and a duck called the goldeneye produces such a loud sweet sound with its wings that hunters call it the "whistler." The woodcock has an elaborate flight song and a good part of the twittering musical sounds are actually produced by air rushing through the special stiff, attenuated outer wing feathers.

579. What bird sings with its tail? One may say the common snipe sings with its tail. On rapidly vibrating wings, it gives its flight song high above the marsh. It circles around and around, periodically dashing downward and producing an eerie ventriloquistic sound, as the air rushes past the unique rigid outer tail feathers.

580. Is it true that young people can hear bird songs better than older people? There is great variation in the hearing ability of humans. Some may hear notes as low as 20 cycles per second and as high as 17,000 cycles per second. Of course an adult with acute ears will hear more than a young person with poor hearing. But in general, young people do hear much better than older people. Young people have ears which are sensitive to high frequencies. As one grows older, he tends to lose the higher notes and in later life all songs based on high frequencies may be unheard.

Some years ago W. E. Saunders, a well-known Canadian ornithologist, wrote an article describing his loss of high-frequency songs. At the age of 60 he could no longer hear the lisp of a golden-crowned kinglet, at 65 the trill of a cedar waxwing became inaudible, and at

68 he could watch Blackburnian and Cape May warblers sing, but not a single note was heard.

COURTSHIP AND FORMATION
OF THE PAIR

581. What is meant by mating? In ornithology this term generally is used in reference to pairing. It includes the entire engagement period when the formation of the pair is being established. It should be distinguished from the actual sex relation which by itself usually is spoken of as copulation or coition.

582. What is courtship? Naturally one cannot talk about mating without including some discussion of courtship. The latter, however, consists of a wide assortment of displays or ceremonies used to attract and stimulate the opposite sex. They are by no means confined to the time of pairing but often are carried on long before, right through, and sometimes long after the period of mating. Some courtship acts may be as simple as the raising of a showy crown, as in the ruby-crowned kinglet, or as elaborate as the amazing pirouetting of a peacock with its incredibly beautiful "tail" fully fanned. (See Question 434.)

583. When does the mating of migratory species take place? In the Northern Hemisphere mating usually follows closely on the heels of spring migration. In the majority of migratory passerine birds, the males arrive first, whereupon most of them immediately establish territories and sing frequently and intensely to announce ownership of their chosen piece of land. As with males, some females may wander for a brief period after arrival, but ordinarily would-be residents are attracted directly to the territories established by males of the same species. As soon as a resident female appears on a territory mating attempts begin. In species other than passerine birds there are great variations. Some, like the ducks and many sea birds, even mate while still on their wintering grounds.

584. What is the average procedure in mating? As soon as the female arrives on an established territory, the male engages in displays and sexual pursuit. Some males seem able to differentiate between transient females and would-be residents and show interest only in the latter.

Although he may attempt copulation during this initial acquaintance, the male is usually unsuccessful, as the female at first is unreceptive. But if the female remains on the territory after these ardent displays and sexual pursuits, and tolerates and then encourages more attention from the male, the pair is formed and mating accomplished. In most passerine birds, within a few days the female usually reaches a phase in the breeding cycle when she is receptive and copulation then takes place.

585. Does the male always select the nesting territory?   In the majority of migratory passerine birds, the males usually arrive first and establish territories. In some migratory species, however, the formation of the pair may take place on the wintering grounds far from the nesting territory. In still others, it may take place immediately after completion of the migratory journey, even before a territory has been established. In all these latter cases the pair together apparently selects the nesting territory.

586. What are the stages leading up to mating in nonmigratory species?   Many nonmigratory species remain mated throughout the year and even from year to year. Consequently, the steps leading to the true initial mating or engagement period, when not repeated annually, are difficult to detect. In fact, they have so seldom been witnessed or recognized that much research is required before any satisfactory detailed sequence of events can be presented.

587. Are all birds monogamous?   The majority of birds are monogamous, faithfulness of the pair to each other during the breeding season ordinarily being constant. This faithfulness is induced by attachment to the sex partner, to the territory, and finally to the eggs or young.

588. Do monogamous birds ever accept different mates during one breeding season?   Although a monogamous bird may be faithful to its mate for an entire season or even several years, it is very practical and usually will mate again as soon as its partner dies.

Remating sometimes takes place after desertion by a partner, or even upon eviction of the partner from the territory by a more aggressive dominant male. In some species mates are changed regularly between broods.

589. How can a bird widow or widower replace a mate after the breeding season is under way? Mortality among birds is high during the nesting season and the surviving individual of a pair must replace its mate quickly if success in raising young is to be achieved. In most species there is a floating population of unmated birds ready and anxious to step in when the first opportunity arises.

If a mated male dies, a wandering male usually takes its place immediately and claims ownership of the territory. If a mated female dies, the male intensifies both his singing and displays to win another mate as quickly as possible.

One female black-capped chickadee is known to have had three successive mates in one season. One scientist collected a mated male indigo bunting. Another male soon took over the territory and mated with the female. Nine males in succession were taken from this single territory and a tenth immediately took possession.

590. Is polygamy rare among birds? Although the majority of birds are monogamous, polygamy is by no means unusual. A number of species such as ostriches, pheasants and various blackbirds are polygamous, an individual of one sex mating during the same period with two or more individuals of the opposite sex.

591. What is polygyny? In polygamous birds usually it is the male that mates with two or more females. This is called polygyny.

592. What are some examples of polygynous birds? Ostriches and rheas are polygynous. They have a unique system wherein each male is mated to several hens. These hens lay their eggs in a single family nest which is supervised by the male.

Many pheasants are polygynous. A single cock may be mated to a half dozen or more hens. Even some small passerine birds such as red-winged, yellow-headed and Brewer's blackbirds may be polygynous if the proportion of females in a given area is high. Frequently one male will control a definite territory which includes several nests.

593. What is polyandry? When a female mates with two or more males at the same time it is called polyandry.

594. Which species of birds regularly practice polyandry? The mating of one female with two or more males is unusual among birds. The phalaropes, which show a sex reversal in courtship and nesting activities, are polyandrous. In these birds the female is more brightly colored than the male and she makes most of the advances in courtship. Indications are that this is true in some other shorebirds. Tinamous follow this pattern. In button-quail the female, which is larger and more brightly colored, lays several clutches of eggs in different nests, and each nest is tended by a single male. Old World cuckoos are polyandrous, while most New World cuckoos are not. In cowbirds, some longspurs and other species, one female will generally be courted and mated with by two or more males. Furthermore, even in species which are normally monogamous, there are times under special conditions when polyandry is used.

595. Why are some birds called promiscuous? This term usually applies to species in which no definite pair is formed and copulation is promiscuous. Most writers include these with polygamous birds. Boat-tailed grackles of the southern United States provide a good example. The males usually stay in groups or small flocks during the breeding season and the females visit these flocks and mate at random with any male. Male prairie chickens, sharp-tailed grouse and sage hens engage in elaborate courtship dances on ancestral dancing grounds. The females visit these dancing grounds and copulate with the first male which stimulates them sufficiently. No pair is formed and courting and copulation are decidedly promiscuous.

In other species such as the ruffed and spruce grouse the males, although performing on individual drumming grounds by themselves, copulate with any willing female. There is no pair formation as such. One male may copulate with many females and one female may visit several males, each performing in his own area.

596. How long do birds remain mated? There are many variations in the length of time birds remain mated. Most monogamous birds stay together for an entire season or as long as it takes to raise their one, two or more broods. Some may even remain mated from one season to the next, though they are less closely attached to each other through the nonbreeding season. In some species the pair may break up soon after the eggs are laid, others after the young are reared, even though a second brood is to follow. In other words, some may change mates between broods. A few species are said to keep their mates for life.

597. Which birds remain mated for life?   It has been proved that some birds remain paired for a long time and it is supposed that some of these mate for life. There are definite records of captive swans and geese that never remated after the partner died. On the other hand, there are cases of Canada geese actually changing mates for no apparent reason, and many cases where the surviving individual of a pair remated. It is obvious, therefore, that the subject needs considerable study before unequivocal statements can be given for a species as a whole. Some ornithologists interpret the term "mating for life" quite loosely to mean that the bird remains faithful as long as the mate lives, and upon death of a mate a new partner may be accepted. Various authors have stated that eagles, hawks, cranes, owls, parrots, ravens, crows, magpies, chickadees, titmice, wrentits and others mate for life. Some of these statements are based on the circumstantial evidence that certain pairs were mated for many years.

598. What is meant by courtship display?   A courtship display is any performance or activity that attracts and stimulates the opposite sex and helps maintain an emotional relationship between the sex partners. Birds present an amazing variety of displays, some so subtle, some so complex, that at present it is impossible to interpret the exact function of many, and difficult to divide them into clearcut, simple, satisfactory types. As a rule, the courtship display stimulates the mate by its sudden, unusual, attractive or sensational nature.

599. Is song part of the courtship performance?   Indeed it is. Although in many birds song is used primarily for proclaiming territory and warning rival males to keep away, it is also used directly to attract the mate. Some songs, though merely weak trills as in the chipping sparrow, are just as effective as the elaborate beautiful music of a hermit thrush. (See Question 552.)

600. What are the most conspicuous types of courtship displays?
Many birds either erect, spread or otherwise exhibit a crest, ruff, tail, modified scapulars, or other showy adornments of plumage. Many flash brilliantly colored patterns on the wings or tail, or present colors of the gape, lores, feet, bill and face which at mating time often assume their most intense color. A few birds inflate sacs on the throat or other parts of the body. In some species the structural modifications of the bill and face may be flushed with color and used to good advantage. Many displays are accompanied by queer body postures, shuffling of the feet or an amazing assortment of dance steps. In some species it involves loud vocal calls, in others mechanical noises, flight exhibitions or aquatic performances.

601. Does the male alone engage in courtship displays? In the majority of monogamous birds a solo display is usually presented by a solitary male. This may indicate the desire for a mate, eagerness to copulate, or devotion to the sex partner. Some females may respond with a less evident and showy display which nevertheless is just as effective. In a few species, both male and female perform before each other in a similar and equally intense manner. This often is referred to as mutual display. A number of species engage in so-called social displays wherein several males perform in the presence of one another. These social exhibitions usually take place on ancestral or traditional dancing grounds where annually the males court the females attracted by the performance.

602. What are some species of birds which indulge in mutual display? Since World War II the mutual display of the gooney birds (Laysan albatrosses) of Midway Island has become known around the world. All species of albatrosses indulge in mutual displays, as do gannets, boobies and cormorants. The mutual display of many grebes, particularly the western grebe, is spectacular.

603. Which species practice social displays? In North America the most dramatic of social displays are performed by prairie chickens, sharp-tailed grouse and sage grouse cocks. These species group on ancient dancing grounds where daily for several weeks the cocks endeavor to secure dominance over their fellows in the winning of hens. In Europe the dancing hills of the ruff are scenes during the breeding season of aggressive but bloodless displays between numbers of ruffs seeking the favor of the reeves.

604. Are there other kinds of courtship displays or performances?
For convenience of discussion and study, ornithologists have attempted to divide the courtship displays or performances into types. One kind, wherein the male pursues the female, is usually referred to as sexual pursuit. In songbirds this is generally carried on in the air. In aquatic birds it frequently takes place on the water. The sexual pursuit occurs most frequently during the mating period, when the male is trying to win a sex partner. The female may not appreciate the initial attention, but if she is a would-be resident she may remain in and around the selected territory and eventually reach a receptive mood.

The mating or engagement period follows, and eventually copulation takes place. Undoubtedly these pursuits tend to create and maintain a high emotional level in both birds, as well as indicate the readiness and eagerness of the male to copulate.

605. What is meant by symbolic display? A symbolic display is just a special type of courtship performance. It may occur during all phases of the breeding cycle and serves to strengthen the bond with the sex partner. One type is usually referred to as symbolic nest building. The male normally plays the dominant role, even though he may take no actual part in nest construction. Some birds may simply play with sticks, twigs or other vegetation, some may pass them to the mate, and still others may bring nesting material and present it to the sex partner each time he comes to take his turn at incubation. Some water birds dive, come to the surface with the bill full of plant growth and proudly show it as if to say, "See what a wonderful nest builder I will be."

Another type of symbolic display is frequently referred to as courtship feeding. Again the male plays the dominant role. He gathers food and presents it to the female, at times even after she is incubating or brooding young.

606. Which birds engage in the most elaborate courtship performances? There are many almost incredible courtship performances. One of the most elaborate is undertaken by the bowerbird of

Australia. The male carefully constructs a shelter of branches, twigs and leaves, and then decorates it with bright petals from flowers. During World War II many of these bowers were gaily decorated with objects discarded or lost by soldiers. Throughout the breeding season, the male goes through elaborate courtship displays in its decorated bower. As is often true with species having such elaborate and intensive courtship performances, the males are so preoccupied with these activities that they have little time to show interest in other aspects of family life.

Some ornithologists may consider the courtship ceremonies of certain birds of paradise even more spectacular. Some of these birds are adorned with unbelievably fantastic and often brilliantly colored plumes, capes, ruffs, false wings, and other strange plumage decorations. This finery should be enough to attract and win any female, yet the male may engage in excited dances and acrobatics, often somersaulting, swinging upside down and leaping about in ecstatic excitement.

But one may well ask if these are more spectacular than numerous other displays such as the strutting and pirouetting of the peacock with its beautiful tail coverts fully fanned, or the ludicrous mutual display of a pair of western grebes running neck to neck across the water.

607. How do birds recognize the opposite sex?   In most cases where the sexes have conspicuously different plumage the bird uses obvious visual clues. At breeding time there should be little difficulty in a male scarlet tanager's recognizing the differently patterned female. That the primary clue is based on distinct plumage is dramatically shown by experiments with yellow-shafted flickers. Females captured and painted with black mustaches were attacked immediately by the resident male. The error was realized quickly, however, since the attacked bird immediately reacted as a female and thus revealed her sex.

When plumages are similar or identical, vision too is used to spot some revealing sex pose or attitude. Another male will show readiness to fight, an unreceptive female will retreat, and a receptive female will indicate her willingness to receive attention. Sex recognition is a complex, interesting problem and much research is needed in this field.

608. When does copulation take place? As in most phases of bird behavior, there are numerous variations. Details of the initiation, frequency, duration and termination are sadly lacking in ornithological publications. In most birds, however, the act usually comes or is concentrated during that brief period between the formation of the pair and egg-laying. In some species it is repeated at frequent intervals throughout the breeding season. Although the male is usually the aggressor, the female often invites the act by a song, call, posture or display. The song of the female cardinal, for instance, seems to serve as an invitation to the male.

In some ducks, hawks, owls and other birds which mate more or less permanently, copulation may begin a month or more before the eggs are laid. In many birds the female may be receptive only during a relatively brief period. On the other hand, in some species copulation, though confined to the annual dance period, may be rather promiscuous. One virile male sage grouse was seen to copulate with 21 different females in a single morning.

609. Why do so many game birds display longer and more intensely than most other birds? In most game birds, the males are not actually paired. They are generally promiscuous, and incubation as well as raising of the young is left to the hens. No sooner does a male copulate with a female than he starts performing again in an attempt to attract and win favor from another member of the opposite sex. Competition among such virile males is always keen, calling for extreme effort if success is to be attained. Naturally the strongest, most excitable, demonstrative and enduring cocks are the most successful. Consequently natural selection has a chance to work, and these favorable qualities are inherited by the greatest number of offspring. The amount of effort entailed in these courtship displays and dances is indicated by the fact that the males lose a great deal of weight during the courting season.

610. Where would be the first place to look to see an example of bird courtship? One of the most universally observed examples of courtship is that of the domestic pigeon. Even people living in towns and cities can observe this elaborate performance in parks or on sidewalks. And what a performance it is! The male with tail spread wide and feathers of the throat fluffed to form a large collar, dances

before the lady of his choice. He walks beside her cooing and dancing with persistence until she touches his bill and indicates her willingness to pair.

**611. Why do some birds fight their reflections in windows or other
mirrorlike surfaces such as hub caps on cars?** This frequently happens during the breeding season. Usually the male bird, discovering
its reflection, believes another male has entered its territory and
attempts to drive it away. Unless the reflection is destroyed by some
means or covered, the bird may continue its futile warfare as long
as the breeding season lasts.

In Florida a snowy egret jealously guarding its special winter
feeding territory spent hours daily attacking its reflection in the windshield of a boat.

THE NESTS OF BIRDS

612. What is meant by the term "nest"? No matter how primitive
and undeveloped the place may appear to humans, all places where
birds incubate their eggs are called nests. Most nests are receptacles
that insure the protection of the eggs during incubation and often
of the young during their early development.

613. How did nest-building develop? No fossil record remains
to give us a clue to the development of the nests of birds. Therefore the theories of scientists must remain purely suppositions. One
theory suggests that nest-building may have evolved from the slight
depressions often formed in the ground during sexual excitement.
For instance, a female tern usually turns around and around with her
breast on the ground as the male circles her. Some female birds
scratch in the ground at this time. From such simple beginnings, the
complicated nests built by many species today may have developed.

614. What leads a bird to build a nest? This is primarily internal.
When the physiological development of the bird reaches the right
stage, the nest-building is carried forward rapidly.

615. How is the nest site chosen? The foremost consideration is
security. The nest must be protected from predators and from the

weather. It must be close to food supplies. Though exceptions are frequent, each species has typical demands for its nesting site.

616. Which sex decides where the nest will be placed? This varies with the species. With some birds such as the terns, the nest is usually made in the place where the female formed a depression during nuptial ceremonies as she turned around and around to face the circling male. Often birds which nest in holes search together for a suitable place to nest. Among most passerine birds, the female selects the site, usually within the territory defended by the male of her choice. In such species as grouse, turkeys and hummingbirds, the sexes meet only during courtship and nuptial ceremonies, then separate, the female alone making the choice. The male knows nothing of the nest or young.

617. Is there any relationship between the nest site and the place where birds feed? Ground-feeding birds usually nest on the ground. In the same way, shrub and tree-feeding birds usually place their nests in those locations. Birds that eat chiefly fish and other aquatic life usually nest close to the water. Birds that feed on the wing show considerable variation in the places they choose to nest. Barn swallows nest in buildings, under eaves or beneath sheltering cliffs. Cliff swallows nest under eaves, bridges, and on the sides of cliffs. Bank swallows dig holes in sheer banks. Tree swallows and purple martins nest in holes in trees or in bird boxes. Rough-winged swallows nest in old kingfisher holes or other ready-made crannies in cliffs or bridges. Nighthawks nest on bare earth. Thus the variety of nesting sites of a few species of air-feeding birds indicates the great variation of preferred nest habitats.

618. When does nest-building begin? The choice of a nesting place is usually the first activity of the newly formed pair. Building may begin immediately after the site has been chosen. This is true among most northern warblers. Starlings, on the other hand, may select their nest site as much as two months before they add any nesting material to the cavity.

619. Which sex builds the nest? Generally the female plays the more important role. Often the male accompanies the female even though she does both the collecting of material and nest-building. Among some of the crows, herons and storks the male does most or all of the material collection while the female weaves the nest. With cedar waxwings nest-building seems to be a co-operative task shared equally.

620. Does the male of any species build the entire nest? Male phalaropes do most of the nest-building with but token assistance from the females. Even among species such as the phalaropes, which show a decided sexual reversal of roles to the point where the male does all of the incubation and most of the feeding of the young, the ovulation of the female makes the nest of primary importance to her. So far as is known, the female always takes some part, though it may be very limited, in the building of the nest.

621. How long does nest construction take? Even within a given species the time of nest construction varies. Usually experienced birds build their nests more quickly than do first breeders. Nests for second and third broods of a single season usually are built consecutively faster. Weather conditions affect the time. Construction is slowed by cold, stormy weather, or a belated spring.

Woodpeckers often take less than a week to chisel their cavities. Carolina wrens have been known to take two weeks to build a nest during stormy weather, while in fine weather they may take but a week or even less. Robins take anywhere from 5 to 20 days, while song sparrows may build a nest anywhere from a low of 3 days to a high of 13 days.

Among many species, the nest is added to even after the clutch of eggs is completed or the young have hatched. Herons, spoonbills, cormorants, pelicans and gulls, as well as eagles and ospreys, continue to add material until the young fly.

622. Do birds work steadily, once nest construction has begun? Not only does the work depend on the physiological development of the female but also on the conditions mentioned before. Lack of rain may slow swallows which must have mud with which to form their bricklike pellets. Woodpeckers often work steadily for hours at a time. Carolina wrens frequently make repeated trips in quick succession during early morning hours, then abandon work for several hours or even days at a time.

623. How do birds collect materials for the nest? Birds that collect their food in their claws collect nest material the same way. Birds that use their bills to collect food collect the material for their nests in the bill. Swifts circle and periodically fly right up to a branch with possible nest twigs, testing one after another until they find one that will break off. Birds often pick up one or several twigs, discarding those unsuitable until they find one that meets their requirements.

624. Nests are often flimsy affairs. Do birds make any effort to strengthen these structures? Hummingbirds, parula warblers (as well as other species of warblers) and blue-gray gnatcatchers are a few of the species which habitually use spider silk to strengthen and tie together the fabric of the nest. Gulls, cormorants, gannets and other sea birds use various seaweeds (algae) which are flexible when wet but harden when dry, to hold their nests together. Creepers use the mycelia of fungi to fasten their nests under the flaps of bark hanging from tree trunks.

625. Is it possible to determine the species of bird that built a nest without seeing the builder? The nests of each species are fairly uniform in their location and structure. Nest-building is an instinctive reaction in birds. Therefore, if an ornithologist studies the location of a nest and its structure and the materials used, he usually can determine the species that built it though he has never seen the bird near the nest.

626. Does each species of bird build its nest in a particular kind of place? Strange exceptions may occur. Nevertheless, it is a fact that each species builds according to a set pattern and also builds in a particular kind of place. While meadowlarks nest from the Atlantic to the Pacific and from Florida to Canada, it is useless to search for their nests anywhere but on the ground in wide, grassy fields. Magnolia warblers nest only in evergreen trees of the North. Loons nest within a few feet of bodies of water. Leach's petrels nest only in burrows on oceanic islands. Birds not only nest within a given range but choose a definite kind of habitat within that range for their nests.

627. Do individual birds ever vary from the normal in this respect? Occasionally birds place their nests in strange places. For several years blue jays nested on a fire escape in Rye, New York. Canada geese, usually ground-nesting birds, have been known to nest high in trees, while starlings, normally tree-nesting birds, have been found nesting in cavities under the ground. Such unexpected nesting places are always interesting but have little bearing on the broad picture of the nesting habits of a given species.

628. Do birds too young to breed ever build nests? It often happens that young birds build nests, which are then abandoned. This instinctive building of nests by young, nonbreeding birds may serve as an apprenticeship for adult duties.

629. By what means do birds try to protect their nests? One of the primary factors in the choice of the nest site is the need for concealment. Most often the nest is concealed by making it of materials that blend inconspicuously into its surroundings. Nests in burrows and tree cavities are fairly safe from many predators. Cactus wrens, curve-billed thrashers, desert sparrows and other birds that nest in desert areas often place their nests in prickly, thorny plants such as acacias, yuccas and cacti generally. Doubtless the thorns of these formidible plants offer considerable protection to the nests. Other birds such as the Baltimore oriole place their nests so far toward the tip of delicate flexible branches that predators cannot reach them. English sparrows and starlings are among the small birds that actually build in the sides of eagle and hawk nests where they are protected from enemies by the watchful-eyed raptores that assiduously drive harmful creatures away from their own eggs and young.

Village weavers in Haiti nest close to wasp nests. Trogons, parrots and barbets in the tropics frequently nest close to big ant or termite colonies and thus receive the protection of those biting insects which for some unknown reason do not attack the birds, which do not feed on them.

630. Cast snake skins are often found in birds' nests, particularly those of the crested flycatcher. Do these help to keep predators away? It is doubtful that snake skins offer any protection to the crested flycatcher or the ten or twelve other species that incorporate them in their nests too regularly for the act to be accidental. More than 30 species of birds are known to use cast snake skins in their nests.

631. What are some other odd materials used by birds in building their nests? Many birds place shiny cellophane, sheets of cleansing tissue, colored yarns and strips of newspapers in their nests. Barn owls increase the size of their nests by the addition of their disgorged pellets. Kingfishers do not elaborate on the burrows they dig for their eggs but as time goes on, the bones and scales of fish eaten by the kingfishers or their young make a prickly bed. Practically any dry plant fibers, from poison ivy tendrils to prickly twigs of chaparral plants, may be used.

632. Do birds ever decorate their nests? Several species of hawks add green leaves to their nests. When these are faded, they are replaced. Occupied red-shouldered hawk nests can be detected in early spring by the presence of the fresh green leaves. Red-tailed hawks, broad-winged hawks and golden eagles frequently place fresh green leaves in their nests. Though attempts have been made to explain the use of these leaves as contributing moisture to the nest or perhaps cooling it through evaporation of moisture from the leaves, no one is sure if such theories are correct. To most people the leaves look like decorations.

633. What are dummy nests? Most, if not all, species of wrens build so-called dummy nests. They are made by the male and are never used by the female. It is believed that these nests play a part in the courtship of the wrens. Occasionally a box already filled by the male will please a female house wren. When this happens, she throws out all the sticks and builds a new nest in the box. Male marsh wrens build dummy nests, sometimes several of them, in the reeds and sedges of their wet habitat, but they are never used as egg receptacles. Some scientists believe the extra nests serve a purpose by attracting predators which then are discouraged by their lack of success in finding eggs or young.

634. Do all birds build nests? Though a particular spot where the eggs are deposited and incubated becomes the nest, among some species no attempt is made to improve the place. Nighthawks, whip-poor-wills and chuck-will's-widows simply choose a suitable place and deposit their eggs without making any attempt to change the area. Murres and auks which nest on the ledges of cliffs also make no pretense of building nests. Parasitic birds depend on other species to provide a safe receptacle for their eggs.

635. What happens to the eggs of parasitic birds? Female parasitic birds skulk about to locate suitable nests before they are ready to deposit their eggs. European and Asiatic cuckoos, like the American cowbirds, are parasitic. They place their eggs in the nests of other species. Since the eggs of parasitic birds hatch quickly, the young usually emerge a day or two before the rightful young of the nest. Parasitic young grow rapidly, and frequently push the young of the species that hatched them from the nest, or consume so much food that the young of their foster parents starve.

636. Do cowbirds prey particularly on any species of bird? The nests of both red-eyed and solitary vireos are often used as repositories for the eggs of brown-headed cowbirds. Chipping sparrows, yellow warblers and redstarts are also frequently preyed upon. In Texas, New Mexico and Arizona, the bronzed cowbird usually parasitizes the nests of the sparrows of that area.

637. Are American cuckoos parasitic? All American species of cuckoo build their own nests and rear their own young.

638. How did parasitism develop among certain birds? This is a matter on which there is no proof and any answer must be considered pure speculation. It has been suggested that cowbirds, which have the habit of feeding near the feet of ruminant animals and eating the insects disturbed by these beasts, may have followed the bison herds on their treks northward in spring and back again in the autumn. Because the herds of bison moved steadily onward, the cowbirds had no time in a given area to build nests and raise their young. Therefore they developed the habit of placing their eggs in the nests of species that are sedentary during the nesting season. Though such a theory appears logical, it throws no light on the development of parasitic habits among European and Asian cuckoos.

639. **Why do some species defend a nesting territory which may cover several acres or even miles, while other species nest in dense concentrations so that each pair has but about a square foot of ground?** Birds that feed on the territory where they nest must establish and defend a territory great enough to feed themselves and their young. Where food is fairly scarce, eagles may have to defend a square mile or more against other eagles. If food is abundant a house wren may defend one garden, while if it is scarce, the same bird may defend an area as large as or larger than a city block.

Birds that feed by sweeping the air as swallows do can nest close together, for they shift their feeding areas daily as flying insects emerge in different places. The same is true of fish-eating birds. They may fly many miles from their nests before they discover a concentration of fish.

640. Why do birds sometimes build one nest on top of another? Reasons for this vary. Occasionally nests remain in place over the winter and a bird may return to the identical place for several successive years and build a new nest on top of those of former years. This would seldom happen in an exposed place, but a robin that builds in a protected place under a porch or overhanging roof may use its old nest as a foundation for the new one.

Second or even third and fourth nests are sometimes built on the first one by yellow warblers or other species that find an undesired cowbird egg in their nests. One such triple-storied nest contained a cowbird egg in the bottom nest, two cowbird eggs and one yellow warbler egg in the second nest, while the third one was not parasitized.

641. Do any birds build communal nests? Smooth-billed anis in Florida and groove-billed anis in Texas build communal nests and several females deposit their eggs in it. All the anis take turns incubating and later in caring for the young. Monk parakeets in South America co-operate in the building of colonial nests that may be as much as nine feet long, but each pair has an individual compartment within the community nest.

642. Is it communal nesting when three chimney swifts care for a single nest? Occasionally three chimney swifts or three cliff swallows not only build a single nest but all three help to feed the young birds. Some scientists think that the extra bird may be an immature individual of the previous year or one from an earlier nesting which is assisting its parents in raising a new family. If this is true, the third bird is in the position of an apprentice rather than a bird taking an equal share in community life.

643. Do birds use a nest for more than one brood?   Most passerine birds, which may have two or more broods in a single season, build a new nest for each brood. In this way each brood begins life in a clean nest, free of disease and insects that may have infested the nest in which the first brood was raised. In the far North where the season for nesting is very short, passerine birds sometimes break custom and use the nest for two broods.

644. Are any nests used for more than one year?   Most passerine birds use a nest but once. However, the same pair of bluebirds or house wrens may return again and again to the same bird box. Hawks, eagles and owls often use the same nest for many years. One bald eagle nest was used for 35 consecutive years until the tree which held it was blown down in a storm. Frequently abandoned eagle nests are occupied in years that follow by great horned owls or hawks. Woodpecker nest holes are often used for many years by other species of hole-nesting birds.

645. Do birds use their nests for shelter in winter?   It is doubtful that birds use their own nests in winter. Most birds move away from their nesting territory when winter comes. Therefore, a chickadee may take refuge in a nest excavated by other chickadees, or a woodpecker find refuge in a hole chiseled by another bird. Old magpie nests and the crevices of large nests, such as those of eagles and ospreys, are sometimes used as a refuge during stormy weather.

646. What are some of the simplest or most primitive bird nests?
Among American birds are several species that make no nest at all. Murres lay their conical eggs on bare rocky ledges. Nighthawks, chuck-will's-widows and whip-poor-wills make no nest but simply place their eggs in some spot they consider suitable.

Fairy terns of the Pacific balance their single egg, with nothing to protect it, on a horizontal branch. Emperor penguins, with no nesting material available, make the best of their frigid situation on the antarctic ice and hold their single egg on their feet.

647. What are some of the extremely complicated nests built by American birds? The carefully woven, pendulous, plant-fiber nests of the Baltimore orioles are among the most complicated found in North America. The tiny bush tits of California build long, pendent bags of oak catkins, bits of dried leaves, lichens and moss woven together with spider webs. These 4½-inch birds sometimes make a foot-long nest.

Perhaps the chiseled nest holes of woodpeckers should be included in this class, as well as the nests of thorny twigs woven into a jug shape and lined with felted plant fibers by verdins, and the goblet-shaped nests made of small pellets resembling tiny bricks, formed of mud and saliva, that cliff swallows build.

648. If the nests of the whole world are considered, which are the most complicated? Many nests are extremely complicated, and ornithologists doubtless would disagree about which one to place first. The ovenbird (no relation to the warbler bearing that same name) of South America weighs less than three ounces but it builds a great, hollow ball of earth sometimes weighing nine pounds which it saddles on the limb of a tree. Broadbills in Asia build large, round nests of grass which they suspend by a single thread, often above water. This nest is entered through the side, and over the opening is a roof which keeps out the rain.

One of the most astonishing nests is built by the tailorbird of Africa. This small bird uses its bill as if it were a needle to pierce holes, usually 16, on each edge of the chosen leaf. Using spider silk as thread, it pulls this back and forth through the holes, tying knots as it sews. The resulting bag is filled with plant fibers and a single egg deposited within.

The big family of weaverbirds of Africa, India and Australia build a variety of complicated nests, using both their bills and feet to weave the hanging, pouchlike structures. The entrance is usually at the bottom. Some of these have two compartments, the back one being used for the eggs and young, while the front one offers a guardroom from which enemies which have gained entrance may be repelled. In some species a long entrance way leads up from the bottom to a platform with a "fence" around it to keep the eggs from rolling out.

649. Which North American bird builds the largest nest? The bald eagle builds the largest nest of any species on the North American continent. Herrick records a nest of a bald eagle at Vermillion, Ohio, which was 12 feet deep and 8½ feet across. It was estimated that this nest weighed about two tons. It was occupied continuously for 35 years until it crashed. Charles Broley measured a bald eagle nest in Florida which was 20 feet deep and 9½ feet wide.

650. Which bird builds the smallest nest? Some hummingbirds are the smallest birds in the world and logically enough they build the smallest nests. These nests usually match closely the branch on which they are placed. Plant down and lichens are most frequently used materials. These are bound together with spider silk. (See Questions 624, 790.)

651. What are the types of nest materials generally used? While plant materials are most generally used, almost anything from pebbles and broken shells to horsehair and sheep wool may be used. A supply of the materials preferred by a species sometimes determines the habitat of the species.

Grasses, twigs and roots are used frequently, some nests being limited to one type of material, while other species incorporate many materials in their nests. Leaves, as in the case of the tailorbird, may be used for the entire nest or for part of it. Dried leaves are particularly desired by ground-nesting birds.

Linings among many species are soft and warm. Animal matter such as down, feathers, wool or fur are frequently used, while spider silk is employed by many species to strengthen the walls of the nest. Chipping sparrows line their nests with animal hair; horsehair if available. Barn swallows use feathers as a nest lining and eider ducks use down pulled from their own breasts. Goldfinches and yellow warblers place soft lining material from catkins, milkweed seed pods, thistledown, or material from the stems of cinnamon ferns in their nests.

Mud is used by swallows, many species of thrush and phoebes. The swallows use little but mud for the outside of their nests (which may be lined with feathers) while robins make a mud cup inside a layer of vegetable materials and then line the cup with soft vegetable fibers. A knowledge of the materials normally chosen by each species is most helpful in identifying a nest. (See Question 657.)

652. What are the chief types of nest placement? 1. *Burrows under ground and crevices under or in rocks.* Kingfishers, bank swallows, Leach's petrels and burrowing owls are among the birds that dig nest burrows in the earth. Black guillemots and razor-billed auks occupy crevices under rocks or in cliffs, while rough-winged swallows use burrows made by kingfishers or small mammals, or utilize holes in bridges or other man-made structures close to water.

2. *On the surface of the earth.* A vast army of species nest on the ground, among them such colonial birds as terns, gulls and skimmers. Shorebirds usually nest on the ground, generally close to water. Ducks nest in marshes or near water, while loons and grebes situate their nests so they can easily slide directly from their eggs into the water. Many species of sparrows, meadowlarks, horned larks and buntings are among the species that prefer broad open fields. Ruffed grouse, whip-poor-wills and ovenbirds are among those that nest on the floor of the forest.

3. *Shrubs and trees.* Birds that nest in these necessarily build fairly sturdy nests (a striking exception to this is the fairy tern; see Question 646). The location chosen helps identify the species. Yellow warblers and catbirds usually choose a dense but often low shrub. Vireos and Baltimore orioles build hanging nests. The nests of robins, wood pewees and blue-gray gnatcatchers are saddled on top of a branch. Myrtle warblers, Blackburnian warblers and golden-crowned kinglets usually nest in the thick foliage on the outer parts of conifer branches.

4. *Marshes.* Pied-billed grebes build floating nests which are usually anchored to reeds. Sand-hill cranes take advantage of tussocks rising above the water as a platform on which to build. Clapper rails and bitterns build their nests on the floor of the marsh. It is not unusual for these birds to have their nests flooded by a rise of but a very few inches of water, so they are forced to build again and lay a

new clutch of eggs. Red-winged blackbirds and marsh wrens build in the low shrubs, reeds or sedges that grow in the marsh.

5. *The trunks of trees, particularly dead ones.* Woodpeckers, chickadees and nuthatches usually, though not always, make their own nest holes. Old woodpecker holes are used by other species of woodpeckers, tree swallows, purple martins, starlings, bluebirds, house wrens and other species of hole-nesting birds. Brown creepers usually build their nests under a loose flap of bark dangling on the trunk of a tree.

6. *Man-made structures.* Barn swallows and cliff swallows have to a large extent left the caves and cliffs where they originally nested, for barns and eaves of buildings. Phoebes frequently nest under bridges or on window sills. Robins often move from trees to window sills or into the shelter of porches. Chimney swifts seldom use hollow trees but now nest almost exclusively in chimneys or inside walls of buildings. In fact, almost any species of hole-nesting bird willing to occupy the ready-made holes of other species may be induced to nest in bird boxes or other human structures. It is surprising to realize that wild, independent birds such as barn owls, screech owls and sparrow hawks accept man's hospitality. Perhaps the most striking adaptation in this respect is the nesting of wild and fierce peregrine falcons on window sills of hotels in great cities such as Montreal and New York, as well as on the tall towers of huge bridges spanning rivers.

Rock wrens have moved from cliffs to the walls of great dams built in Texas and other western states. Carolina wrens often choose the pockets of coats or pants left hanging on a line or perhaps on a scarecrow, and have nested in such odd places as paper bags, clothes-pin bags, cigar boxes and even a human skull.

7. *Cultivated lands and gardens.* Aside from the use of man-made structures, many species of birds have moved into gardens to build their nests. Probably such species as robins, catbirds, chestnut-sided warblers and chipping sparrows are more numerous today than when the Pilgrims arrived because they have adapted their nesting habits to man's gardens. Mockingbirds have increased in numbers and extended their range, for as man cleared the land he created a wealth of suitable places for this species and others that demand the same kind of habitat.

It is believed that the abundance of golf courses has been largely responsible for the extension eastward of horned larks as nesting birds.

653. What proportion of nests are successful? Dr. Arthur Allen of Cornell University believes that less than 20 per cent of nests are successful, that is, that the eggs laid in the nest hatch and the young leave the nest at their appointed time. The reason for this is clear. Over thousands and even millions of years, the earth has been able to support a limited number of the higher forms of life. Only so much food and shelter are available. Therefore many of the eggs and young of birds become food for other creatures. Should all of the birds' eggs laid in North America in a single season not only hatch but the young mature, the continent would be so crowded with birds than man himself would suffer acutely. Therefore the fact that a garden which has one family of house wrens this year will have but one next year is not a regrettable fact. Should the pair have three clutches of eight eggs in each and raise the young, at the end of the nesting season there would be 26 house wrens where two had been in spring. Multiply this by all the house wrens on the continent and the figures become astronomical. It is easy to understand why the laws of nature, always struggling for balance, operate in favor of the survival of all species by wiping out the surplus in each.

654. What should be the attitude of a person who discovers a nest?
A nest should be left strictly alone. While many eggs and young birds become food for other forms of life, man does not need these creatures in his diet, and it is against the ideals of sportsmanship and the principles of conservation to encourage the destruction of a nest by leading predators to it. Birds have enough difficulty in maintaining their numbers without the interference of man.

655. Is it legal to collect abandoned birds' nests? It is illegal to collect the nest of birds, abandoned or otherwise. It may be done only if a permit has been obtained from the Fish and Wildlife Service in Washington, D.C. Another permit should be obtained from the state where the collection is to be made.

656. Do birds ever use the nests made by other species? The use of woodpecker holes by other species has already been discussed (see Question 652). Hawks and great horned owls often use the nests of eagles or other hawks as platforms for their own nests. Among colonial birds nest material is stolen from neighboring birds. Occasionally several birds will drive a neighbor from its nest and take all the material away. Herons, white ibises and wood ibises are given to this kind of thievery. Dr. Olin Sewell Pettingill has described the stealing of nest stones by some of the penguins on the Falkland Islands. Cedar waxwings have been observed tearing apart old Baltimore oriole nests and placing the soft fibers in their own nests. The same is true for old goldfinch and yellow warbler nests.

657. Are any nests of birds useful to man? Some swallows and swifts secrete a sticky saliva at the time they build their nests and this is used to strengthen their structures. Some species of Asiatic swifts develop particularly large glands at this time and build a nest composed of little but hardened saliva. The nests are gathered, cleansed and used in making the famous bird's-nest soup of the Orient. In spite of the enlarged glands, it often takes these birds from 33 to 41 days to build their shallow little cup nests.

Gila woodpeckers and gilded flickers frequently make their nests in the giant saguara cactus. In self-defense, the cactus secretes a sap which rapidly builds up a hard scar tissue that prevents evaporation in the dry desert heat. The scar tissue around the gourdlike cavities hardens and seems impervious to age. It remains intact long after a fallen saguara has disintegrated to a mere skeleton of dried ribs. Long ago the Apaches used these hard, dry, indestructible woodpecker nest shells as water jars. Now when one of these is found in a fallen saguara it is usually hung up as a bird box.

Among American and European birds, the nest of the eider duck is most valued. The down of this duck is not only one of the warmest animal substances known but it is amazingly tough and resilient. The female eiders pluck down from their breasts to form a large fluffy ring around the eggs. When the eider leaves the nest to feed she pulls some down over the eggs. Because this down is in great demand for quilts, sleeping bags and arctic clothing, nests were robbed of down for centuries. Fortunately the collection of down in Canada is now controlled rigidly by law, and the ducks themselves are protected during the breeding season. In Iceland, where much eider down is produced, the birds are carefully protected, and they have assumed almost the status of domestic fowls. If down is taken before the eggs have hatched, only a small portion of it may be removed. After the young have hatched and left the nest, all of the remaining down is gathered, cleansed and used for its unequaled insulating qualities.

658. Do birds always desert if their nest is moved? Ordinarily most birds will desert their eggs and even their young if the nest is moved. A few confiding species such as chickadees, kinglets and certain warblers may hear the calls of their young if the nests are not moved far, and attend them.

A few strange tales of birds that nested successfully even though their eggs and young moved about are interesting because they illustrate that living creatures sometimes fail to stay within the behavior pattern expected of them. For many years a ferry plied a one-mile course across the St. Lawrence River between Ogdensburg, New York, and Prescott, Ontario. Tree swallows found suitable cavities on this ferry for their nests, and in these laid their eggs and reared their young, sometimes gathering insects in Canada, sometimes in New York, for their much-traveled young.

In British Columbia, barn swallows nested in the open baggage car of a train for many years. This train made regular two-mile runs between Atlin Lake and Tagish Lake, yet the birds nested successfully, following the train about on its journey.

THE EGGS OF BIRDS

659. What is an egg? An egg is composed chiefly of storage materials or food on which the fertilized cell is nourished during incubation.

660. How does the embryo develop? Once incubation begins, development of the embryo is rapid. Respiration takes place through the porous shell. Near the end of the incubation period, the young bird almost fills the shell, having used the egg white and the yolk, except for what remains in its abdomen for sustenance immediately after hatching.

661. Do birds ever lay unfertilized eggs? Unfertilized eggs are frequently laid by domestic fowls but infrequently by wild birds.

662. What is the largest known bird's egg? An extinct, flightless bird of Madagascar, the *Aepyornis maximus,* known variously as the elephant bird, giant bird and roc, laid the largest known egg. Some of these eggs measured as much as 13.5 inches in length and 9.5 inches in diameter. (See Questions 784, 785, 786.)

663. How was knowledge of the eggs of an extinct bird acquired? The eggs of the *Aepyornis maximus* were first discovered when natives brought two of the shells to a trading post to have them filled with rum. They had a capacity of more than two gallons. Some nearly complete shells and many fragments of these huge eggs have been found.

664. How do Aepyornis eggs compare in size with eggs of living birds? It is estimated that an *Aepyornis* egg would hold the equivalent of 6 ostrich eggs, 148 hen's eggs or more than 30,000 hummingbird eggs.

665. What is the largest egg laid by living birds? The ostrich egg is the largest egg laid by birds today. One of these eggs will hold from 12 to 18 hen's eggs. They are 6 to 9 inches long and 5 to 6 inches in diameter. Their shells are a quarter of an inch thick. Ostrich eggs are so large that it takes 40 minutes or more to hard-boil them.

666. What bird lays the smallest egg? Hummingbirds lay the smallest eggs of any bird. The egg of a ruby-throated hummingbird is scarcely half an inch long, or about the size of a pea. Some of the smaller species lay even smaller eggs. The vervair hummingbird of Haiti and Jamaica lays eggs only ¼ inch long.

667. Do only birds lay eggs? By no means. Insects, spiders, most fish and many other marine animals, turtles, many snakes, and lizards are among the creatures that lay eggs. Any animal which lays eggs that hatch outside the body is called an oviparous animal.

668. Does any mammal lay eggs? The strange little duckbill platypus (*Ornithorhynchus anatinus*) of Australia, which measures from 18 to 20 inches in length, lays two eggs at a time, each about ¾ inches long. These eggs are but slightly larger than the eggs laid by the 5-inch-long blue-throated hummingbird.

669. What birds lay the most eggs? Domestic fowls, bred for that purpose, lay the most eggs. An Australorp hen of Australia won the world's record in 1946 when it laid 361 eggs in 365 days. A domestic duck won the world's record for its race in 1927 when it laid 363 eggs in 365 days.

670. Among wild birds of the United States, which lays the most eggs? Ducks and gallinaceous birds such as prairie chickens, bob-whites and grouse usually lay the largest clutches of eggs. These may contain anywhere from 8 to 15 eggs or more.

671. Can birds be induced to lay abnormal numbers of eggs? This is possible among some species. Scientists have prolonged egg-laying of certain birds by removing, day after day, an egg from a nest under observation. Under this artificial condition, a flicker once laid 71 eggs in 73 days, and a house wren laid 72 eggs in a single nest. The same conditions caused a wryneck in Europe to lay 62 eggs in 62 days.

672. Can all species of birds be induced to lay abnormal numbers of eggs? Some species lay exactly the same number of eggs each year and cannot be induced to lessen or increase the number of eggs in a clutch. Sandpipers normally lay four eggs in a clutch. Scientists have attempted to lessen the number by placing a strange egg in a sandpiper nest after three eggs have been laid. Nevertheless the sandpiper laid its full quota of four eggs. Though an egg or two is removed from the nest, the sandpiper lays its four eggs and does not replace any that are removed. Should all eggs be taken, the sandpiper would desert and apparently make no further attempt to nest until the following year.

673. What is a clutch of eggs? A clutch or set of eggs is the total number of eggs laid by one bird for a single nesting. While the size of the clutch may vary slightly with individuals, the average number of eggs in a clutch is known for all birds native to North America. However, the larger the normal number of eggs in a single clutch, the greater the individual variation may be.

674. Can the eggs of birds be identified without supporting evidence? Thousands of eggs of most species of birds in the United

States have been collected for museums, universities and so on. Therefore their average colors, sizes and shapes are well known. Nevertheless a careful examination of the trays of eggs in a museum reveals a striking similarity in the size, shape and color of the eggs of many species of birds. It is evident at once that the identification of an egg may be difficult, for not only are the eggs of many species similar but there is considerable variation in the characteristics of the eggs of a given species.

Few eggs are as distinctive as the species that laid them. If one cannot observe the bird that laid the egg under consideration, the nest, its materials and location may be important clues to the identity of the egg. While it is possible to make a fair guess as to the species that laid it, a positive identification of most eggs depends on corroborative evidence.

675. How many clutches of eggs do birds lay each year? When a whole clutch of eggs is destroyed, the majority of passerine birds lays another, but the number of eggs in the second clutch is often less than in the first one. Most small passerine birds, particularly those nesting in the temperate zone, lay two, three or even four clutches of eggs annually.

Some species of birds never lay but one clutch of eggs a year. Among the less fecund birds are albatrosses, shearwaters, fulmars and petrels. These birds lay but one egg each year and if this single egg is destroyed, it is not replaced.

676. Hummingbirds lay the smallest eggs and ostriches the largest. Does this progression in egg size in relation to the size of the bird that laid it hold true throughout all species of birds? The size and weight of eggs is not strictly correlated with the size and weight of the bird that lays them. Precocial birds, whose young are hatched covered with down, with their eyes wide open and able to run about as soon as they are dry, lay much larger eggs than those of altricial birds, whose young are hatched blind, naked and helpless. (See Questions 741, 775.)

Upland plovers and meadowlarks are approximately the same size, yet the precocial plover lays eggs 1.80 inches long and 1.30 inches in diameter. In contrast, the eggs of the altricial meadowlark measure about 1.15 inches in length and .80 inches in diameter.

677. Which bird lays the largest egg in relation to its size? A kiwi, one of the flightless birds found in New Zealand, probably lays the largest egg in proportion to its size of any bird in the world. This bird normally lays but one egg annually, but the weight of that single egg is about 25 per cent of the weight of the kiwi.

678. Which bird lays the smallest egg in relation to its size? Strangely enough, the ostrich, which lays the world's largest egg, lays the smallest one for its size. The egg of an ostrich weighs only 1.5 per cent as much as the bird that lays it.

679. What American bird lays the largest egg for its size? If not actually laying the largest individual egg for its size, the ruddy duck lays the greatest total weight of eggs in relation to its size of any North American bird. A ruddy duck lays an egg as large as does a canvasback, which is three times the size of the smaller duck. Though a female ruddy duck weighs scarcely a pound, it is known to lay as many as 14 eggs in 15 days. Such a clutch of eggs weighs three pounds, about three times as much as the duck that laid them! Tiny golden-crowned kinglets may lay 11 eggs, their total weight being about 125 per cent of the weight of the kinglet.

Among English cousins of the American chickadees, up to 18 eggs have been found in blue tit nests and up to 20 eggs have been found in a long-tailed tit's nest. In both species the number of eggs usually varies between 8 and 12 eggs in a clutch, which generates a suspicion that two females may lay in a single nest where abnormal numbers of eggs are found.

680. What factors control the shape of a bird's egg? Of course the oviduct through which the egg travels molds the shape of the egg, but sedentary birds such as owls usually have almost round eggs while extremely fast-flying birds such as swifts and swallows are likely to have long, narrow eggs. Birds such as murres and auks that frequently lay their eggs on the bare rock of narrow ledges usually have conical eggs which roll in a circle like weighted salt shakers when disturbed. The shape of these eggs actually keeps them from rolling off their precarious platforms above the surf.

Eggs of most shore birds and other species that customarily lay a clutch of four are tapered to fit easily, the small ends in the center, within the nest. The eggs of nighthawks, normally laid on bare, flat earth, are long and almost equally rounded at both ends.

681. What purpose can the colors of eggs serve?   It is believed that the first birds laid white eggs as do reptiles today. Undoubtedly the pigmentation, developed over the ages, was a factor in the survival of the eggs and therefore of the race. The pigment is deposited on the shell as the egg travels through the egg duct.

Eggs that are placed in burrows, cavities or other well-concealed places, and also eggs that are incubated by both parents so they are continuously covered, are usually white. The more the eggs are exposed, the more likely they are to fade into their surroundings due to the pigmentation of the shells. Often pigmentation is heaviest on the larger end, which leads in the oviduct.

682. Does the color of an egg remain the same throughout incubation?   The color of an egg often changes during incubation. Part of this change is due to the tarnishing of the surface and staining but part of the change is caused by fading of the colors.

683. Are most eggs colored in such a way that they tend to blend into their surroundings?   While most eggs laid in the open are marked in such a way as to render them inconspicuous, there are many exceptions. The beautiful greenish-blue eggs of robins and other thrushes are well known. There is a warbler in Japan which lays red eggs, and curiously enough, a cuckoo that puts its eggs in the nest of this warbler lays red eggs also.

South American tinamou eggs are variously colored in blue, green, brown, yellow and purple. The emu of Australia usually lays dark green eggs but they have been known to lay black ones.

684. Do birds always recognize their own eggs?   Birds appear to recognize their nest sites better than they do their eggs. Domestic hens will incubate duck, turkey, bobwhite, grouse and glass eggs. Cowbirds, which lay their eggs in the nests of other small birds, can be fairly certain that the owner of the nest will care for the eggs and young. This is true also of the cuckoos in Europe, which lay their eggs in the nests of other birds. Pheasants and ducks have been known to lay their eggs in other pheasant and duck nests, upon which the owner of the nest broods the strange eggs.

Oddly enough, not all birds can tell whether an object in the nest is an egg or not. Black-crowned night herons have been known to brood children's square blocks. A black-headed gull in England incubated an empty gun cartridge. A bald eagle in Florida spent long weeks sitting on a large white rubber ball.

685. Does the texture of eggs vary? Ducks' eggs as well as those of grebes and other water birds are oily or greasy. This must be a safety device when eggs are placed in moist or wet situations. Some egg shells, the Leach's petrel's, for example, are so thin and delicate that the contents within can be seen when first laid. Cormorant and gannet eggs are covered with a chalky layer. Ostrich eggs have a pitted surface. Emu and cassowary eggs are rough and grainy, while the eggs of tinamous are as smooth as polished metal or fine china.

686. Do all members of a species lay the same-size clutch of eggs? While the egg clutch of a given species is fairly constant, there appears to be a variation in the size from the tropics to the arctic. The farther north a species nests, the larger the clutch is likely to be. For instance, a redwinged blackbird nesting in Costa Rica may lay but two or three eggs in a clutch, but the same species, nesting in Alaska or Mackenzie, may lay up to five eggs or more.

687. Why does the clutch of some birds vary from year to year? Food supply may control the number of eggs in a clutch. For instance, snowy owls may lay as many as ten eggs when mice are abundant in their arctic nesting grounds, but only three or four when mice are scarce. Barn owls may have two or more broods in a year when the meadow mice are at peak abundance, but when the mouse cycle reaches its lowest ebb, they slow down or even skip a breeding season altogether. In general there also seems to be a correlation between the size of the clutch of a given species and the replacement necessary to maintain a stable population of its race.

688. Do birds lay every day until their clutch is complete? Most passerine birds and many of the smaller birds in lower orders lay an egg each day until the clutch is complete. Barn owls usually lay every second or third day.

689. Do any large birds lay an egg each day? Many ducks average about an egg daily until the clutch is complete.

690. Is there an orderly sequence of egg-laying among birds that do not lay daily? Grouse average an egg every day and a half. Many hawks and owls lay every other day. A megapode in Australia, the malee bird, is said to lay every third day. Its relative, the maleo bird in Celebes, lays its 6 to 8 eggs at 10- to 12-day intervals, taking 2 to 3 months to complete its clutch.

691. Do birds have a preferred time of day for egg-laying? Generally the morning seems to be the favored time for egg-laying. In Europe the cuckoo, which is parasitic like the American cowbirds, seems to exhibit great cunning, for it waits to deposit its egg until afternoon when the nest owner is away.

THE EMBRYO

692. When does the development of the embryo begin? When an egg is laid it is really no longer just an egg. During its passage through the oviduct, the first development of the embryo is begun in the warmth of the bird's body.

693. Is development of the embryo constant after it begins? The cool air stops the development of an embryo when the egg is laid. It continues development only when incubation starts.

694. How long does the minute embryo remain alive without incubation? A hen's embryo remains capable of development for three to four weeks after the egg is laid if it is kept under 75° F. For this period of time it can be lowered to freezing without harm. Doubtless this is fairly typical of the embryos of most birds.

695. What happens inside the egg as the embryo develops? The single living cell becomes a living organism. The single cell divides, and each cell, after creation, divides again. This process continues until thousands upon thousands of cells grow and give form to the complete bird.

696. What are the primary needs of the growing embryo? Oxygen and warmth are the foremost necessities of the growing embryo.

697. Are there waste products from the use of oxygen and the assimilation of the yolk and white of the egg as food? Some urates and carbonic acid are formed.

698. Why does the egg become lighter during incubation? Most of the change in weight comes from the evaporation of water through the porous shell. Fresh-laid eggs sink if they are placed in water because their specific gravity is then high. After incubation has been carried on for a fairly short time the eggs will float.

699. Does the same thing happen to unfertilized eggs? Unfertilized eggs will sink when they are fresh, but if they are incubated, water evaporates from them and they soon float even though there is no life, no developing embryo, within them.

700. What is the temperature of an egg during incubation? This varies slightly, but an average temperature is about 93.2° F. The temperature may drop a degree or more when the bird is off the nest, then rise almost a degree higher when the bird is incubating the eggs.

701. What happens to the yolk and white as the embryo develops? These are used slowly as nourishment by the growing embryo. By the time the bird is ready to hatch, all the white and part of the yolk have been used by the embryo. From $\frac{1}{7}$ to $\frac{1}{3}$ of the yolk remains in the abdomen to sustain the bird immediately after hatching.

702. What part of the young bird develops first? The first to develop is the vascular system. Within 24 hours an embryo has laid down the beginnings of vascular, nervous and digestive systems. Within 36 hours the heart begins to beat. By 48 hours the eye, ear, and brain lobes can be detected.

703. Does breathing begin early in embryonic life? Breathing does not begin until a day or two before hatching. The chick bursts the sheath that surrounds it and pushes its bill into the air chamber which at that time occupies about $\frac{1}{4}$ of the space within the egg.

At once breathing begins. This is accompanied by a sharp rise in combustion, which in turn causes an abrupt drop in weight.

704. While changes go on within the shell, do any changes take place in the shell itself? The shell is much more brittle by the time the bird is ready to hatch. During the incubation, the embryo extracts lime from the shell as the skeleton is built. (See Question 682.)

INCUBATION

705. What is incubation? Incubation is the warming and care given an egg during the development of the embryo. Either or both parents sit more or less regularly on the eggs until the embryo is fully formed and breaks out of the shell. In some situations, such as sandy beaches, and in torrid climates, keeping the eggs cool is more important than warming them.

706. When do birds begin to incubate their eggs? Most frequently birds begin incubation soon after the final egg of the clutch is laid. However, certain birds begin to incubate as soon as the first egg is laid. The barn owl is one of these birds and if it lays a clutch of six eggs, the first and last egg may hatch from 12 to 18 days apart. The last egg may not hatch until the first bird is quite large. The oldest young owl has been known to eat its newly-hatched brother or sister.

Canada jays and great horned owls, which often nest in winter in the North, must begin incubation as soon as the first egg has been laid in order to keep it from freezing.

707. What is meant by "incubation patch" or "brood patch"? Incubating birds develop bare areas on the ventral surface of the body; feathers and down fall out, the skin becomes more delicate and a concentration of blood vessels insures warmth for the egg when in contact with this part of the bird's body. There may be one, two or three of these patches, depending on the species of bird.

708. Does the male as well as the female develop an incubation patch? If both male and female incubate the eggs, both develop incubation patches. In some species, though the male may occasionally cover the eggs, he does not develop an incubation patch; so, strictly speaking, he cannot be said to incubate the eggs. In some species of birds, such as the phalarope and dotteral (a European shorebird), only the male develops an incubation patch and he alone cares for the eggs and young.

709. Does any species of bird lack an incubation patch? Geese and ducks do not have automatically made incubation patches. They have to make them by pulling the down from their bodies. This is added to the nest and pulled over the eggs whenever they are left alone.

710. Emperor penguins which nest on antarctic ice and snow have nothing with which to build nests. How do they keep their eggs from freezing? These penguins roll their eggs onto their feet and a thick, warm fold of skin covers the egg almost as snugly as if it were in a pouch.

711. What is the longest period of incubation known? A royal albatross incubates its single egg from 78 to 80 days. Other long incubation periods are like those of the kiwi, which incubates for about 75 days, while that of the emperor penguin may last from 7 to 8 weeks.

712. What is the longest incubation period of any North American bird? Probably the longest incubation period is that of the Leach's petrel, which lasts from 48 to 54 days.

713. What is the shortest incubation period known for birds in the United States? As a whole, the wood warblers probably incubate their eggs for the shortest times, but it appears that even within a species the time of incubation is not stable. Eggs are likely to hatch more quickly in warm weather than when the weather is cool. Most passerine birds in North America incubate their eggs from 10 to 20 days, the average being between 12 and 14 days. Some scientists suggest that records of extremely short incubation periods of 10 or 11 days may result from the egg's having been held within the oviduct for an extra day.

Eggs of both black-billed cuckoos and English sparrows have hatched in 10 days. Those of a flicker, a horned lark and a cedar waxwing have hatched in 11 days. In each instance the eggs of these species normally require longer incubation. Cowbirds, which are parasitic, have eggs that usually hatch in a slightly shorter period than those of the natural eggs in the parasitized nest.

714. Do most small birds have short incubation periods? As a general rule, small birds have short incubation periods. Nevertheless there are some striking exceptions, for hummingbirds, the smallest birds in the world, have an incubation period of nearly three weeks. The Leach's petrel, a slim, eight-inch bird about the size of a purple martin, probably has the longest incubation period of any North American bird. (See Question 712.)

715. Aside from size, are there other known factors that affect the length of incubation? Precocial birds' eggs require longer incubation than do the eggs of altricial birds. Though robins and killdeers are almost the same size, the large eggs of the precocial killdeer must be incubated about 26 days, while the small robin eggs need about 13 days of incubation. It must be kept in mind that egg size alone does not determine the length of incubation, for a cowbird egg is usually larger than those of the parasitized bird, yet it generally hatches first. (See Questions 740–42.)

716. Is the incubation period known for all North American birds? Comparatively few species of North American birds have been studied so thoroughly that extremes and the average incubation periods are fully established. For the majority of species, records of incubation periods are confined to relatively few individual nests. Much study remains to be done in this field.

717. Is incubation constant, once it has begun? Not necessarily. Scientists call the times when the eggs are being incubated "attentive periods," and the times when they are abandoned "inattentive periods." These periods may vary with the weather, with individuals and with species. Inattentive periods usually are most frequent or longest when one sex does all of the incubating.

As the end of the incubation period approaches, many species of birds become attentive for longer and longer periods while others, as with some ducks, actually abandon the eggs for the last day or last few days before hatching.

718. Which birds customarily have short periods of attention and inattention? Usually these are found among the smaller birds in the passerine group. Black-capped chickadees frequently average about 24 minutes on the eggs and 7 minutes away from the nest. Song sparrows usually are attentive for approximately 20 to 30 minutes, then inattentive (off the nest) for 6 to 8 minutes. However, a red crossbill has been known to stay on its eggs for more than 14½ hours and then take little more than half an hour away from them.

719. What birds have the longest periods of attentiveness? Sea birds appear to have the longest periods of attentiveness of any birds. A Leach's petrel nesting in a burrow on an oceanic island off the coast of Maine may incubate its single white egg continuously for 48 hours while its mate feeds far at sea. The mate returns at night to fulfill an equally long vigil. There is a record of an albatross that incubated its egg for 24 days without relief. Female eider ducks occasionally remain on their eggs constantly throughout the entire 28-day incubation period.

720. People have been watching birds since the days of Aristotle. Why is there such ignorance about the length of incubation periods? Perhaps the most important reason for the lack of, and disparity between, incubation records results from lack of proper scientific methods on the part of observers.

The period of incubation may be variable because weather (rain, heat, cold and so on) retards or accelerates the rate of incubation. Extremely long periods of attention or inattention on the part of the parent birds for whatever reason (abnormality in the birds themselves, fear, disturbance, etc.) may also affect the rate at which the embryo develops.

Though amateurs and scientists who study birds number in the millions today, comparatively few have the time to follow a nest from beginning to conclusion, let alone the many nests of a single species which would lead to definite conclusions about incubation of that species.

721. If the female assumes all the incubation duties, does the male have any responsibility during that period? The males of some

birds, among them hummingbirds, eider ducks, wild turkeys and
prairie chickens, take no responsibility whatever for the nest, female,
eggs or young.

Males of other species, such as Canada geese and mute swans, will
bravely defend the female and eggs. They even do their best to protect
them against such overwhelming odds as dogs and men. Kingbirds
attack hawks, eagles or other birds much larger than themselves that
threaten their territories.

Less spectacular duties of nonincubating males include challeng-
ing songs sung from various points of the territory to warn off intruders; bright colors may be flaunted to attract and lead predators
away from the nest; while the feeding of choice bits of food to the
female as she sits on the eggs is part of the work carried on by male
finches, jays and cedar waxwings.

**722. What male bird has the heaviest duties while his mate incu-
bates?** Surely the duties of no male bird at such a time surpass
those of the hornbills of tropical Africa. The female, sometimes alone
and sometimes with the help of the male, walls herself into the
cavity of a tree, using mud to block the entrance until only the end
of her bill can be thrust through the tiny opening. There she remains
imprisoned throughout the laying period, the incubation and at least
part of the time while the young remain in the nest. Through this
long period, the female is fed exclusively by the male. When at last
the female breaks out of her voluntary imprisonment, she is in fine
condition and her feathers are beautiful, for she has molted her old
ones. But the exhausted male is tattered and weary. Instances are
recorded of male hornbills that died of overwork when their labors
were finished. (See Question 260.)

723. Do birds other than the parents ever incubate the eggs?
Among some penguins, particularly the emperor penguins, any bird
that can secure an egg incubates it. Sometimes fierce squabbles over
an egg take place, and when this happens the precious egg may be
broken.

**724. Do a chick and its shell weigh at hatching time as much as
the fresh egg?** The shell of an egg is porous and evaporation of
from 10 to 20 or more per cent takes place between laying and

hatching. In incubators for domestic eggs, loss of weight is somewhat controlled by increasing the amount of humidity. Birds sometimes sprinkle water on their eggs, either deliberately or accidentally. The birds may be hot and therefore dip into nearby bodies of water, then return to the eggs with their feathers wet.

725. How do the eggs of desert birds survive the dry conditions?
Even in desert areas birds must have water. Sand-grouse are desert birds in Asia and Africa which fly long distances to reach water. It is said that they not only wet their feathers in order to dampen their eggs but that the young birds actually suck water from the dripping plumage of the adults. Dew probably helps supply moisture to the eggs of desert birds. Gambel's quails, which nest on American deserts in the southwest, must make their nests near enough water so the young can reach it quickly or they will die of thirst.

726. When a bird arrives at the nest to assume incubation, what is its first act? As soon as a bird arrives at the nest to incubate, it turns the eggs carefully, using the bill to do so. Usually the bird stands from time to time to repeat the turning process during its period of attentiveness.

Incubators used for the artificial hatching of the eggs of domestic birds turn the eggs mechanically at least three times during each 24-hour period. It is believed that turning the eggs prevents adhesion of the embryo to the shell. A pheasant that incubated 23 eggs was watched from a blind and observed to turn all of the eggs frequently. Its entire head was covered with the eggs as it shifted them about.

727. Do all species of birds turn the eggs regularly? While turning the eggs seems almost universal, it is apparently not essential in all species. The palm swift of the South Pacific glues its eggs firmly to the nest as soon as they are laid.

728. Is incubation such a fundamental need that no bird eggs would hatch without it? There is a family of gallinaceous birds called megapodes or mound-birds found in the forests of Australia, New Guinea and the Malay Peninsula which do not incubate their eggs. Some species bury their eggs in warm sand; others take advantage of the heated earth near volcanoes and still others pile up vegetation that generates heat as it decays.

Some of these birds lay their eggs in cavities on the top of mounds which they build. These may be as much as 8 feet high and 24 feet in diameter. The birds are about the size of a domestic hen, yet the mass of material they pile up is said to weigh in some cases as much as five tons.

Once the eggs are deposited in a suitably warm place, the megapodes usually leave them forever, though in some species the male may control the temperature slightly by altering the amount of material covering them. He may help the young to dig their way out of the heap upon hatching after eight to ten weeks. When the young megapodes hatch they are able to feed and care for themselves. Some of them actually fly away when they hatch, completely and immediately independent from the day of their birth. (See Question 355.)

THE YOUNG BIRD HATCHES

729. How does the young bird break out of the shell? The egg shell gradually weakens during incubation. When the embryo is fully developed, increasing pressure by the young bird results in the pipping of the shell. A star-shaped crack appears, generally on the side of the larger end of the egg. This is enlarged by the movements or scraping of the "egg tooth." The egg tooth continues to enlarge the crack until the shell breaks apart and the young bird emerges.

730. How can a young bird possibly have an egg tooth, since one of the characteristics of birds is their toothless mouth? The so-called egg tooth is not really a tooth at all. It is a small, rough, horny spike on the tip of the upper mandible. This temporary growth is most useful in making and enlarging the opening through which the young bird finally breaks from the shell. The egg tooth falls off within a few days after the bird hatches.

731. How long does the hatching process take? Though some eggs, particularly those of shorebirds, appear to hatch quickly, it usually requires from several hours to a day or even as much as 48 hours for the bird to hatch.

732. Can any changes in the eggs be noted as the end of incubation nears?   Young birds, especially ducks, chickens and gulls, may often be heard cheeping within the eggs during the last day or so before hatching.

733. Are young birds conscious of outside influences before hatching?   Scientists have found that young birds cheeping within their shells become quiet immediately if the parent birds give an alarm note.

734. Do all eggs of a clutch hatch at once?   This varies greatly among different species. Among birds that begin incubation as soon as the first egg is laid, there may be a difference of from a few days to a couple weeks or more in hatching. By the time the last egg in a large barn owl clutch has hatched, the first owl to emerge may be quite fully grown.

Among birds such as pheasants, ducks and shore birds that lead their young away from the nest soon after hatching, all eggs must hatch virtually at once, or even living embryos are left behind to perish. The eggs of most passerine birds hatch within a single day, though frequently three eggs will hatch on one day and the fourth not until the following day.

735. Do the parents help young birds to emerge from the eggs?   Occasionally some species, especially among the rails and cranes, help to enlarge the hole made by the young bird. Too much interference might result in the rupturing of blood vessels in the lingering remains of the yolk sac.

736. What happens to the empty eggshells?   Because there is considerable odor connected with the shell and its membrane during hatching, the birds usually dispose of it quickly. Some birds eat the shells, though there is little or no food value left in them; other species carry them away, and some break the shells and add the fragments to the nest lining. Young flamingos take care of the shells themselves, for they swallow their erstwhile covering.

737. If an embryo dies or does not develop, what happens to the egg?   Unless the young birds break it, such an egg usually remains in the nest even after the young have left. Should none of the eggs hatch, the parent birds usually continue to incubate them until long after the normal hatching period has ended.

738. Do parent birds realize the significance of the hatching eggs? It often appears that they do. The parent birds are likely to exhibit considerable excitement at that time. Perhaps the female signals the male when hatching is taking place, for both parents frequently attend the nest at that time. Occasionally the male bird develops parental instincts too soon and brings food for the young before they are out of the shells.

Many species of birds refuse to leave the nest when the young are hatching. Wood thrushes, blue jays and catbirds are particularly attentive to the eggs at that time and scientists studying them have often been able to touch a normally shy bird as she sits on the nest, or lift the bird to examine the condition of the eggs without driving her away. At hatching time there is great reluctance among terns to surrender nest duties when the mate comes to relieve the incubating bird.

739. Young birds frequently do not eat the same food that their parents eat. Do the parent birds recognize the needs of the young birds?   The parents must know by instinct what the young birds need to eat. A cedar waxwing which attentively fed fruit to the female throughout incubation immediately collected a mouthful of small insects to feed them as soon as he saw the young in the nest.

740. Into what classes are young birds divided?   Young birds are divided into two major classes: precocial birds and altricial birds.

741. What is meant by precocial birds?   They are born covered with down, with their eyes wide open, and are able to run about as soon as they become dry after hatching. They either help to find part of their food or all of it.

742. What are altricial birds?   Altricial birds are hatched blind, naked and helpless.

743. What are nudifugous birds?   Nudifugous birds leave the nest soon after hatching and join their parents in search of food. Typical precocial birds are also nudifugous. Young grouse, chickens, and ducks are nudifugous precocial birds.

744. What are ptilopaedic birds? A ptilopaedic bird is covered with down, usually dense, both above and below, when it hatches. Typical precocial birds are also ptilopaedic.

745. What are nidicolous birds? Nidicolous birds remain in the nest for an extended period. The parents bring food to the nest for these birds. Typical altricial birds are also nidicolous.

746. What are psilopaedic birds? Psilopaedic birds are born either naked or very sparsely covered on the back with down. Typical altricial birds are psilopaedic.

747. What precocial birds in North America are not typical members of that group? Gulls, terns and members of the alcid family hatch with their eyes wide open, they are covered densely with down, and are able to walk, but they remain for a few days to several weeks in or near the nest, where they are fed by their parents.

748. Does the kind of food eaten by young precocial birds indicate whether they are typical precocial birds? Apparently the kind of food eaten by the birds plays a very important part, or perhaps it would be better to say the way the food is obtained has a bearing on whether the young birds are typical precocial birds or not.

Precocial birds which feed on land, either by scratching on the ground or searching it for food, are accompanied by their young as they seek the food.

The precocial young of most sea birds which seek food on or in the water, or which fly far from the nesting place to obtain food, naturally cannot follow their parents. That must await the growth of the primary wing feathers.

749. Which North American altricial birds are not typical of that group? There are many altricial birds that do not conform to the typical characteristics of this group of birds. The albatrosses, shearwaters, fulmars, petrels, herons, storks, ibises, spoonbills, flamingos, hawks, owls, nighthawks and whip-poor-wills are among the birds which are not typical altricial birds. All are hatched helpless and dependent on their parents for food and shelter. However, instead of being hatched naked, they are more or less covered with down. In other words, they are ptilopaedic, which is one of the characteristics of precocial birds.

750. Can any bird fly as soon as it hatches? Some species of megapodes pass through the down stage in the egg and when they hatch they already are wearing juvenile plumage and can fly away from their empty eggshells. (See Question 728.)

751. Do birds recognize their own young? Passerine birds usually accept any birds that hatch in their nests. They feed cowbirds as carefully as they do their own. Hens which hatch duck eggs care for the young ducklings and become greatly upset when they go in the water. Pheasants and ducks usually kill any young birds or at least refuse to care for them if they look too much unlike their own. In Europe, owls and buzzards have hatched domestic chicken eggs and reared the young. Herring gulls will feed any young of the same age as their own for the first four days, but after that they recognize their own young and will kill strangers that are put in the nest.

752. What is the gravest danger to newly hatched birds? Probably prolonged rain poses the greatest threat to young birds. They survive cold very well if they are fed regularly the large amounts of food their bodies demand. But during rainy weather they do not always receive as much food as they need and they become chilled when left uncovered while the parent birds search for food. During prolonged rains it is not unusual for all the very young birds from more than a thousand tern nests on a single Maine island to perish.

753. Do young birds recognize their parents? For the first few days young passerine birds apparently do not know their parents. They readily accept foster parents. Any movement suggests food to them and they will beg for it from humans. If a stick is moved close to them, they open their mouths and beg. Wild birds reared by humans accept their caretakers as parents. Dr. Konrad Lorenz, the great animal behaviorist, discovered that when he learned certain call notes of mallards, graylag geese and other birds, and gave these notes when the eggs hatched, the young birds accepted him as their mother and followed him in complete confidence.

YOUNG PRECOCIAL BIRDS

754. What is the appearance of a young precocial bird? Precocial young are thickly covered with down that dries within two or three hours after hatching. The eyes are open and vision and hearing are well developed. The body temperature control is partially developed, but the bird must be brooded in cold or wet weather. The egg tooth is conspicuous on the tip of the upper mandible. The wings are relatively small and undeveloped. Gulls, terns and alcids are not typical precocial birds, for the young stay from a few days to several weeks in or close to the nest.

755. How do young precocial birds develop? The period of development may be divided into two phases: the time between hatching and the development of flight; and development after flight is attained.

756. What activities occur during the first period? This period is less complex than with the altricial young, where complicated nest behavior occurs. Anywhere from three to twenty-four hours after hatching, precocial young (with many exceptions) follow the parents from the nest. They are brooded frequently and respond to the often-given brood call of the adult. They sun, preen, swim (if aquatic), hunt food and so on.

757. How long after hatching does flight, indicative of the second period, become possible? This varies from 14 to 20 days or more with land birds and between 6 and 12 weeks with most water birds. The larger the birds, usually the longer the time elapsing before flight begins.

758. What activities occupy the young during the second period? The family bond as a rule holds strongly until the brooding is no longer needed and flight is well developed. Frequently the family bonds remain well into the first autumn or winter. Chasing, fighting and pecking often occur between the young at this period.

759. Are the soft parts of young precocial birds brightly colored, as are those of altricial young? The fleshy parts of young precocial birds are no more brightly colored than those of the adults, and sometimes are even duller.

760. Why do precocial birds not need brightly colored mouth parts? The young feed themselves from the beginning. Even birds such as gulls, terns and alcids, which are not typical precocial birds since they feed the young for a while at the nest, bring food and drop it beside the young birds, which then pick it up. Typical precocial parents may lead the young to food and indicate its presence, but the young pick it up themselves.

761. When the precocial bird first takes flight, how does its weight compare with that of the female? When a typical precocial chick first flies it is much smaller in proportion to the female than is the young altricial bird on its first flight. The precocial land birds weigh about 60 to 70 per cent less than the female at this time.

762. Is the precocial bird considered a primitive or advanced form of life? The precocial bird is considered more primitive than the altricial bird. The species of megapode that flies from its nest soon after hatching is most like its reptilian ancestors of any young bird. Though all birds high in the evolutionary scale are altricial, not all birds low in the evolutionary scale are precocial. Cormorants, pelicans and gannets are examples of altricial young among the lower orders of birds.

763. Do the precocial young of water birds have to be taught to swim? Swimming with these birds is an instinctive act. A young black guillemot that has hatched under rocks in a place where it is impossible to see the ocean will, when the time comes, scramble over and between the rocks and enter the pounding surf without fear, swimming and diving with superb skill.

764. Do these birds know instinctively which objects are good food? Apparently good judgment must be learned. At first young precocial birds that follow their parents may pick at anything and everything. The parents show them which objects to eat by picking these up in front of them. They also take up seeds and drop them again in front of the youngsters as if to encourage them to take the right food.

765. Do the parent birds ever carry their young? Young grebes frequently climb on the back of the parent bird and snuggle in her feathers when they are cold, wet or tired. Cygnets climb on the backs of the old swans as they swim about. Ducklings also climb aboard for a free sail. Eider ducks have been observed to dive with the young still nestled in the feathers of the back.

THE DEVELOPMENT OF ALTRICIAL YOUNG

766. What is the appearance of a newly hatched altricial bird? A young altricial bird has an enormous head and abdomen. Its wings are tiny and its legs are weak and helpless. Its eyes are swollen and closed. Its mouth is very large and opens widely, usually in a diamond shape. Most of these birds have a mouth lining that contrasts sharply with their naked bodies or it is brightly colored, usually with red, orange or yellow. A young meadowlark shows not only all of these colors in its mouth but blue in addition to them. The mouth lining of young cedar waxwings is bright red and violet-blue, while that of young nighthawks is smoky blue. Even though the inside of the mouth is not conspicuously colored, the edge of the mouth and bill are usually bordered with bright yellow.

767. What are papillae? Some young altricial birds have small knobs in the mouth which reflect light. All young altricial birds do not have papillae; some have only two as in some thrushes, while some titmice have many. These, together with the bright colors of the mouth, the wide, yellow-edged gape, and the cheeping and the waving or quivering of the head attract the parent birds and guide them to the correct placement of the food.

768. What do young altricial birds eat? Their food is as varied as their appearance. Members of the crow family, for instance, will eat almost any animal or vegetable food. On the other hand, young ospreys will eat only fish. Usually very young birds are fed some form of animal life, even though their parents eat vegetable food almost exclusively. Goldfinches are one exception to this. The adults partially digest seeds and feed these to their young. But sparrows and cedar waxwings, which as adults eat little but fruits and seeds, feed worms and insects to their very young nestlings. Hummingbirds give their young a combination of tiny spiders, insects and nectar from flowers. Many species of altricial birds, among them herons and petrels, swallow and partially digest the food which they regurgitate to feed the young. Roadrunners collect snakes and lizards for their nestlings, while kingfishers dive for fish or tadpoles to feed theirs. Certain species of pigeons and doves secrete a liquid called pigeon milk that the young birds take from the throat of their parents. (See Questions 251, 252.)

769. How do birds carry food to the nest?   Many birds bring food in their bills and place it directly in the mouths of the young birds. Hawks and owls, with few exceptions, carry the food in their talons. Other birds, among them hummingbirds, herons and goldfinches, partially digest the food in their crops. Thus they come to the nest bringing no visible food with them. While there are many exceptions, as a general rule birds that catch their food in their claws carry it in their claws, while those that collect food with their bills carry it in the bill.

770. How much food do the nestlings require?   Passerine birds develop rapidly, usually doubling their weight in a single day after hatching. This is possible only because they eat tremendous quantities of food. It is said that a young robin eats 14 feet of earthworms daily. Many species of birds eat at least half their weight in food each day and some actually eat the equivalent of their weight.

771. How often are young birds fed?   Goldfinches feed their young by regurgitation about every half hour. Scientists have recorded a house wren that made 491 feedings in a day, and a phoebe that brought food to the nest 845 times in a single day. Starlings average about 17 trips to the nest in an hour. Some thrushes make as many as 26 feeding trips, swallows average about 30 feedings, and some titmice feed as many as 70 times in an hour. It must be kept in mind that all young birds in a nest do not receive food at each trip to the nest. Some swifts make but one feeding trip an hour to the nest, but may then give a collection of anywhere from 150 to nearly 700 insects at a single feeding.

Among some families of birds, feeding occurs much less frequently. Often when the young are fed they gorge themselves. Roadrunners have been seen with the tails of lizards hanging out of the bills for some time after feeding, for their capacity has not been equal to their greed. In the same way owls have been observed with the tails of rats dangling from their bills. Birds that catch large prey often leave the carcasses on the nest so the young may feed themselves whenever hungry. Wallace writes of one barn owl nest he observed in which there were four young owls, and beside them 73 mice had been deposited.

Sea birds often search for food many miles away from their nests. Therefore their young may be fed only at long intervals. Some are fed but once daily, while certain petrels may have intervals of as much as ten days between feedings in the latter part of their nestling period. There is a European swift which feeds largely on a particular species of insect that does not fly in rainy weather. Since these swifts, like those in our country, feed exclusively on the wing, they do not try to feed in adverse weather. When this happens, the young birds become torpid, almost like woodchucks in hibernation. While this torpid period seldom lasts as much as 10 days, there is a record of these birds surviving a 21-day fast.

772. How are young birds fed?   All those who have raised a crow or other young wild bird know that the food must be placed deep in the throat where strong muscles are able to swallow it. The strong pull of those muscles can be felt when fingers holding the food are thrust into the bird's throat.

The bright colors and papillae in the mouths of young birds apparently act as guides for the parents when they bring food to thrust into the throats of their young. Among birds which open their mouths wide so that the young birds can reach in for food, the mouth of the adult is usually brightly colored and guides the youngster to the food supply.

Some parents stimulate the young birds to beg for food by swaying their bills while others give a food cry, upon which the nestlings open their mouths. The young bird that begs the loudest and opens widest gets the food. In this way, as the hunger of one young bird is satisfied, it subsides and the next one begs hardest and obtains the food, until each has had a turn.

Young herons take the adult's bill in a scissor-hold and shake it vigorously until the parent regurgitates food into the nest, or as the nestlings mature, directly into their throats. The feeding of young hummingbirds is an awesome sight. The female thrusts her needlelike bill deeply into the throat of the young bird and pumps it rapidly up and down until the observer wonders how she can avoid impaling the nestling.

773. Do all young altricial birds swallow their food whole? Most birds of prey tear apart the food they bring to the nest. Then the young birds help themselves. Among some hawks the male catches the prey when the nestlings are very small and the female, which stays on guard at the nest, tears it apart for them. So rigidly is this division of work observed that if the female is killed while the nestlings are too young to tear apart their own food, they starve in the midst of plenty, for the male delivers ample food but does not prepare it for the young birds.

774. How long must altricial birds stay in the nest? This varies with the family and species. As a whole, large birds stay in the nest longer than small birds but this does not hold true in many instances. Hummingbirds, the smallest birds of all, stay in the nest for about three weeks, though they have been known to remain for 27 days. Bitterns remain in the nest about two weeks.

Birds such as swallows, swifts and woodpeckers, which develop in the nest to a point where they can immediately fly long distances upon leaving it, remain longer in the nest than do sparrows that spend several days hopping after the adults and learning to fly rather slowly.

However, most passerine birds remain in the nest from 10 to 20 days, with 12 to 14 days being the average. Woodpeckers stay in their nest holes from 3 weeks to a month, while hawks and owls spend approximately 6 weeks in their nests. California condors remain in their nests for about 6 months. It is said that some young royal albatrosses have stayed in their nests as long as 9 months.

775. How rapid is the growth of young altricial birds? Most altricial birds grow extremely fast. In fact, the rate of growth exceeds that of any other vertebrate. A European cuckoo 3 weeks after it hatches weighs 50 times as much as when it left the egg. A great blue heron at the end of 6 weeks weighs almost 38 times as much as when hatched.

Strangely enough, some altricial birds weigh more at some time before they leave the nest than they ever will again. Swallows near the end of their nestling period are heavier than their parents. Pelicans, too, weigh more than their parents for a period before flight.

Of all the altricial birds, those in the Procellariiformes order (albatrosses, shearwaters, petrels) show this trait most. Young birds in this order are cared for and fed until they are extremely fat and considerably heavier than their parents. It is said that they are then deserted by their parents, though some scientists maintain that the adults visit them at long intervals. In partial or complete solitude, these birds finish their development, using their reserves of fat as they do so. Finally, when they have become much lighter and very hungry, they take off alone on their first flight.

Thus we see that while birds grow very rapidly, they may actually shrink again before maturity.

776. Do songbirds weigh as much as their parents when they leave the nest?   Songbirds usually weigh about 20 to 30 per cent less than the female when they begin to fly. A few may weigh as much as 50 per cent less than the adults when the nest is abandoned.

777. Are all young birds careful to preserve nest sanitation?   Most passerine birds are careful to keep the nest sanitary. At each feeding, the parent usually waits for the fecal sac to appear. Among many species, the fecal sac is swallowed by the adults during the first days after the young birds hatch. Later the fecal sac is carried away and dropped at a distance from the nest.

Certain passerine birds, among them the goldfinch, swallows and phoebes, permit the nest to become very dirty. This is particularly unpleasant when swallows or phoebes nest near houses.

The "whitewashing" around heron, cormorant, pelican and gannet colonies makes them very conspicuous. These birds customarily discharge the excrement over the edge of the nest. The fact that guano can collect in dry climates instead of being washed away as it normally is has resulted in the fabulous guano industry of Peru, with an annual income in the millions of dollars.

778. What changes take place as the young bird develops?
When an altricial bird hatches, it closely resembles its reptilian ancestors in that it is really a cold-blooded creature. Its "heating system" does not begin to function until several days after hatching. In most passerine birds, this does not happen until approximately the ninth day. Therefore the young birds must be brooded by one of the adults when the weather is very hot or very cold or they would perish.

In the first few days after hatching, young birds are likely to stretch their necks, open their mouths and beg for food whenever anything moves near the nest. By the midperiod of their nestling life, not only can they see but they "freeze" when anything other than their parents approaches the nest.

As young passerine birds grow, they preen, exercise their wings, and jostle one another in the nest. Their bodies become covered with down and finally with feathers. Usually these birds are colored in such a way that they blend unobtrusively into their surroundings.

Frequently the young of the larger altricial birds not only grow up in conspicuous nests but may be black or white as their down and later their juvenile plumage develop. These birds (hawks, eagles, owls) may place their large nests very high in inaccessible trees, or they may be hidden in less obvious places. Pelicans, herons, gannets and other species usually nest in large colonies, often on islands, and trust to this isolation by surrounding water or the security of numbers to protect the nests from enemies. Such protection usually serves them well except when man becomes their enemy.

779. How do scientists know what and how much birds are fed?
Scientists may conceal themselves in blinds (hiding places) where they can watch birds from morning until night. They are able to count the number of visits made to the nests by the parents. Often they can identify the food that is brought and estimate the amount of each kind of food. More often the kind of food and its weight are measured from the contents in the crops of birds that have been killed. Some scientists have made imitation mouths of nestlings and placed them in nests that they wished to study. The parent birds, seeing the wide-open mouth colored just like those of their young, stuff food into them. Then all the food can be removed, weighed and identified.

IX. THE SIZE OF BIRDS

780. What is the largest bird living today? The ostrich, which may stand nearly eight feet tall and weigh as much as 300 pounds, is the largest living bird. The ostrich is a native of Africa but man has taken the species as a zoo or domestic bird to all continents.

781. What is the largest living native bird in North America? The trumpeter swan is the largest wild bird. The males average almost 28 pounds and the females about 22 pounds in weight. They have a wingspread measuring from 8 to nearly 10 feet. Whooping cranes are the tallest birds, standing almost five feet tall, but they weigh between 8 and 17 pounds and their wingspread is under 8 feet.

The California condor (the Andean condor is no larger) averages about 21½ pounds and has a wingspread that varies between 8 feet and 9½ feet. Much greater wingspreads, up to 14 feet, have been reported but never verified.

782. What is the largest bird known to have lived? The giant moa of New Zealand which apparently became extinct about five centuries ago stood, according to reconstructions of their skeletons, as much as 12 feet tall. They were flightless birds built for running. The giant moa belonged to a large family that ranged in size from the 12-foot giants down to small species about the size of turkeys.

783. What caused the extinction of the giant moas? The cause of their extinction about the fourteenth century is not known. However, some were eaten by the primitive people who then inhabited New Zealand. Others died in "graveyards" containing hundreds of skeletons of moas, which suggests that they may have been herded together by some catastrophe, perhaps fire, that caused simultaneous death to great numbers. In Pyramid Valley of South Island a very sticky lake deposit over which a thin film of humus and vegetation spread trapped many moas. The heavy birds broke through the surface and were caught in the treacherous mire where they floundered helplessly and died.

784. Have any other birds approached the giant moa in size?
The elephant bird (*Aepyornis maximus*) may have weighed as much
as 1,000 pounds and reached 11 feet in height. Like the giant moa it
was flightless and somewhat resembled an ostrich in form.

785. Where did the elephant bird live?   On the island of Madagascar off the east coast of Africa. (See Question 662.)

786. When did the elephant bird become extinct?   It is believed
that early navigators, stopping off for food supplies, caused the
extinction of this species. Probably this happened some time in the
twelfth or thirteenth century. It is generally believed that the elephant
bird gave rise to the legendary tales of the roc. (See Questions
663, 991.)

787. What is the smallest bird in the world?   The bee hummingbird of Cuba, measuring a tiny 2¼ inches in length, is the smallest
bird in the world.

788. Which is the smallest bird found in the United States?   The
Heloise's hummingbird, often called the bumblebee hummingbird,
measures but 2¾ inches in length, thus winning for itself the diminu-
tive crown among North American birds. It is found chiefly in
Mexico, Guatemala, and the Honduras but occasionally strays into
southern Arizona.

**789. Heloise's hummingbird so rarely enters the United States that
it can scarcely be claimed as a native of that country. Among those
that regularly nest in the United States, which is the smallest?**
The calliope hummingbird, which measures three inches in length, is
the smallest bird that regularly nests in the United States. This species
nests from the southern part of British Columbia and Alberta southward in the Rockies to Wyoming and Utah and in the mountains of
eastern Washington, eastern Oregon and in parts of California.

**790. How does the ruby-throated hummingbird of eastern United
States compare in size with the calliope hummingbird?**   Some individuals of the ruby-throated hummingbird are scarcely any larger

than the calliope but large individuals may measure as much as 3¾ inches. Its tiny nest, covered with bits of lichen so that it looks like a small knot on the branch, is so small that the cap of a Coca-Cola bottle will cover it. The two white eggs are about the size of peas. (See Questions 624, 650.)

791. Which North American bird has the greatest wingspread for its weight? The man-of-war bird or magnificent frigate bird weighs only 3½ pounds, but its narrow wings stretch 7½ feet.

792. How is a bird measured? Length (L.): The bird is placed flat on its back and gently stretched. A ruler measures from the tip of the bill to the tip of the longest tail feather.

Width or Extent (W. or Ex.): The bird is placed flat on its back and the wings are grasped at the joints. Then the distance from tip to tip of the longest primary feathers is determined with a ruler.

Wing: The measurement is taken from the bend of the wing to the tip of the longest primary while the wing is folded in the normal position of rest.

Tail: The distance from the tip of the longest tail feather to the point where it emerges from the skin.

793. Bird books give the same length for robins and bobwhites, yet they do not appear the same size. How is this explained? The length of both robins and bobwhites is taken as directed above. But robins have fairly long tails and their bodies are slim. Bobwhites have extremely short tails and their bodies are quite round. It is the shape of these birds that deceives the eye and makes them appear quite unlike in length whereas scientific measurements show them to be the same.

When observing birds, note their shape, the length of the bill and the tail, and the form of their bodies when comparing them with birds already known. Such careful observations are more valuable to the bird student than the sizes given in bird books.

794. Is there as great variation in the size of mammals as there is among birds? The variation between the greatest and smallest mammals is much greater than between birds. The blue whale, largest of the mammals, weighs about 200,000 pounds while the smallest mammal in the world, the masked shrew, weighs but $\frac{1}{7}$ of an ounce.

Ostriches, the largest living birds, average about 150 pounds (the greatest weight attained is about 300 pounds) while the smallest hummingbird weighs only $\frac{1}{10}$ of an ounce. Mammals vary in mass more than a thousand times as much as do birds.

X. NUMBERS OF BIRDS

795. How many birds are there in the United States? Various scientists have estimated the number of birds in the United States and each has found a different answer. However, the number usually falls somewhere in the region of six billion.

796. How many birds are there in the world? The answer to this question must remain in the realm of conjecture. Many scientists, however, consider the estimate of 100 billion birds made by the English ornithologist, James Fisher, as quite reasonable and based on sound computation.

797. How many species of birds are there in the world? Scientists are not in complete agreement as to which birds are distinct species. Therefore there is disagreement as to the number of species of birds in the world. Dr. Ernst Mayr of Harvard University believes there are about 8,600 species of birds on the earth.

798. How many species of birds have been found in the United States? There are about 650 species of birds in the United States, though some scientists count another 100 or so accidental species.

799. What are accidental species? An accidental species of bird is one that occasionally wanders outside of its normal range. It may be carried away by a storm or stray for unknown causes.

800. Which family of American birds has the most species? The Tyrannidae, the New World flycatchers or tyrant flycatchers, is the largest family. It contains 365 species. They are found in all kinds of habitats from Tierra del Fuego in extreme southern South America to tree line in the arctic.

801. Why are these birds called tyrant flycatchers? These birds which catch their insect food on the wing are well named, for many of them, though small, are ever ready to fight. They will not hesitate to attack crows, hawks, and even eagles that enter their territory.

802. How many larks are native to North America?   Only one species of native lark, the horned lark, occurs in North America. The meadowlark is not a lark but a member of the blackbird family. Skylarks from Europe have been introduced in several places on the North American continent, but the only successful establishment of these birds is on Vancouver Island.

803. Where are the most birds found in the United States?   Roger Tory Peterson in *Birds over America* lists the following great concentrations of birds:

A farm in Maryland where 59 pairs of birds have nested on one acre in a single season.

The walls and eaves of a single barn near Deerfield, Michigan, where in one summer 2,015 cliff swallow nests have been counted.

In a single acre of marsh in California between 5,000 and 10,000 nests of tri-colored redwings were concentrated.

On Bush Key in the Dry Tortugas 14,620 pairs of sooty terns nest on a single acre. They average three nests to the square yard.

On Three Arch Rocks off the coast of Oregon, 750,000 murres are said to nest on a 17-acre tract. This averages out to about one bird for every square foot.

804. Is there any other place in the world with as dense a bird population as the Three Arch Rocks of Oregon?   On one of the Chincha group of islands off the coast of Peru between four and five million guanay cormorants nest. This may be the densest breeding bird colony in the entire world.

805. What place in the United States has the fewest birds?   Strangely enough, the place most barren of bird life is not in the midst of one of the great cities but in an area not inhabited by man.

The glistening white Bonneville Salt Flats of Utah are practically destitute of birds.

806. What species of bird in the United States is most numerous?   Speculation necessarily enters into this matter but judging by the nearly 9,000,000 redwings listed on Audubon Christmas bird counts which cover but about 500 fifteen-mile diameter circles, or approximately $\frac{1}{132}$ part of the entire country, this is the most numerous bird in the United States in winter.

Redwings occur in every state, and nest beside streams of all sizes, around the borders of lakes, in swamps, sloughs and salt marshes, and even in brush-tangled damp areas too dry to be called swampy. This species may be proposed as the most numerous in the United States, in summer as well as in winter.

807. Has any bird in the past outnumbered any present species of bird on the North American continent? In the last century both Alexander Wilson and John James Audubon estimated more than a *billion* passenger pigeons in a single flock. These birds must have constituted a large part of the land bird population of the continent at one time. Dr. A. W. Schorger in *Passenger Pigeon* states that nesting areas of 31 square miles—3 miles wide and 10 miles long—were typical and quotes Alexander Wilson as saying that in 1808 in Kentucky there was a nesting area several miles wide which extended 40 miles north and south. Remains of 90 nests were found in a single tree.

Dr. Schorger who made a thorough study of the literature concerning the Passenger Pigeon reported a nesting site in Michigan which was 40 miles long and 6 miles wide. In Oneida County, New York, there was a nest area 30 miles long which averaged 3 miles in width. In Cattaraugus County a 30-mile long nesting area averaged 6 miles in width. In 1863 there was in Pennsylvania a nest area which extended for 60 miles.

808. What is the most numerous land bird in the world? This is a matter open to dispute. A study of habitat may be helpful in forming an opinion. House sparrows adapt readily to both urban and rural habitats. They have been taken to all continents of the world and everywhere they have thrived and multiplied enormously. The same is true of the European starling. It may be that one of these species is the most numerous land bird in the world.

On the other hand, all around the Northern Hemisphere where the largest land masses occur are vast stretches of grasslands and prairie country. Wherever this type of open country occurs, horned larks are found. This species may outnumber the artificially colonized European starlings and house sparrows.

809. What water bird is most numerous? While dovekies are incredibly numerous in parts of the arctic, many scientists believe the Wilson's petrel, which breeds in the Southern Hemisphere and visits the Northern Hemisphere during its summer, is the most numerous species. Others speak strongly for the guanay cormorants of western South America.

810. Which species of bird in the United States has the most restricted range? If the dusky seaside sparrow is regarded as a full species (and not just a race of the seaside sparrow) its range is the most restricted, for it is nonmigratory and breeds only in the scattered salicornia fields of a small section of Merritt Island, and at nearby Salt Lake and Persimmon Hammock in Florida.

However, many scientists regard the dusky seaside sparrow as a mere race or subspecies. A species about which there can be no dispute is the Kirtland's warbler. This warbler nests in a very limited area and in a limited type of habitat within that area. Burning must keep the pine trees at a particular height if these birds are to breed. They nest chiefly in three counties in Michigan within an area about 60 miles wide and 100 miles long.

811. What are the rarest birds in the United States? The ivory-billed woodpecker, whooping crane, California condor, Everglades kite and Bachman's warbler.

812. Are these species in danger of extinction? All five species are in grave danger. Of the three first mentioned, each is the largest member of its family in the United States. Each demands a certain type of habitat in which to feed and breed. To each of the three species, man has not only been a serious threat because large birds are easy target for thoughtless gunners, but he has also destroyed or reduced the habitats which these birds demand. The California condor has suffered not only through invasion of its territory by man, but as a carrion-eater, it has often died from eating poisoned carcasses placed as bait for coyotes and other mammals.

813. Have any species of birds once occurring in the United States become extinct in the twentieth century? The last passenger pigeon died in the Cincinnati Zoo in 1914, the lone surviving individual of a race that once occurred in such fantastic numbers that the flocks actually darkened the sun as they passed. Sometimes the passage of a flock took many hours. The last heath hen was seen on Martha's Vineyard in 1931. This bird was a race of the greater prairie chicken.

No one knows when the last Carolina paroquet died. Dr. Frank M. Chapman saw a flock of 13 near Taylor Creek northeast of Okeechobee, Florida, in 1904. He collected four birds from the flock. Though reports of living Carolina paroquets continue to circulate, when traced to the source all have proved unfounded.

The Eskimo curlew, the smallest American curlew, may still exist. One was collected at Battle Harbor, Labrador on August 29, 1932. In the October issue of the *Auk,* Joseph M. Heiser, Jr., reported having observed two Eskimo curlews near West Bay on Galveston Island, Texas, on April 29, 1945. Overshooting during migration and on their breeding grounds accounts for the virtual or complete disappearance of this species.

814. What other species of birds are known to have become extinct in North America since Columbus discovered the western world? The Labrador duck was last collected at Elmira, New York, on December 12, 1878. The cause of its extinction is unknown but is generally attributed to its limited range and the fact that, though considered inferior in taste, it was often shot by market gunners.

The last great auk was taken on Elderry Island, Iceland, in 1844. These good swimmers were flightless. Often they were herded into pens where they were killed with sticks and then salted down, or carried alive on board ships to provide fresh food for the voyage. Their eggs were eaten and their oil was considered valuable. They were chopped up for codfish bait. When feather beds became fashionable, the doom of these densely feathered, easily collected birds was sealed.

815. What can be done to prevent more birds from becoming extinct? It must be understood that a part of the evolutionary picture of this earth is a constant upsurge of some species while others decrease in numbers and perhaps vanish forever. Evolutionary change is always at work. It is inevitable that certain species should disappear from the earth. Nevertheless man can do much to delay this usually slow process of evolution. He can protect threatened species by laws, by wise and flexible hunting codes, and most of all, by preserving adequate nesting and feeding habitats for all wild creatures. A boy with a BB gun does not begin to do the damage to wild life that a well-meaning but shortsighted and unwise civic program of marsh drainage may do. Great blocks of every type of habitat should be maintained undisturbed so that all species of birds (and other animals as well) may find ample space in which to live. It was man's ruthless destruction rather than evolutionary change which sent the birds mentioned above to sudden extinction.

816. Are the numbers of birds in North America decreasing? On the contrary, the actual number of birds is probably increasing. But many of the big, showy birds whose grace and beauty thrill all who see them suffer most from the pressures of increasing human population. The small birds, particularly those that prefer open farmland and suburban habitats, have undoubtedly increased with the destruction of the wilderness. Few people today can watch the majestic flight of whooping cranes and trumpeter swans or hear their glorious, ringing voices. But from all sides come the chirping sounds of English sparrows and the whistling of European starlings.

817. In what habitat are birds most in danger of extinction? Generally speaking, island birds are most easily destroyed. Through countless ages island birds found safety in their insular isolation. They therefore developed few means for the protection of their nests and young. Their boundaries were limited.

Now man is invading the islands in increasing numbers. He takes along dogs, cats, foxes and other mammals. Inadvertently he also introduces rats to the islands. Birds long accustomed to safety are vulnerable to quick destruction, once mammals inhabit islands formerly free of them. Some mammals kill and eat the birds, while others compete with them for food and shelter.

818. Why did the vast company of passenger pigeons disappear? The beech forests which provided a large part of the food of these birds and offered them nesting sites, and the oak forests of the South which provided much of their winter food, were quickly reduced in number and extent as the white population swelled and surged ever farther west and south. Moreover, domestic mammals such as pigs competed with the pigeons for beech and oak mast.

Vast numbers of passenger pigeons were killed for food, sometimes trainloads of them being collected at once and shipped to eastern markets. No doubt many factors entered into the final abrupt extinction of this once spectacularly abundant species. These birds had developed such strong colonial habits that disrupted small groups probably were unable to breed. In a few decades the passenger pigeon passed from incredible abundance to total extinction.

819. How does the world's population of birds compare with that of other vertebrates? Most scientists consider birds, at least numerically, the most successful vertebrates in the world. If subspecies as well as species are counted, there are about 25,000 kinds of birds, while there are about 15,000 species and subspecies of mammals, and about the same number of species, plus subspecies, among the fish.

XI. BIRDBANDING

820. What is meant by birdbanding? Birdbanding as it is done today means the placement of identification bracelets on the legs of birds. In the British Isles this is known as ringing.

821. Why are birds banded? Only by banding can the scientist discover the longevity of a species and hope to follow its wanderings on migration. Does a bird breed in the same area each year? Does it winter in the same area? Does it use the same routes every time it migrates north or south? At what age do certain changes in the color of plumage, eye, bill, legs or feet occur? Banding answers these questions and aids those making detailed life history studies of specific species, and helps students keep track of the activities of individual males, females, and young. In the latter type of research, however, an additional colored band or combination of colored bands is frequently used to facilitate recognition in the field.

822. When was the first bird banded? Apparently the first record is that of a great gray heron captured in Germany in 1710 and found to be wearing metal rings or bands which had been placed on its legs several years previously in Turkey.

823. When was the first bird banded in North America? Probably the first birds banded in North America were marked by John James Audubon, who tied silver threads around the legs of a brood of eastern phoebes at Mill Grove, Pennsylvania, in 1803. Subsequently he discovered that at least two of these birds returned to the same locality the following spring.

824. When was the first intensive systematic banding begun? There are numerous records of birds banded, tagged or otherwise marked during the nineteenth century, but most of these were rather haphazard. Little of particular importance happened until 1899, when a Danish schoolmaster-ornithologist named Mortensen commenced systematically placing aluminum rings on storks, teal, starlings and hawks. His results were so interesting that birdbanding rapidly spread through Europe, and within a decade a couple of dozen projects were in operation in a score of countries.

825. When was birdbanding in North America organized under one central agency? In the first two decades of this century there were scattered individual banding projects, but they lacked organization. There was no guarantee that the same number was not being used for several different birds. Moreover, banding in quantity was too expensive for most individuals to afford, and the inevitable mass of clerical details became too great for mere hobbyists to handle. Finally in 1920 all birdbanding was organized under the supervision of the United States Biological Survey, a governmental body now called the United States Fish and Wildlife Service. This agency assumes all responsibility for issuing banding permits, supplying bands, offering guidance, and keeping careful files for the ever-growing mountain of records.

826. What types of bands are used? In North America serially-numbered light aluminum bands issued by the United States Fish and Wildlife Service are used. Each band has its own individual number as well as engraving indicating it was issued by the Service. The bands come in assorted sizes from 0 to 8. The zero-sized bands are used for small species such as kinglets and wrens, the number 8's for birds with heavy legs such as pelicans.

827. Can anyone band birds? It is against the law to capture wild birds for any reason whatsoever without a permit. Anyone planning to band must first obtain an official permit from the United States Fish and Wildlife Service in Washington, D.C. In spite of what many may assume, most banding is not done by museums or universities. Governmental agencies, strangely enough, concentrate almost entirely on game species. Most banding is done by interested teachers, doctors, farmers, engineers, artists, insurance men, housewives and others from virtually every walk of life.

828. How is a birdbanding permit obtained? The first step is to write to the United States Fish and Wildlife Service, Department of the Interior, Washington, D.C., fully stating the reasons for wanting the permit, your qualifications in bird identification, and your ability to devote a good deal of time to the project. Chances of obtaining a permit will be greater if you can include recommendations from several nationally known scientists, preferably ornithologists.

Once the Federal permit is obtained you must get an additional permit from the state or states in which you plan to operate. This is usually issued by the conservation department of the state.

829. Why is such careful screening of all licensed operators necessary? It is important that only well-qualified persons receive permits, for several reasons. If everyone requesting a license were granted one, the project would become just a plaything. What good would a record be if one were not 100 per cent sure of the identification of the species banded? The cost of providing bands for a multitude of people and the clerical work involved in keeping track of all banders and their data would be prohibitive. Many people would soon lose interest and do no work during the year, yet the upkeep for such people would be as high as for conscientious banders. Furthermore, some not even interested in banding might use the permit to cover up their collecting of birds for illegal purposes.

830. What does the accepted bander receive, what is he expected to do, and what does he have to supply himself? The official bander receives *A Manual for Bird Banders,* an assortment of bands as requested, and periodic releases concerning birdbanding activities and discoveries. Each bander is required to abide by rigid standards and report his activities regularly to the Federal headquarters. He must submit a list of all the birds banded, giving the species, the number of the band, the place, date, and wherever possible the age and sex of each individual. The bander must supply his own pliers for tightening the bands on the birds' legs, a record book, and traps and bait for capturing his subjects.

831. How and where do Canadians and Mexicans obtain a banding permit? Whereas the United States, Canadian and Mexican governments issue their own banding permits and supervise banding activities in their respective countries, they co-operate fully in ornithological investigations. All bands used in North America are issued from Washington. Thus by control of the serial numbers from a single source each band used in North America has its own individual number. In Europe, with a multitude of separate banding enterprises in each country, there are frequent duplications in numbers and consequently ensuing confusion.

People living in Canada and Mexico who wish to band birds should write to their own fish and game departments for a permit.

832. Do any women band birds? Some of the most energetic and famous banders have been women. Mrs. Margaret M. Nice in Ohio; Mrs. F. C. Lasky in Tennessee; Mrs. Marie V. Beals in New York; Mrs. F. M. Baumgartner in Oklahoma and others have been responsible for much scientific data now gathered from a study of banded birds.

833. How are birds captured so they may be banded? A great many young birds are banded. The young of passerine species are lifted from the nest, banded, and then carefully replaced. The young precocial birds are captured as they attempt to hide and immediately after banding are liberated on the territory where they were caught. Adult birds generally are captured with traps, each bander often inventing his own ingenious devices.

834. What types of traps are used to capture adult birds? Every conceivable type of trap for catching birds without hurting them has been used or tried. Some have been baited with food, some with dripping water, some even with begging young birds to lure the parents.

Mist nets, made of such fine thread that they are almost invisible, prudently placed, will ensnare numbers of migrating birds.

Traps for birdbanding are described in a government manual which may be obtained from the Superintendent of Documents, Government Printing Office, Washington 25, D.C.

835. How many birds does one individual band in a year? Naturally this varies considerably from individual to individual. It depends not only on the energy and enthusiasm of the bander, but also on the amount of time he can devote to the project, and the type of birds he bands. Some who do a great deal of banding of young birds in large colonies often band thousands in a single month. Those who do most of their work in a woodland back yard cannot hope to equal

such numbers, and an annual total of several hundred birds banded
is more likely. Some banders concentrate on special local population
studies, some on life history studies of a single species.

836. Is it possible to read band numbers on free wild birds? In
some large species under the most unusual circumstances this may be
possible, but ordinarily the bird must be captured alive in some manner or else found dead.

837. Are many banded birds ever heard of again? Naturally most
dead birds are never found. Some may fall into the ocean, some are
buried by drifting sands or leaves, and others are devoured by
animals. In large, conspicuous birds a recovery of 3 or 4 per cent is
considered high, while in small passerine birds 1 per cent is more
likely. These recoveries, though small, constantly add to the wealth of
information accumulating in the files of the United States Fish and
Wildlife Service.

838. Why do birdbanders prefer to band adult birds? Adult birds
are preferred, especially in small species, since the percentage of recoveries for birds banded as adults is much higher than that for birds
banded when young. The mortality among young birds before they
leave the nest, or even the nesting area, is extremely high. Once they
are on the wing and have had even a few months of experience in
avoiding dangers, their chances for survival are greatly increased.

As a rule, in banding young, only large, conspicuous birds like
cormorants, pelicans, herons, geese, ducks, hawks, gulls and terns
yield sufficient returns to make such a project worth while. At Kent
Island off New Brunswick, Canada, Bowdoin College students banded
23,000 herring gulls in a five-year period to achieve the rich result of
800 discoveries.

839. How are most recoveries made? Some banded birds are
caught in the same or in another banding trap. A few are found injured. But the great majority of records come from birds found dead.
In many instances the cause of death is reported as unknown. Among
the causes of death most frequently listed are shot, struck by a car,
caught by a cat, killed by striking a wire, antenna, lighthouse, ceilome-
ter or other man-made structure.

840. How many birds have been banded in North America? Since North American birdbanding was officially organized in 1920 over $7\frac{1}{2}$ million individual birds representing more than 600 species have been banded. At present about half a million additional birds are banded on this continent annually. The extensive files cataloging all data on the birds banded and numerous recoveries are now kept at the Patuxent Research Refuge at Laurel, Maryland.

841. Of the seven and a half million birds banded, how many have been recovered? More than 600,000 of these have been recovered or their return to the place of banding recorded.

842. How many people band birds in North America? According to the files of the United States Fish and Wildlife Service more than 2,000 co-operators in the United States and Canada now use official bands supplied by that agency.

843. What should be done if a banded bird is caught or discovered? If the bird is alive, carefully copy the number of the band and liberate the bird. If the bird is dead remove the band. Send either the band or the band number together with information concerning the date, place and circumstances of the recovery to the United States Fish and Wildlife Service, Department of the Interior, Washington, D.C. This service in turn will check the files, notify you of the species and the place and date the bird was banded, and inform the bander of the date, place and circumstance of your recovery.

844. How is the band size for young birds determined? The band placed on the leg of a young bird is the size required for the adult. The band is never placed on the leg of a very young bird as it would slip off. By the time a bird is large enough to band, its leg is usually swollen and fleshy and often as large as, if not larger than, the adult's leg. The band is so light and fits so perfectly that it does not handicap the bird in any way.

845. Can birds as small as hummingbirds be banded? Many hummingbirds are banded annually. Their legs are so tiny, however, that even number 0 size slips off. The operator has to trim his zero-

218   BIRDBANDING

size bands to fit these smallest of all birds. One has to be very careful
in handling these pennyweight birds, and use even greater care in
placing the bands on the pin-sized legs.

846. Is there a publication that deals specifically with bird-banding? Everyone interested in ornithology should subscribe to
Bird-banding, an excellent, stimulating periodical published four times
each year. Not only does it print articles dealing with new techniques
in banding operations and analyses of banding records, but it publishes some of the most thought-provoking articles on ornithology in
general. For subscription write to E. Alexander Bergstrom, 37 Old
Brook Road, West Hartford 7, Connecticut.

In addition, several local and state banding associations publish
their own magazines, newsletters or mimeographed leaflets con-
centrating on discoveries and projects of particular interest to that
locality.

**847. Do bands last and remain legible as long as the bird is likely
to live?** Unfortunately, bands tend to wear with age and the numbers become illegible. This is particularly true of bands placed on
sea birds. Due to the corrosive effect of salt water, the light bands
used on small species may wear off in a matter of five to ten years. A
Leach's petrel banded by Joseph Cadbury of the Audubon Camp of
Maine, on Eastern Egg Rock in Muscongus Bay, was recovered on the
same island nine years later. The band was as thin as tissue paper and
would not have lasted much longer. Of course the bird was rebanded
and released and this information immediately sent to headquarters
at Patuxent.

On the other hand, a European black-headed gull was captured 24
years and 10 months after it had been banded, and though the band
was thin it was still legible. It should be pointed out that this latter
species spends a good part of its life on fresh water.

**848. Have any birds banded in Europe been recovered in North
America?** Records of birds banded in Europe and recovered in
North America are steadily increasing. Space permits mention of
only a few. More than half of the recoveries of kittiwakes banded
in England have come from the western side of the Atlantic. A
lapwing banded in England in May, 1926, was found in Newfound-

land on December 27, 1927. A black-headed gull banded in Germany in July, 1911, was recovered in Mexico in February, 1912. A skua banded in Scotland on July 3, 1939, was recovered in Massachusetts on February 4, 1940. A black-legged kittiwake banded in Russia on August 9, 1939, was recovered in Newfoundland on November 14, 1939. A gull-billed tern banded in Denmark on June 17, 1937 was recovered in the West Indies on September 5 of the same year.

849. Has banding helped prove that some North American birds move eastward across the Atlantic to the Old World? Since in the latitude of the United States the prevailing wind across the Atlantic is eastward, the number of American land birds that cross to Europe apparently is greater than the number of Old World land birds that cross westward. Observations and discoveries of foreign passerine birds on both sides of the Atlantic verify this. On the other hand, banding recoveries tend to contradict this statement, but one must bear in mind that most banding recoveries are of large water birds. Excluding the arctic tern, more recoveries of ocean-crossing sea birds have come from the west side of the Atlantic than from the Old World.

A Caspian tern banded in Michigan on July 14, 1927, was recovered in England in August, 1939. Perhaps the greatest story is the one verifying the fact that arctic terns breeding in North America first cross the Atlantic before heading south to their near-antarctic wintering grounds. A young arctic tern banded on Eastern Egg Rock in Muscongus Bay, Maine, on July 3, 1913, was found dead at the delta of the Niger River, South Africa, in August, 1917. An arctic tern banded at Turnevik Bay, Labrador, on July 23, 1928, was found dead in Natal, South Africa, on November 14, 1928. Another banded at Turnevik Bay, Labrador, on July 22, 1927, was picked up dead at La Rochelle, France, on October 1, 1927.

850. Are many birds banded in North America recovered in South America? It is common knowledge that many birds breeding in North America spend part of the year in South America. There are numerous banding records to verify this. A purple martin banded at Winona, Minnesota, on May 30, 1934, was taken near Itaituba, Brazil, in December 1936. A barn swallow banded at Muscow,

Saskatchewan, on July 7, 1929, was retaken at El Carmen, Bolivia, in June, 1935. A bank swallow banded at Clear Lake, Indiana, on June 12, 1932, was found near Yquitos, Peru, in June, 1936. As examples of large birds: a roseate tern banded at Chatham, Massachusetts, on July 6, 1938, died at Maiguetia, Venezuela, on September 12, 1938. A blue-winged teal banded at La Batture aux Loups near L' Islet, Quebec, on September 5, 1930, was shot at Georgetown, British Guiana, on October 2 of the same year.

851. Has banding helped prove that many migratory birds return to the same breeding area year after year? Quantities of adult migratory birds banded on their breeding grounds have been found in subsequent years in the same area, often the same acre, and sometimes even in the same nesting cavity. A few examples will suffice. An American redstart banded at Groton, Massachusetts, on May 18, 1929, was recovered at the same place on May 11, 1932, and May 17, 1933. Another American redstart, banded at Wolfville, Nova Scotia, on July 2, 1929, was retrapped at the same banding station on June 30, 1930, and June 25, 1931. A chipping sparrow banded at Treesbank, Manitoba, on May 26, 1930, was retrapped at the same place on May 10, 1934, and May 14, 1935. (See Question 141.)

852. Has banding helped prove that many migratory birds winter in the same place year after year? Substantial proof of this has been established. Probably the best example that can be given is the case of W. P. Wharton of South Carolina who reported that of 11,886 birds banded, 1895 or 15.9 per cent were recaptured during some subsequent winter. The highest returns, 19.6 per cent, came from chipping sparrows. Rufous-sided towhees and white-throated sparrows tied for second place, both with 18.4 per cent.

853. Have banding records indicated whether migratory birds follow the same route each year? It is still too early to give any definite answer. Several semipalmated sandpipers banded at North Eastham, Massachusetts, during July and August have been recaptured at this banding station in subsequent years. A yellow-bellied flycatcher banded at Groton, Massachusetts, on May 29, 1931, was caught by a cat near Groton about May 18, 1934. But such records are few. Some banding stations have banded hundreds or even thousands of migratory birds, yet never have had a recovery in their area. One station in Illinois banded 15,000 white-throated sparrows during 20 years of operation, yet never retrapped a single bird. But this should not be taken as conclusive evidence. Many birds may well follow the identical route year after year but drop down at different spots along the way. Some may even occur only a fraction of a mile from the banding station, yet not be recorded.

854. Have banding records helped give some idea of how fast migratory birds travel? A dowitcher banded at North Eastham, Cape Cod, Massachusetts, on July 31, 1935, was captured 1,800 miles away on the island of Guadeloupe in the French West Indies on August 26 of the same year, indicating a migration speed of at least 70 miles a day. Another dowitcher banded at the same station on Cape Cod on August 24, 1935, was shot on September 12, 1935, near Fort Randolph Reservation in the Panama Canal Zone. Since this is a distance of nearly 2,300 miles, the bird must have traveled at a minimum rate of 125 miles a day. A lesser yellowlegs banded at this same Cape Cod station on August 28, 1935, was killed on the island of Martinique in the West Indies on September 3, 1935. In five days it had traveled 1,930 miles or an average of 386 miles a day.

855. Have banding records helped to give an idea of the longevity of birds? As the years pass and data increase, it will be easier to give some statement as to the longevity of a species. There are already some interesting records. An osprey banded as a nestling on Gardiner's Island off the eastern end of Long Island, New York, on June 19, 1914, was found freshly dead on the same island on June 1, 1935. Thus it is known that this bird lived to be almost 21 years old. A European black-headed gull banded as a nestling was captured in central Europe 24 years and 10 months later. At present a Caspian tern banded in Michigan and killed in Ohio 26 years later holds the record for longevity among banded birds.

856. Is there any method of identifying individual banded birds without capturirg them? Some scientists making special studies use variously colored celluloid bands in addition to the aluminum bands issued by the government. If the bander uses five different colors and places up to three celluloid bands on each bird, 300 birds can wear their individual identification tags. By using five bands of seven different colors the bander can obtain 14,406 different combinations.

Several years ago herring gull colonies were assigned different color combinations. In winter, after the gulls had left these colonies, one could go to a New York garbage disposal area and accurately identify birds from the St. Mary Islands in Quebec; from Muscongus Bay, Maine; from the Isles of Shoals, New Hampshire; and other large colonies. Since different color combinations were used each year and since only birds hatched each summer were banded, it was possible not only to record where the bird came from, but also its year of birth, and its progress in acquiring the plumage, bill color, leg color and eye color of the adult.

857. Are bands other than the official Fish and Wildlife Service aluminum bands, and the colored bands used for special studies, ever placed on birds in North America?   In order to keep records of individual birds, pigeon fanciers, as well as farmers who raise domestic fowl, often band their stock. These bands usually look quite different from the official ones used for wild birds and they are quickly recognized for what they are by any ornithologist.

858. If a banded pigeon is found, should a report be sent to the United States Fish and Wildlife Service?   The United States Fish and Wildlife Service is interested only in bands placed on wild birds. Generally a local pigeon breeding or flying organization will welcome information concerning the banded pigeon. The nearest local chamber of commerce usually will know if there is such an organization in the area.

859. Aside from banding, what other methods have been used for marking birds?   For special projects certain harmless dyes are sometimes used. In recent years ducks have been trapped at their winter quarters, dipped in yellow, red or green dyes and released. Subsequent reports of these birds on their way north add light to the flyways and breeding grounds being used by the wintering birds of a certain area. Imagine the astonishment of some person who discovers a pink scaup on his lake! Most people report such strange observations.

In addition, birds have been marked by gluing brightly colored feathers on tails, tying colored threads on legs, spotting them with quick-drying brightly-colored lacquer, painting the legs white, ad infinitum. Since it is against the law for anyone to capture wild birds without a permit, any person wishing to carry on a project should first discuss it with the banding director of the Fish and Wildlife Service.

XII. ATTRACTING BIRDS TO THE GARDEN

860. How can one attract birds? The best approach is to maintain the type of habitat preferred by the species you wish to attract. This can be supplemented by (1) increasing the amount of natural foods used by these birds, (2) artificial feeding, (3) meeting water requirements, and (4) erecting suitable houses for species habitually nesting in cavities.

861. Is it really necessary to feed wild birds? In most situations it is unnecessary, as wild birds know all the tricks for obtaining sufficient food. Nevertheless it is an advisable project, even if done solely for the pleasure it affords, to have an abundance of birds frequenting the yard, garden, farm or estate. Moreover in northern climates feeding may well tide birds over periods of deep snows and severe ice storms when natural foods are buried or encased.

862. When should one start feeding? Some people maintain feeding stations all year round, some only during the coldest winter months, most from midautumn to early spring. If you plan to run a feeding station throughout the winter, it is advisable to start it in the midautumn before the great majority of wintering birds decide on their choice of territory and have formed rather fixed feeding habits.

863. What kind of food should one use to attract birds? Birds visiting feeding stations generally fall into three major groups: those which feed primarily on seeds, those which feed chiefly on insects, and those which are rather omnivorous. A mixture of cracked corn and popular bird seeds will attract most of the first group; beef suet and meat scraps will be devoured by the insectivorous group; while the omnivorous birds will partake of practically all foods placed on the feeder. Broken nuts, peanut butter, bread crumbs, pancakes, doughnuts, pie crusts, broken dog biscuits, raisins, shelled cocoanut and various fruits will prove satisfactory. The more variety one offers, the more kinds of birds will be satisfied.

864. Which kinds of seeds are most frequently used for feeding wild birds? Finely cracked corn or scratch-feed, besides being relatively cheap and available in most areas, is quickly accepted by the great majority of seed-eating birds. Mixtures of carefully selected seeds are good. These may contain millet, hemp, buckwheat, rape, clover, sunflower seeds, wheat, barley, oats, rye, wild rice and canary seeds. Sweepings of weed, grass and grain seeds from the floors of barns, or sweepings from factories using peanuts, pecans and various grains will provide a quantity of attractive bird food.

865. Is salt injurious to birds? In spite of the widespread belief that salt is injurious to birds, a little of it is required. Sufficient salt ordinarily is obtained from natural foods or from peanut butter, bread crumbs and other man-made offerings.

Many winter finches, especially pine siskins, pine grosbeaks and crossbills, seem to crave salt, for they are observed regularly taking salt sprinkled on roads to melt ice, or the salt left at the edges of ocean tide pools by evaporation. When these birds are present, therefore, salt should be offered. A concentrated solution of salt in water may be flowed gently over a rough board which is then dried. Salt crystals will remain on the board which may be placed near the feeding shelf so species demanding salt may obtain it.

866. Is feeding ever harmful? A few people have suggested that the feeding of wild birds prevents them from devouring their usual amounts of insects or weed seeds and consequently should not be practiced. Anyone who carefully watches birds around the yard, however, will notice that most birds visit the feeders only periodically and spend the rest of the time gathering their normal foods. It is doubtful that artificial feeding keeps most birds from doing their duty in the control of insects and weeds.

The only real harm that can be done in feeding birds is to stop putting out food once winter has arrived. Feeding stations tend to influence certain species to remain far north of their normal wintering grounds. Consequently, once a feeder has been established and birds induced to stay in an area for the winter, the station should be maintained well into spring when natural foods are once again abundant. Even a day of neglect during zero spells, heavy snowfalls or severe ice storms can be disastrous, as the wintering guests may be entirely dependent on your food for survival.

867. What is the best type of feeder to use? The birds visiting a feeding area are interested only in the food and not in the architectural beauty of the station. In fact, some of the most successful feeding stations are those where the grain is merely scattered on the ground or sprinkled in the cracks of a log, and the suet tucked into natural cavities in trees. Most ornithologists advocate the natural type of feeding area.

In city and suburban yards, however, many people find a manmade feeding shelf easier to keep neat. Such shelves, covered or uncovered, are screwed to tree trunks, suspended from branches, supported by poles, attached to clothes lines, or fastened to windows. There are numerous commercial feeders on the market, but one will have as much success with a simple shallow home-made tray.

868. Should feeding shelves be covered? The major advantage of a cover is its tendency to keep food from being soaked by rain, buried by snow or encrusted by ice. Soaked grains quickly spoil, especially in warm weather. Snow- and ice-covered foods often become completely buried from the birds during inclement weather, when most vitally needed.

869. How can jays be kept away from the feeder? Jays are among the most beautiful, active, amusing and clever of our native birds, and it is difficult to understand anyone's not wanting them around the garden. They are no more dominant than other birds of similar size and they make no effort to keep other birds away from the neighborhood. If anything, their activities often cause passing birds to inspect an area and discover the food. The best answer is to have several small feeders rather than a single large one. Then, if a jay is at one, the nuthatch, chickadee or purple finch merely flies to another.

People who welcome all species at their feeders have the most enjoyable experience with wild birds, for all are interesting. Those who wish to feed particular species and exclude all others must supply a limited kind of food desired only by those species, or make a feeder which will exclude undesired birds. If sparrows, starlings or any other species are too dominant at a feeder, a permit may be obtained to trap these birds, which can then be transported some distance and released unharmed. All who feed wild birds are urged to accept all comers and enjoy each species for its particular characteristics.

870. How does one prevent wild mammals from reaching bird feeders? Most naturalists derive as much pleasure from the wild mammals visiting feeding stations as they do from the birds and consequently make no effort to keep them away. The best plan is to put up several small feeders rather than one large one, thus allowing all visitors to enjoy their stay.

However, if one is inclined to keep wild mammals away, the feeding stations suspended by a strong thin cord or placed on a tall, smooth, slippery pole can be easily protected by placing a smoothly painted wobbly metal collar, disc or cone on the pole or cord just above or below the feeder. Some have found a collar of dense thorny twigs wired in a similar position to be equally effective.

871. What kind of suet is best for feeding birds? Hard, firm white beef suet, particularly that from around the kidneys, is most satisfactory. Birds do not care for yellow suet if it contains any stringy connective tissue. By all means avoid mutton suet, for birds will not eat it.

872. What are the best devices for offering suet? If a large piece of suet is offered to birds, the first mammal or crow that comes along will go off with it. Even pieces carefully tied to branches or placed in holders made of knitted string or ordinary wide-meshed wire netting will quickly disappear. The most satisfactory method is to drill numerous small holes in an eighteen-inch-long log, firmly suspend it from a branch with strong string, and then tightly pack suet in each hole. The wobbly log will discourage most mammals from trying to reach the suet, and prevent others from emptying the small holes. Most birds readily cling to such logs and obtain the suet they wish.

873. Is it true there is danger in using wires and metals for food containers? Many people find wire screen containers or metal soap shakers very convenient for holding suet. Those living in northern areas are advised not to use such devices in frigid weather as the birds' wet feet, wet feathers or even eyes may freeze quickly to cold metal.

874. What is meant by a weather-vane feeder? The weather-vane feeder is generally a well-proportioned box with one side completely open and the top gently slanting away from the open side. It has weather-vanelike flaps projecting from the open side and is mounted on a sensitive swivel perch so that the slightest breeze swings the open side of the feeder away from the wind. This prevents snow and ice from covering the food and keeps most rain from pouring in.

875. How can one attract hummingbirds? An abundance of flowers growing in the garden, especially those with colors near the red end of the spectrum, is the best way to attract hummingbirds. The following flowers seem to be particularly favored: trumpet creepers, nasturtiums, columbines, delphiniums, sweet peas, touch-me-nots, cardinal flowers, bee balms, coral bells, scarlet runner beans, scarlet sages and gladioli.

At times when the flower supply is limited, small bottles, vials or nectar cups about an inch and a half to two inches long filled with concentrated sugar water and hung in the garden will prove successful. It is preferable, though not imperative, to have the vials red. Some companies even sell bright red vials with the tops shaped to resemble flowers. A solution made from one part honey to three parts of water will prove just as effective as one part of sugar to four parts of water.

876. Can plantings supply bird food? Plantings of carefully selected fruit-bearing shrubs, trees and vines not only supply food for birds, but offer shelter and nesting sites as well. They should be chosen to provide food over the entire year, but particularly during the winter months when food is scarce in most areas. The kinds of plants to use will depend largely on the geographical location of the garden. By far the best plan is to select native plants popular with the birds of the particular area. The use of native plants gives assurance that they will grow well. If exotics are to be used, seek the advice of a local nursery or carefully read one of the numerous books on attracting birds, now on the market. In most sections of the United States a variety of viburnums, mulberries, birches, cherries, elderberries, dogwoods, barberries, hawthorns, grapes and bayberries will prove successful. Patches of popular grains and seeds, though requiring considerable annual work, will also be attractive.

In Florida callicarpa bushes, camphor trees, cabbage palms and wild figs are extremely popular.

877. When planting for birds should one completely cover an area with trees and shrubs? Fortunately most birds do not like extensive, dense, uniform stretches of trees and bushes, but prefer the generally accepted principles of landscaping used by man. Clumps of trees, bushes and dense thickets, separated by numerous lawns and open spaces, attract the largest number of species. Bear in mind that most birds prefer the periphery of dense vegetation, the margins between two types of habitat. Where uniform vegetation already covers an area, one can attract more birds by cutting a network of broad paths and planting them to grass or at least keeping them open.

878. Can any bird desired be induced to nest in a birdhouse? With rare exceptions, the only birds that will accept birdhouses are species which normally chisel nesting holes for themselves, and those which ordinarily nest in holes excavated by other species, in hollow trees, or other cavities. One should not expect birds such as Baltimore orioles, scarlet tanagers and rose-breasted grosbeaks to utilize birdhouses.

879. How many species of birds in the United States and Canada have nested in birdhouses? About 50 species of birds in North America have nested in man-made birdhouses or other artificial devices.

880. Why is it necessary for man to erect birdhouses? In natural wilderness areas there are generally quantities of tree cavities in which birds may nest. As man settles an area, he tends to prune dead branches, remove hollow trees, and even fill in cavities in tree trunks. Thus he eliminates sites formerly utilized by cavity-nesting birds, and if he wishes to keep these species around he must offer them substitute birdhouses.

881. When was the first birdhouse erected in North America? No one can give a definite date. The first white settlers on this continent found purple martins using hollowed gourds hung on tall poles by the Indians.

882. What type of birdhouse is usually most successful? The simpler the box the better. The more it resembles an old hollow limb or a hole in a fence post, the more success it is apt to have, and the more appropriate it will look in the garden. Brightly colored, fancy-looking houses with chimneys, steeples, frescoes, porches, balconies and other absurdities should be avoided. Houses with several compartments are not advisable, unless specifically designed to attract purple martins.

883. Should the birdhouse be concealed in dense vegetation?
This will depend on the species of bird desired. Most cavity-nesting species prefer their nesting holes to be in the open and easily entered. Thus boxes for such species as purple martins, tree swallows and bluebirds are more successful when placed on dead trees, poles, fence posts, or sides of buildings.

884. Is it necessary to include drainage and ventilation holes in a birdhouse?   Since such features seldom are found in natural or bird-drilled cavities, most authorities feel they are unnecessary. On the other hand, natural cavities usually have thicker walls than bird-houses do and thus the insulation against excess heat is greater. Some natural cavities have cracks permitting water blown into the cavity to escape. So for insurance, it is advisable to drill a couple of small holes in the floor of the box and add three or four more tiny openings just under the overhanging slanting roof.

885. At what height should one place a birdhouse?   Naturally this will vary according to species. For birds such as bluebirds, tree swallows, house wrens, and black-capped chickadees, the greatest success is achieved by placing the houses only 5 to 10 feet above the ground. Birds such as wood ducks, screech owls, flickers, crested flycatchers and purple martins seem to prefer houses placed 10 to 30 feet high. There are exceptions, however, and wood ducks may nest from 1 to 60 feet above the surface, while tree swallows have been known to nest from 2 to 40 feet above the ground.

886. What material is best for birdhouses?   In general wood is preferable to any other material, especially if the house is to be placed in an open situation. The summer sun beating on houses made of metals or pottery often turn such cavities into ovens which ruin eggs and kill young birds.

887. How many birdhouses should be placed on one acre?   This will vary considerably according to the species involved, the amount of food and cover offered each species in the given area, and the local population pressure. For wide-ranging territorial birds like screech owls, one birdhouse for each dozen acres ordinarily is sufficient. For such species as house wrens, a half acre may support a pair, while for downy woodpeckers and crested flycatchers one birdhouse per species on every three to five acres ordinarily is the maximum used.

On the other hand, for virtually nonterritorial species, the number of houses may depend largely on the local abundance of the species. On a two-acre tract at Worcester, Massachusetts, a population of 600 tree swallows was built up over a 50-year period.

888. Should one clean out birdhouses annually? The general practice is to clean out birdhouses annually, although the necessity or even advisability of this is questionable. Birds usually will do their own renovating if they wish to use a house. If one feels he must clean a box, it is better to do this in early spring, just before the nesting season. Leaving the old nesting material in the box over the winter possibly reduces bird ectoparasites by permitting their own parasitic enemies to develop.

889. Is it advisable to put nesting material in the birdhouse? An inch to an inch and a half of coarse sawdust placed in a birdhouse is advisable. In fact, it is necessary for such birds as woodpeckers and screech owls, which gather no nesting material. The sawdust provides a good base for such nests and prevents the eggs from rolling about. No grasses, feathers, sticks, cloth, paper or other nesting material should be inserted in any box. Such materials placed conveniently near the birdhouse, however, may encourage nesting.

890. How many entrances should there be in a birdhouse? Only one, except in apartment-type houses constructed for purple martins, in which case an entrance is required for each individual compartment.

891. What shape and size opening should one make in a birdhouse? Birds which excavate cavities usually dig round holes just large enough for them to go in and out without any difficulty. But the majority of hole-nesting species will accept natural cavities of great variety in internal size as well as in size and shape of entrance.

Naturally, therefore, one does not have to be too particular in bird-house construction.

However, except in certain multichambered houses designed for purple martins, it is suggested that the entrances be circular. Species ranging in size from the flicker to the sparrow hawk will readily accept an entrance 3 inches in diameter. For species approximately the size of a hairy woodpecker or crested flycatcher a 2-inch diameter is preferable, while for smaller birds such as wrens, chickadees and bluebirds an entrance $1\frac{1}{2}$ inches in diameter will prove satisfactory.

892. How can birdhouses be made to last for many years? A good insurance is to use cypress, redwood or cedar and thoroughly treat all wood with a reliable wood preservative. A slanting roof overhanging on all sides and carefully covered with a thin sheet of copper will assure quick, thorough runoff of water. The floor, the most vulnerable part of a box, will have better protection if the sides of the box extend down just a bit beyond its base, and if holes are drilled in the floor to encourage quick drainage of any water that may work its way inside. Screws, preferably brass, should be used instead of nails. Three brass eyes screwed into the back of the box to form a broad isosceles triangle enable one to easily attach the box to brass hooks screwed into the tree or post in a similar pattern. This will not only hold the box away from any rainwater pouring down the tree trunk, but it will also allow some roof overhang in the rear, and permit easy removal of the house for inspection and repairs when necessary.

893. What are the best types of purple-martin houses? Hollow gourds with circular entrances $2\frac{1}{2}$ inches in diameter are used with great success throughout the southern United States. A tiny hole drilled in the floor is advisable to drain any water blown in by wind. Sometimes as many as a dozen such gourds are suspended side by side from crossbars on a tall supporting pole.

Whether a single or multifamily conventional house is constructed, each compartment should have a floor approximately 6 x 6 inches, a cavity depth of roughly 6 inches, and the entrance with a $2\frac{1}{2}$-inch diameter should be placed only one inch above the floor. Martin houses frequently contain as many as two dozen compartments, and occasionally twice that number.

894. How high should purple-martin houses be placed? The great majority of purple-martin houses are placed on poles or iron pipes between 15 and 20 feet above the ground. Some purple martins, however, regularly nest in hollow trees only two feet above the water, others in the crevices of buildings or in natural cavities of trees as high as 30 to 40 feet. Therefore it seems unlikely that there is a set height at which martin houses must be placed.

895. Do ducks sometimes nest in birdhouses? Any species of duck that normally nests in natural cavities in trees is a potential user of a birdhouse.

896. Has man succeeded in increasing a local duck population by erecting birdhouses? In some areas birdhouses erected for wood ducks have been very successful in restoring this beautiful species. It is estimated that in recent years the wood duck population in Massachusetts has almost doubled, due to this project. In one study 45 per cent of the 2,000 houses erected by state personnel were used by wood ducks. In Europe similar projects for goldeneyes have proved successful.

897. What is a good size for a wood-duck nesting box?
1. Floor of cavity: 10 x 10 inches
2. Depth of cavity: 24 inches
3. Height of entrance above floor: 18 inches
4. Elliptical entrance 4 inches wide by 3 inches high keeps out raccoons.

898. Should one help birds by supplying nesting material? Though seldom necessary, putting out plenty of easily available nesting material may induce some birds to nest locally. Moreover, it is an interesting project, and often has been used to arouse local interest in birds. Imagine the fun of watching a Baltimore oriole gather soft strings or yarns from the lawn, a tree swallow snatch chicken feathers from a window sill, or a yellow warbler pull cotton from a handful wired to a tree! At Avery Island, Louisiana, where a large colony of egrets and herons nest on long racks erected above the water, the owners have laborers gather piles of twigs far afield and pile them near the colony for the birds to use.

899. In the preceding discussion it says "seldom necessary." Does this imply that an artificial supply of nesting material is sometimes necessary? Occasionally under drought conditions such species as phoebes, barn and cliff swallows and robins may have difficulty in obtaining sufficient mud with which to build their nests, and they readily utilize mud puddles created for them by man. In Wisconsin one farmer increased the size of a cliff swallow colony on his barn to 2,000 by providing a quantity of convenient mud when the birds arrived each spring.

900. Are there other devices one can use to encourage birds to nest around one's home? Convenient shelves built inside barns and sheds, as well as covered shelves open at the sides and nailed to trees, buildings or the under side of porches and eaves are frequently used by such species as barn swallows, phoebes and robins. In many sections of the United States, ospreys are attracted by erecting platforms and wheels on which they may nest. Likewise, storks in Europe are attracted by supplying similar platforms, placed on roofs, chimneys and towers.

Rainproof boxes, a foot and a half high with floor space 2 x 2 feet, which are firmly braced against the side of a barn, garage or shed, or erected in a tree, sometimes attract barn owls. The entrance should have an 8-inch diameter. Even peregrine falcons have been induced to nest in the largest cities when human admirers placed large shallow boxes of gravel on outside ledges of tall buildings.

901. How large should a birdhouse be? There is no unalterable standard. Naturally a house should not be so small as to cramp the bird entering it, or so large as to create much waste space. Three sizes of boxes will take care of most birds habitually using birdhouses. The complex meticulous directions for specifically satisfying the imagined whims of each individual species which have been published in recent years only have served to discourage many people from constructing birdhouses.

To be assured that meticulous measurements are unnecessary, one only has to notice the great variety of natural nesting cavities used by a species in wilderness areas. The amazing assortment of mail boxes, newspaper receptacles, and other man-made gadgets used by nesting birds further supports the belief that birds are not as particular about sizes and shapes of nesting cavities as many people imagine.

Moreover, it is common experience to have a birdhouse built specifically for one species, taken by another. The authors have had both great crested flycatchers and red-bellied woodpeckers nest in a screech owl box. On another occasion, red-bellied woodpeckers enlarged the entrance to a bluebird house and nested within. Sparrow hawks, screech owls, flickers, starlings, Carolina wrens and even tiny house wrens have been found nesting in boxes erected for wood ducks.

902. What dimensions are recommended for the three most useful sizes of birdhouses? Dimensions follow for three sizes of birdhouses which will satisfy most species frequenting these sites:

Species	Inside floor space (inches)	Depth of cavity (inches)	Entrance above floor (inches)
Sparrow hawk Screech owl Saw-whet owl Flicker	7 x 7	16	10
Red-bellied woodpecker Red-headed woodpecker Hairy woodpecker Crested flycatcher Starling	6½ x 6½	11	7
Downy woodpecker Western flycatcher Violet-green swallow Tree swallow White-breasted nuthatch Red-breasted nuthatch Black-capped chickadee Carolina chickadee Tufted titmouse House wren Bewick's wren Carolina wren Bluebird Prothonotary warbler House finch	5 x 5	8	5

903. Why are bird baths or drinking fountains necessary in a garden if one wishes to attract birds? In most wilderness areas there are numerous ponds, streams or at least springs and small pools where birds may drink or bathe. If such sources of fresh water are present in an area, then artificial pools are superfluous. But in extensively built-up areas, most water is usually drained off or covered and birds are hard put to find an adequate supply. Under such conditions one can induce a great many birds to frequent his grounds by creating small pools of fresh water where birds may conveniently drink and bathe.

904. What kinds of bird baths are most successful? Birds seem to show no preference as long as water is always available and the receptacle is large enough and shallow enough to permit bathing. A simple nonslippery trough varying from one inch in depth at one end to two inches in depth at the other is recommended. One will have as much success with a cheap homemade cement basin as with a thousand-dollar fountain. In summer most birds prefer some shade over the bathing area and at all seasons birds should be provided with close, dense vegetation in which to flee if danger appears.

In a formal garden or suburban yard, well-designed cement or pottery baths set on graceful pedestals are appropriate as well as effective. In general, however, a one- or two-inch deep hollow in the ground lined with cement or concrete and planted to resemble a natural pool will be most effective.

An additional attraction is some device that allows a trickle of water to splash into one corner of the bath. The sound of dripping water seems to induce birds to bathe and immediately informs migrants dropping down of the presence of water.

905. Do birds require water in winter? Most birds habitually drink and bathe during the winter, regardless of the severity of weather, as long as open water is available. In northern areas drinking requirements are usually satisfied by picking at snow and ice. Nevertheless, one will find that any water supplied at this season will be used readily by birds.

906. How can freezing of water in bird baths be prevented when temperatures fall? Except in the severest climate some of the water in bird baths will be in liquid form, especially at noon. In most areas water constantly dripping from a home outlet into a bird bath will keep a sufficient supply open for birds to use. A cement bath, placed in an open spot on the south side of a slope, ordinarily will pick up enough heat from the sun to keep the water open, at least around midday. In recent years some people have run waterproof electric wires to the bird bath from the house and attached water temperature regulators designed particularly for tropical fish fanciers. Finally, some supply houses even offer electrically heated bird baths.

907. What is meant by a bird dust bath? Frequently birds flutter in a dry dusty area and go through all the motions of bathing. They do this to help rid themselves of external parasites, particularly the so-called bird lice. Knowing this, bird watchers offer dusting areas in the yard by filling a very shallow box with two or three inches of roadside dust. Some people even attempt to make the dust more effective by mixing it with one-tenth the amount of powdered sulphur.

908. When a bird is stunned by hitting a window or other obstruction, should first aid be given? Leave the bird strictly alone, but keep cats and dogs from the vicinity. If the bird is not fatally injured, it will rest as long as necessary and fly when sufficiently recovered. Picking up such a stunned bird often causes its death. The fright from being handled when in such a weakened condition often induces a rupture of blood vessels or heart failure.

909. How can birds be prevented from hitting picture windows? Birds living near a house quickly learn the lay of the land and learn not to fly against windows. Migrating birds dropping down for the first time frequently strike windows, often with such force that they are sometimes stunned, occasionally killed.

If this happens repeatedly it means that particular window is a special hazard, and the owners can take one of several steps. A temporary screen can be placed outside the dangerous window, pieces of cloth or strings may be hung in front of it, or a pattern may be drawn on the window with glass wax, Bon Ami or other window cleaner which dries to a white powder.

XIII. BIRD CONSERVATION

910. What is meant by ecology? Ecology means the study of the house. To the scientist it is the study of a complete plant and animal community. In particular, it includes the governing physical factors of light, heat, water, atmosphere and soil; the relationships among the various plants growing there; among the animals living there; and of the plants and animals to one another. This is the only sensible way to study a biotic community in order to understand its complexities. (See Questions 67–73.)

911. Why do naturalists object to draining of marshes? Marshes are not wastelands, as so many people believe. They are part of nature's reservoir system. Not only do they help store water and maintain a good water table necessary throughout the surrounding countryside, but they also serve as emergency storage basins during periods of heavy rain or melting snow, and prevent, or at least reduce, flood damage.

Moreover some specialized birds such as bitterns, rails and gallinules, as well as certain herons and ducks, demand marshes in which to breed and live. If the mania for draining marshes continues, the populations of such birds will be greatly reduced and possibly some species will be wiped out altogether.

912. Are not other types of habitats just as necessary to birds as marshlands? Indeed they are, but marshes form a relatively small, restricted type of habitat and one which is being quickly reduced by man.

Each species of bird is particularly suited to a special niche. Many find existence tolerable only in very specialized surroundings. Some require a particular type of deciduous woodland, some a certain kind of marsh, some even a specialized desert community. The best conservation practices recognize the necessity for preserving all types of habitat.

913. Is conservation of bird life a new concept? While skyrocketing human populations have made it more and more imperative that definite regulations be established immediately to preserve bird life, this conservation concept is by no means new. Perhaps the first mention of bird conservation was written in Deuteronomy 20:6 when Moses decreed that a nesting bird should not be killed, though the young might be taken for food. Even in those ancient times wise men recognized the necessity for not destroying the breeding stock.

914. When was the first law enacted to protect birds in the United States? Probably the 1818 law giving seasonal protection to the game birds of Massachusetts was the first one enacted in the United States. It pointed out the necessity for such legislation, and other states not only passed similar laws, but soon gave protection to most songbirds.

915. When did the United States Federal Government first show interest in wild life? On February 9, 1871, a Commission of Fish and Fisheries was established by the Federal government. This later became the Bureau of Fisheries in the Department of Agriculture. Finally, on June 30, 1886, the Division of Economic Ornithology and Mammalogy was created. This later became the Biological Survey.

916. Were these first Federal agencies instructed to protect wildlife? At first the only function of these agencies was research. Then through the years management and regulatory functions were added either by Congressional action or through the inherent powers of the President.

917. What is the Lacey Act? The Lacey Act, passed by the United States Congress in 1900, prohibited the shipment of "game" taken illegally across state boundaries, and gave the involved states powers to prosecute violators. It was designed to terminate market hunting which was inducing more and more men to slaughter waterfowl and shorebirds by every possible means.

918. Where was the first National Wildlife Refuge established in the United States? In 1903 Theodore Roosevelt by executive order made Pelican Island in the Indian River a National Wildlife Refuge. This tiny island near Sebastian on the east coast of Florida may be considered the birthplace of the United States National Wildlife Refuge System which now includes about 280 sanctuary areas.

919. What is the Migratory Bird Treaty Act? This is a unique international agreement in which the United States, Canada and Mexico agree to co-operate fully in giving adequate protection to those birds which migrate from one country to the other.

920. When was the Migratory Bird Treaty Act ratified? The Weeks-McLean Migratory Bird Law established by the United States in 1914 was ratified at a convention of officials of the United States and Great Britain on December 8, 1916. It went into complete effect as a Migratory Bird Treaty Act in 1918. A similar agreement with Mexico on March 15, 1936 extended this treaty to include that country. Thus for the first time in the history of man international co-operation promised protection to the bird life of an entire continent.

921. What major protection measures are included in the Migratory Bird Treaty Act?

(1) With a few exceptions all migratory insectivorous birds are protected at all seasons.

(2) Each government is to establish open seasons, closed seasons, and issue special regulations for the hunting of migratory game birds.

(3) All other migratory nongame birds are to be protected unless the government feels that a particular species or group is locally destructive or annoying.

922. What jurisdiction in bird protection does a state have? Every state has to obey the regulations established by the Federal government for all migratory birds. Each state, however, must enact its own laws regarding nonmigratory game birds, as well as decide whether or not to give protection to those nongame migratory species not specifically protected by Federal statute.

923. Which government agency is responsible for waterfowl hunting regulations and the maintenance of wildlife refuges in the United States? All such matters are directed by the United States Fish and Wildlife Service, Department of the Interior, Washington, D.C.

924. When was the United States Fish and Wildlife Service established? The President of the United States under authority by Congress to reorganize the executive branch of the government established the United States Fish and Wildlife Service in 1939. In this reorganization the Bureau of Biological Survey in the Department of Agriculture and the Bureau of Fisheries in the Department of Commerce were combined to form the United States Fish and Wildlife Service which was placed in the Department of the Interior.

925. How many wildlife refuges are managed by the United States Fish and Wildlife Service? There are now some 280 wildlife refuges managed by the United States Fish and Wildlife Service. These range in size from tracts of a few acres to those of over 4,000 square miles. Over 200 of these are primarily for waterfowl. This constitutes the largest and most carefully managed system of wildlife refuges in the entire world.

926. What is meant by the Migratory Bird-Hunting Stamp Act? This act passed in 1934 requires all shooters of migratory birds to buy a one-dollar stamp each year. In 1948 this was amended raising the price to two dollars.

927. How is the money collected from the sale of migratory bird-hunting stamps used? Receipts from such sales are placed in a fund specifically designated for the acquisition and management of inviolate waterfowl sanctuaries, for research to improve such areas, and for law enforcement.

928. Is strict protection given to birds on all Federal refuges? In the beginning strict protection was afforded birds on Federal refuges. However, in 1948, when the Migratory Bird-Hunting Stamp Act was brought up for amendment to raise the price of the stamp to two dollars, hunting interests managed to attach a provision authorizing the director of the Fish and Wildlife Service to open up 25 per cent of any refuge area to public shooting if and when the waterfowl population justified it. Severe opposition defeated the passage of any bill containing such a provision.

In 1949 a new amendment was proposed in which no shooting would be permitted on any refuges acquired with stamp funds prior to July 1, 1949. The bill, however, slipped through the House of Representatives with this safeguard omitted. Though the Senate bill included the safeguard, the House version was enacted into law.

929. Are birds nature's chief agents in controlling insect populations? Although birds undoubtedly consume quantities of insects and are part of nature's system for suppressing insect populations, in the past their role has been somewhat exaggerated. Weather, predatory and parasitic insects probably should be given more credit as important limiting factors. Birds, however, are of incalculable help, and at times may well be the deciding factor in curbing potential insect outbreaks, or in preventing the spread of insect plagues.

930. What is the source of lead poisoning in birds? Shotgun shells annually scatter multitudes of small lead pellets in ponds and marsh areas frequented by water birds. Each year the total of these pellets increases. While gathering food an astonishing number of birds accidentally swallow some of these lead pellets. Sometimes but a few pellets lodged in the digestive tract may cause death. Scientists examining ducks picked up dead have found over 70 lead pellets in a single individual.

931. How can lead poisoning be prevented? This problem is more serious than many people realize. It is being studied carefully by research biologists. The only answer seems to be that some nonlead alloy be used in manufacturing shotgun pellets.

932. What is botulism? Botulism, a disease which destroys thousands of birds annually, is caused by a certain bacterium (*clostridium botulinum*) living in decaying organic matter. These bacteria are most numerous in alkaline marshes, especially in times of drought when the water is low and decaying material is most abundant.

933. How can botulism be controlled? On some of the large United States government wildlife refuges ducks have been captured and inoculated against this disease, but obviously mass inoculation of wild birds is impractical. It seems more logical to concentrate efforts on controlling the water level on all major waterfowl refuges, thus preventing the sudden dying of great masses of aquatic vegetation.

934. Are fish-eating birds a menace to fishing? The modern attitude is to consider these birds as fishing companions rather than competitors. Aside from the interest and pleasure that a plunging osprey, a stalking heron, and a yodeling loon add to an outing, scientific investigations reveal that these fish-eating birds are valuable allies in maintaining a healthy condition in the waters, with resultant good fishing. Not only do these birds fertilize the waters, but they control many fish, especially nongame species, which are competitors for food and space, and thus in the overall picture permit more game fish to grow to an attractive edible size. This is another example of the complexities of prey–predator relationship. Fish-eating birds once thought to be detrimental to fishing are now found to be nature's agents for maintaining a healthy, well-balanced fish population.

935. Is DDT harmful to bird life? Already there has been considerable damage to bird life by DDT spraying, especially when heavily concentrated applications have been used. This insecticide is an accumulative poison and consequently it is potentially more dangerous with each application. Apparently some species are affected much more easily than others. Bobwhites are said to be three times more susceptible than ducks, and nestlings are much more susceptible than adults. Moreover, the elimination of insects from any piece of land is bound to affect the birds living there. Unless firm controls in the use of DDT are established, it may have disastrous effects on bird life.

936. Are other sprays potentially dangerous to birds? It has been estimated that there are now more than 2,000 different brands of insecticides, fungicides, herbicides, and combinations of these on the market. Used very cautiously, some of these can be of benefit to man. Consequently, some are here to stay. Used unwisely, most of them can result in extensive damage to wildlife. Public opinion should insist that a careful overall study of a situation be made before any sprays are permitted, and that all spraying campaigns be carefully supervised by personnel understanding the potential dangers.

937. Are any insecticides more dangerous to wildlife than DDT? One of the most deadly of modern insecticides is dieldrin. Tests by the United States Fish and Wildlife Service show that one pound of dieldrin has sufficient toxicity to kill approximately four million quail chicks. The California Department of Fish and Game reports that only 1½ pounds of dieldrin per acre caused the death of pheasants, quail, gophers, snakes, jack rabbits, dogs, chickens, geese and turkeys. In spite of such reports the United States Department of Agriculture still proposes to apply this deadly insecticide at the rate of two pounds per acre.

938. Are any of these insecticides, fungicides, herbicides and so-called pesticides injurious to man? The use of all highly toxic sprays and dusts carries with it a much higher potential of harm to human beings than is generally recognized. If continued, it may rank in seriousness with the dangers of radioactive fallout. The use of these toxic chemicals has increased to a point where cumulative secondary poisoning of humans and wildlife, which already exists to some extent, may become catastrophic.

Tests conducted by the United States Fish and Wildlife Service reveal that in the second generation of exposure to insecticides in their diet, birds invariably become incapable of reproduction. Since these poisons well may have a similar cumulative effect on the human system, mass spraying or dusting with such potentially dangerous chemicals should be prohibited until conclusive evidence gives indisputable proof that there is no such risk to the human race.

939. Can't the amount of chemical to be applied to an acre be controlled so that no harm to humans or wildlife will occur? Most of these so-called pesticides are applied in mass sprayings or dustings from aircraft. Experience shows that it is impossible to apply chemicals from the air without multiple doses occurring in many areas.

940. If a hunter is interested mainly in bobwhites, and he sees a marsh hawk capture one of these birds, why shouldn't he shoot the hawk? One might simply state that the hunter is shooting the bobwhites merely for recreation while the hawk is capturing the bobwhite because it requires food to live.

But from another approach it must be pointed out that man may often arrive at erroneous conclusions. It is true that a marsh hawk occasionally captures bobwhites. But for every bobwhite it takes it destroys dozens, sometimes hundreds, of rats and other rapidly multiplying rodents. Once the hawk and owl predators are eliminated, the chief control is gone and the rodents multiply to such an extent that they destroy most, if not all, of the bobwhite eggs and young, and the game species actually decreases or disappears altogether.

941. Does any actual research support the preceding statements concerning marsh hawk–bobwhite relations? Many a game-hunting preserve has embarked on a campaign of eliminating hawks and owls, only to change opinion and prohibit the shooting of these birds of prey.

On a Georgia game preserve, Dr. H. L. Stoddard collected and examined 1,098 marsh hawk pellets. In this entire collection only four pellets contained bobwhite while 84 per cent contained cotton rats, which are extremely destructive to bobwhite nests, eggs and young.

942. What was the first significant effort to inform the public of the usefulness of predators? In 1893 Dr. A. K. Fisher in a publication of the United States Department of Agriculture entitled *Hawks and Owls of the United States in Their Relation to Agriculture* presented the findings of a study of the feeding habits of 32 species of hawks and 17 species of owls. This report, based on a study of the stomach contents of 2,690 birds, urged protection of most hawks and owls because of their usefulness in rodent control. This was the first major publication referring to hawks and owls as beneficial. It served as an eye-opener even to naturalists and influenced the thinking of conservationists for the next half-century.

943. Is the stomach-contents method still used to explain the role of the predator in nature? This approach is often used, but generally with modifications. At the end of the last century public opinion was so prejudiced against hawks and owls that Fisher's approach (see Question 942) was good. It gave obvious, easily-understood reasons for protecting many maligned predators. At that time it was unique to have anyone champion a hawk or owl. The word *ecology* was not known. Man's understanding of the role of predators was vague. Many old-timers could accept the idea that there were some, but only some, good hawks and owls.

As research in predation advanced it was obvious that this explanation was much too simple, and that the labeling of some birds as good and others as bad was erroneous. Careful studies prove that even those species of hawks and owls eating other birds are useful in the complex overall scheme of nature. Today naturalists try to eliminate the unsound concept that some birds are good, others bad.

944. Aren't sportsmen's groups like Ducks Unlimited against all hawks? More and more sportsmen are reading the reports of research biologists and thus acquiring an understanding of the complex interrelationships in nature, and the useful role of predators. Ducks Unlimited has gone to the expense of publishing a bulletin on hawks which ends with this statement: "Unless any of them [hawks] are doing harm to you—let them go their way in peace. They have their place in nature. . . . Do not allow your sympathies for their prey to turn your heart and hand against them. There is more to this predator–prey relationship than meets the eye. Dame Nature fitted them for their roles and she is a wise old Dame and knows what she is doing."

945. How did the prejudice against predatory birds develop? This prejudice was created by the gamekeepers of Europe. There hunting was confined almost entirely to the estates of very wealthy families. Special gamekeepers were employed to try to maintain an unnatural concentration of game in small, unsatisfactorily confined areas. The gamekeepers considered anything which competed with the game (even for food) as vermin. Under such unnatural, overcrowded situations game was very vulnerable to predation and consequently all hawks, owls and other predators were labeled as vermin which should be wiped out.

946. Is there a special sanctuary for hawks? Hawk Mountain Sanctuary was established in the Kittatinny Mountains of Pennsylvania near Drehersville in 1934. Before this sanctuary was established, hunters gathered at this vantage point annually during migrations and slaughtered hundreds and thousands of hawks. Today birdwatchers from all over the northeastern United States (12,000 visitors annually) gather here to observe and enjoy the hawk flights.

As more and more visitors came to see the sanctuary and spent more and more money locally, the initial hostility of the nearby residents shifted to friendliness.

947. What is a vermin campaign? In years gone by, numerous campaigns were carried on with the avowed purpose of exterminating so-called vermin. Certain animals were labeled villains and advertising urged everyone to go out and purify the countryside of these species.

948. Are vermin campaigns recommended by trained biologists? The old-fashioned vermin campaigns invariably proved to be bad and all progressive state fish and game departments have abandoned this approach. Today most states insist on employing personnel thoroughly trained in biology and game management. Such men understand the complexities in the web of life and realize the danger involved in tampering with it.

All biologists agree that nature's system is fundamentally sound. Unless exacting scientific study of a situation is made before any control is permitted, man's efforts to remedy a situation invariably ends in a worsened condition. The interrelationships in nature are extremely complex, and what at first may seem to be an annoyance may well prove to be a blessing.

949. What is meant by the bounty system? Until the last decade it was common practice for state fish and game departments to offer a monetary reward or bounty to anyone bringing in proof that he had destroyed an animal labeled by these departments as unwanted pests.

950. Why have most states discontinued the bounty system? Time after time, use of the bounty as an inducement to people to kill an "unwanted" species has proved inefficient. In most instances it has been a farce. Such projects are not only extremely costly to the taxpayer and difficult to administer, but they also induce a multitude of people to shoot who cannot, or do not care to, differentiate between one creature and another, and indiscriminate slaughter follows.

In most cases the bounty system has led to fraud, graft, wholesale destruction of native songbirds, damage to property, and on occasions even to loss of human life. Invariably even those people initiating the campaign have begged for its cessation.

951. What is the National Audubon Society? Founded in 1905, the National Audubon Society is the oldest and largest national conservation organization in North America. Its annual budget is more than $750,000. It is entirely privately financed and does not receive any governmental funds. The Society is supported primarily by membership dues, contributions and bequests. Its endowment is $2,500,-000. The Society is governed by a board of directors composed of prominent men and women in various walks of life. The officers of the organization are elected every year at the Annual Meeting. The national headquarters occupies its own six-story building, Audubon House, at 1130 Fifth Avenue, New York. The major purpose of the Society is to advance public understanding of the value and need of conservation of wildlife, plants, soil, and water, and the relation of their intelligent treatment and wise use to human progress.

952. What is the philosophy of the National Audubon Society? The following is a statement of National Audubon Society philosophy:

We believe in the wisdom of nature's design.

We know that soil, water, plants, and wild creatures depend upon each other and are vital to human life.

We recognize that each living thing links to many others in the chain of nature.

We believe that persistent research into the intricate patterns of outdoor life will help to assure wise use of earth's abundance.

We condemn no wild creature and work to assure that no living species shall be lost.

We believe that every generation should be able to experience spiritual and physical refreshment in places where primitive nature is undisturbed.

So we will be vigilant to protect wilderness areas, refuges, and parks, and to encourage good use of nature's storehouse of resources.

We dedicate ourselves to the pleasant task of opening the eyes of young and old that all may come to enjoy the beauty of the outdoor world, and to share in conserving its wonders forever.

953. Does the National Audubon Society maintain any wildlife sanctuaries? Wardens of the Society currently patrol more than 1,000,000 acres of land and water in the United States, chiefly in areas where they can afford protection to great concentrations of nesting, roosting and feeding birds that otherwise would be subjected frequently to damaging disturbance.

954. With the existence of Federal and state wildlife agencies, why is such sanctuary work required by a privately financed organization? Eventually such activities probably should be assumed by the Federal and state governments, but at present their agencies are concerned almost exclusively with the welfare of game species. Consequently the National Audubon Society has seen fit to furnish protection to nongame species, particularly such threatened groups as egrets, ibises, and spoonbills.

955. How many wardens are employed by the National Audubon Society and how are their activities financed? The Society maintains a group of some 15 wardens, and their activities are financed by the contributions of members to the Sanctuary Fund of the Society.

956. Can anyone join the Audubon Society? Everyone in the United States interested in the outdoors and the conservation of wildlife should be a member of the National Audubon Society. Information regarding membership and the organization's activities may be obtained from Audubon House, 1130 Fifth Avenue, New York 28, New York. Canadians should join the Audubon Society of Canada, which has headquarters at 181 Jarvis Street, Toronto 2, Ontario. The Society keeps a complete, up-to-date list of all bird clubs in the United States and Canada.

957. Who was Audubon? John James Audubon, a great American ornithologist, born in Haiti on April 26, 1785, spent most of his life exploring the eastern United States and painting the birds he observed on these trips. His great work, *The Birds of America,* containing 435 hand-colored plates with 1,065 life-sized figures, did much to arouse people's interest in the spectacular bird life of North America.

958. An alligator will eat a bird if it can catch one. Why aren't those near bird colonies shot? It is true that an alligator will eat a bird when it can catch one. But catching a healthy, alert bird is seldom possible. The great majority of birds caught by alligators near bird colonies are young which have fallen from their nests. In most cases the young would have died anyway, as most parent birds would not descend through the canopy of overhead branches to feed the unfortunate youngster. On the other hand, the alligators carefully patrol the water around the island, and any raccoon, opossum, wildcat or other mammal predator trying to swim to the bird colony is quickly eliminated. Thus alligators are often referred to as the guardians of the southern bird colonies.

959. Of what use are owls?   There is an incalculable esthetic value to owls. Excluding the few still believing in outmoded superstitions, most people today enjoy looking at owls and listening to their stirring calls. In fact, they are the favorite birds of many people and one sees as many, if not more, porcelain and silver images of owls than of any other family of birds.

Furthermore, owls may well be called nature's flying rat traps. They help keep the fast-multiplying rodents in check. Certain species such as barn owls, short-eared owls and long-eared owls live to a great extent on rats and mice. Dr. A. K. Fisher, in a study of 200 barn owl pellets (the regurgitated indigestible remains of prey), found 454 mammal skulls, among which were 225 meadow voles, 179 house mice, 20 rats and 20 shrews.

960. Aren't great horned owls decidedly destructive to game birds? As pointed out repeatedly, interrelationships are complex. Many hunting clubs planning to increase game have concentrated on attempts to eliminate horned owls. Much to the chagrin of these clubs, the diminution of horned owls, which eat relatively few game birds, resulted in a rapid increase of skunks (a favorite food of great horned owls) and fast-multiplying rodents which in turn destroyed all eggs and young of the game birds. Though the horned owls occasionally take birds, they are in the overall picture extremely helpful to game birds.

961. Is it true that oil and oily bilge water dumped on the ocean by ships often destroy thousands of birds? On occasion the destruction has been almost unbelievable. Mile after mile along the coast has at times been stippled with thousands of oil-soaked loons, grebes, ducks, geese and other species dead or dying.

962. How does the oil cause this destruction? Birds do not know that oil is sticky, and dangerous to their well-being. Swimming through it, they are quickly covered with heavy, sticky oil, which prevents them from flying. It hinders their diving ability and saps their vitality until they are unable to capture sufficient food and consequently starve to death. In others the oil allows the cold water to strike the body between the masses of clotted feathers and this brings on pneumonia. Furthermore, many birds in their attempt to pick off the oil with their bills swallow so much of it that they are poisoned.

963. Can't the government do something to prevent this destruction? A federal law prohibits the dumping of oil within three miles of land. Such a law, however, is difficult to enforce, although the wide use of airplanes and helicopters now makes checking and conviction more feasible. International law should prohibit the dumping of oil anywhere on the waters. Some far-sighted, considerate companies have voluntarily instructed their captains to dump oil only in large containers made for that purpose alongside the docks. Some companies have even devised systems for reclaiming the usable oil. If every sea captain could visualize the destruction caused by the dumping of oil, surely each one would gladly obey the all too lenient Federal law.

964. Is it true that flocks of gulls saved the Mormon settlers from starvation in Utah? Thousands of California gulls suddenly gathering to feed on the armies of crickets devouring the Mormon crops are said to have saved the settlers from starvation. In appreciation of this service, the Mormons erected in Salt Lake City a now famous $40,000 monument to the gulls. (See Question 1001.)

965. Is it true that migratory and wintering waterfowl in California often devour considerable quantities of grain and garden vegetables? Yes, this is true. Federal as well as state refuges often plant extensive areas in grain solely for the birds, hoping in this way to keep them off privately owned lands.

To indicate the complexities of evaluating such depredations, examine one report issued in California. It estimates that the damage done in one year amounted to $1,500,000. No one can deny that this is an impressive sum.

But the same report goes on to estimate that the meat value of the birds shot in one season was $4,000,000, and the amount of money spent in the state by waterfowl hunters was $500,000. Simple mathematics credits ducks and geese with offsetting their destructive habits with immediate monetary assets alone of $3,000,000!

XIV. BIRDS IN MYTHOLOGY, TRADITION AND HISTORY

966. Why have birds figured so prominently in the imaginative life of both primitive and modern man? Certainly birds have exercised a wide and profound influence. Their effect on the superstitious and religious sides of man probably stems from many factors. Perhaps the voices of birds, particularly those that call at night, evoked the deepest response. Superstitions related to night sounds, especially those of owls, have lived on through the centuries and persist today among people of little education.

Other characteristics of birds, such as their powers of flight, their appearance and disappearance due to migrations, their brilliant plumage, and certain humanlike habits all played a part in giving them a prominent place in the lives of men through the ages. The degree of man's ignorance may be measured by his belief in the significance and omens related to the traits and behavior of birds.

967. Do any traces remain in modern culture that indicate the influence of birds on man? There is little doubt that the sounds made by birds influenced human speech. Probably birds also had a deep influence on written language. Primitive men left many pictures of birds on the walls of caves. As the human race matured, the first pictographs and ideographs employed birds or bird forms. Later these were refined in hieroglyphs and early alphabets.

968. What is the most ancient evidence of man's interest in birds? Paintings of birds on the walls of caves prove that ancient man took accurate note of birds and their habits.

969. How old are the cave paintings? Paleolithic or Stone Age man spanned between 500,000 and 1,500,000 years of the earth's history. In certain parts of the world, Stone Age cultures persisted into the present century. In Europe this period ended about 10,000 years ago. It was during the upper part of the paleolithic period in Europe, or more than 100 centuries ago, that some of the cave paintings in both France and Spain were made. The oldest of these were merely etched or scratched in the stone, while the later ones had color added.

970. Did any early paintings of birds have genuine artistic merit? Many of the early paintings showed great vigor and strength but most of them are interesting chiefly because they indicate something of the skill and life of the men who painted them. However, a painting of white-fronted, bean and red-breasted geese called the geese of Medum, Egypt, was created at least 3,000 years ago and has genuine artistic merit. The original is in the Museum of Cairo but many museums around the world, including the Metropolitan Museum of Art in New York, have faithful reproductions of this beautiful painting.

971. What is the earliest known literary reference to birds? It is believed that the book of Genesis was first written in the tenth or ninth century B.C. In this book (1:20) is the account of the creation of birds on the fourth day as follows: "Let the waters bring forth abundantly the moving creature that hath life, and fowl that may fly above the earth in the open firmament of heaven."

972. Do birds have a leading role in any Bible stories? In the story of Noah and the ark (Genesis 7 and 8) the dove and raven both play a part. Noah, at the end of forty days, sent forth a raven and a dove to see if the waters of the flood had abated. The raven went to and fro until the waters were dried but the dove returned to the ark, was sent forth again in seven days and again returned, this time bearing an olive branch in its bill. Again the dove remained in the ark for seven days and when sent forth at the end of that time did not return, so Noah, all the people and all the animals emerged from the ark.

Elijah, the Tishbite, in I Kings 17:1–24, was sent by God to hide and dwell by the brook Cherith. There the ravens brought him bread and flesh in the morning and again in the evening until the brook dried up and he was forced to find shelter elsewhere.

973. What is the best-known reference to birds in the bible?
Probably the exquisite verse in the Song of Solomon (2:11–12)
which refers to the coming of spring:

For, lo, the winter is past, the rain is over and gone;
The flowers appear on the earth; the time of the singing of birds is
come, and the voice of the turtle[dove] is heard in our land.

974. Aside from those in the Bible, what is the most ancient reference to birds in well-known literature? The Greek epic poet
Homer (born about 850 B.C.) described in the *Iliad* the Trojan advance "like the cranes which flee from the coming winter and sudden
rain and fly with clamor towards the streams of the ocean."

975. Did birds play a leading part in any early literature? Aesop
(about 550 B.C.) wrote many fables based on his knowledge of animal
behavior, including man's. Translations of these fables are read today.
One of the fables, "The Jay and the Peacock," includes several observations on behavior that are frequently quoted. Among these are,
"It is not only fine feathers that make fine birds," "Be content with
your lot" and "One cannot be first in everything."

976. Did birds have a leading role in other ancient literature?
Aristophanes (about 448–385 B.C.), the great Athenian dramatist
and poet, often used natural forms in his comedies. *The Birds* is one
of his finest. His references in this play to superstitions then current
are interesting today:

> For every oracular temple and shrine,
> The birds are a substitute equal and fair
> For on us you depend and to us you repair
> For council and aid when a marriage is made,
> A purchase, a bargain, a venture in trade.
> Unlucky or lucky, whatever has struck ye,
> An ox or an ass that may happen to pass,
> A voice in the street, or a slave you may meet,
> A name or a word, by chance overheard,
> If you deem it an omen, you call it a Bird,
> And if birds are your omens, it clearly will follow
> That birds are a proper prophetic Apollo.

More than 2,300 years have passed since Aristophanes voiced these superstitions, yet birds remain in our folklore. Inherited traditions concerning birds and their significance remain today.

977. Did Socrates ever speak of birds? The last words of the Greek philosopher (470?–399 B.C.) referred to a bird: "I owe a cock to Aesculapius; do not forget to pay it." (See Question 985.)

978. What effect did Aristotle, the great Greek philosopher and scientist, have on the study of ornithology? Aristotle (384–322 B.C.) described the food territories of eagles and ravens about 350 B.C. He studied the anatomy of birds, their eggs, and many of their habits. It is not surprising that his bird studies as well as those in other phases of natural history were full of errors and unfounded theories. Nevertheless, for centuries his words were regarded as truth and they continued to influence the western world for more than 2,000 years. Aristotle believed masses of birds hibernated in winter and this superstition became so deeply rooted in folklore and literature that it was hotly debated as late as the time of Linnaeus, Buffon and Gilbert White. William Bartram was the first distinguished writer (1739–1823) to express strongly in literature the absurdity of this notion, and he backed up his opinion with personal observation.

In spite of his shortcomings, Aristotle contributed much to the study of birds. He detected, among other things, the red palpitating speck in an egg incubated for 36 hours and recognized it without the aid of a magnifying lens as the beginning of a living embryo.

Today his remark, "One swallow does not make a spring" from his *Nicomachean Ethics* is frequently quoted, as it has been throughout the centuries since he wrote it, though in popular usage *summer* frequently replaces *spring*.

979. Did any Romans contribute to contemporary bird lore? Though he contributed little factual bird lore, Pliny the Elder, a Roman naturalist (23–79 A.D.), expressed the current superstition concerning owls. This is still alive among people susceptible to superstitious ideas. He wrote, "The Screech Owl always betokens some heavy news and is most execrable and accursed. In summer he is the very monster of the night, neither singing nor crying out clear, but uttering a certain heavy groan of doleful mourning and therefore if it be seen to fly in any place it prognosticates some fearful misfortune."

980. Were owls always feared by ancient people?   Among the Greeks owls were revered as creatures of great wisdom. Minerva, goddess of wisdom, usually was pictured with an owl perched on her shoulder or hand.

981. What birds aside from owls had a widespread place in mythology?   Both swans and eagles had a part in the mythology of both ancient Greece and Rome. Their place in folklore lasted into early medieval times. Wherever they occurred in the world, these species were leading figures in local legends.

982. What is the connection between swans and Helen of Troy?   According to Greek mythology, Zeus once took the form of a swan and coming to earth, met Leda, Queen of the Spartan King Tyndareus, and became through her the father of Helen of Troy and of Pollux.

983. Who were the swan knights of mythology?   In early medieval mythology a knight such as Lohengrin was often drawn by a swan to any land or maiden he planned to succor. According to some legends the swan is the swan-knight's brother who either has lost or injured his magic necklace through the wicked acts of his grandmother and is therefore unable to transform himself back into human form.

984. Who were the swan maidens?   A swan maiden was an elf or fairy capable of becoming a maid or a swan at will by putting on or taking off a magic garment known as the swan shift, a covering of swan's feathers. Swan maidens and the swan song provide the theme for Tchaikovsky's *Swan Lake Ballet*. Beings similar to swan maidens occur not only in European mythology but also in Japan and among some American Indian tribes.

985. What is meant by the swan song?   The belief that a dying swan sings a beautiful song arose behind the curtain of prehistory. Socrates wrote, "Will you not allow that I have as much of the spirit of prophecy in me as the swans? For they, when they perceive that they must die, having sung all their life long, do then sing much more lustily than ever, rejoicing in the thought that they are going to the god they serve."

The swan song reappears frequently through the ages. At least three times Shakespeare mentions the song of the dying swan (*Merchant of Venice, Othello,* and *King John*) but most vividly in Act V of *King John* when he wrote:

>'Tis strange that death should sing.
>I am the cygnet to this pale faint swan,
>Who chants a doleful hymn to his own death,
>And from the organ-pipe of frailty sings
>His soul and body to their lasting rest.

Today *swan song* is used to describe the final production of an artist or a musician, or the end of a period.

986. What place did the eagle hold in mythology?   In almost all cultures the eagle was regarded as the personification of bravery and courage. It was regarded by the Romans as the personification of Jupiter or Jove. Ancient drawings show the eagle gripping the thunderbolts of Jupiter in its claws. Later the conventionalized war eagle was used to represent many of the European countries.

987. Were Jupiter and Minerva the only mythological characters of the classic countries represented by birds?   The beauty of peacocks made them the birds of Juno. Mercury was always represented with winged feet but he was not identified by a specific species of bird.

988. Do birds act as symbols today?   Many birds and feathers play an important part as symbols in the language of contemporary life. They appear so frequently that only a few will be mentioned:

Bluebird: happiness
Cuckoo: rain prophet
Dove: gentleness and peace
Eagle: bravery, courage and as the emblem of war
Game cock: aggressiveness
Goose: stupidity

Kingfisher (European): calm seas and still air
Jay: false pride
Little Bird: carrier of secret information
Ostrich (from the mistaken belief that it hides its head in sand):
   self-deception
Owl: generally wisdom, sometimes ill omen
Pelican: loneliness ("I am a pelican of the wilderness"—Psalm
   102:6)
Peacock: pride and vanity

A feathered arrow represents war, while a quill pen stands for peace. A white feather indicates cowardice. Wings are given to angels, the flying horse Pegasus, many dragons, Mercury, and the United States Air Force men, in each instance indicating mastery of the air.

989. How did the folk tale that storks bring babies arise? The origin of this superstition is not known but it is very ancient. According to the folk tale, a stork passes over the house when a birth is about to take place. From that grew the allusion that storks bring babies, which has passed into popular use today.

990. Did such a bird as the dodo actually live? The dodo was a heavy flightless bird related to the pigeons but larger than a turkey and was once found in great numbers on the island of Mauritius. It is now extinct, having been exterminated by European settlers. The dodo was a forest bird and laid its single large white egg in a grass nest. It was recorded as late as 1681.

991. Was there ever such a bird as the roc? This was a fabulous or mythical bird of Arabia. It was so huge it bore off elephants to feed its young. The legend of the roc was current in the East, and appears in several tales from the Arabian Nights. Some authorities believe the elephant-bird of Madagascar may have given rise to the legend of the roc. Others, also locating the source of the legend on Madagascar, say that it stems from the fact that the gigantic fronds of the raphia palm native to that island look like the quills of birds. It is said that one of these palm fronds was presented as a feather to the Great Khan. (See Questions 662, 781–784.)

992. What is the legendary phoenix?   This was a mythical bird sacred to the sun. It was believed to have bright-colored plumage of fabulous beauty. Stories about the phoenix arose sometime before the fifth century B.C. and belief in the existence of the bird lasted well into the Middle Ages. While accounts of the bird have varied, it was generally believed to be of tremendous size. Only one sex, the male, lived. At the age of about 500 years, the phoenix made a nest for itself in a spice tree and settling itself on the nest, made a tremendous fire and burned itself alive. From its ashes came forth another phoenix. When strong enough, the young phoenix took its father's ashes to the altar of the sun.

993. Was the thunderbird also legendary?   In Australia a species of thickhead is called the thunderbird. The male is marked with black and yellow and has a black crescent on its breast.

Though a species called the thunderbird actually exists, some African and North American Indian tribes have legends of a fabulous thunderbird which caused thunder. Among these widely separated people was a common belief that the thunderbird had had a red bill, tail and legs. A conventionalized form of the thunderbird with widespread wings often appeared in Indian art.

994. Is the harpy a genuine species?   In Central and northern South America there is a double-crested raptore called the harpy eagle. In the Philippine Islands another species is also called the harpy eagle, and is said to live chiefly on monkeys.

The Harpies of mythology, particularly of Greece, were creatures having the heads of women but the wings, tail, legs and claws of birds. Originally they were thought to be the personification of devastating winds but later they became ghoulish creatures that carried off the souls of the dead.

995. How did the goatsucker family win that odd name?   The name is derived from the mistaken belief in Europe that these birds obtain their food by sucking milk from goats. This belief arose from the fact that nightjars (European goatsuckers) frequently fly around goats and other domestic animals. Insects gathered around the animals and those flying up as they move through the grass provide easy feeding for these birds.

996. Do any other families or species of birds represented in North America have names based on incorrect folklore? It is believed that petrels were named for St. Peter who, according to the Bible, walked on the waters. Petrels do not actually walk on the water but when feeding they flutter close to the surface and sometimes their feet patter on it.

Swifts and hummingbirds belong to the order Apodiformes, which means "footless." Proportionately they have the smallest feet in the bird world but the idea of their being without feet is based on folklore and this idea was fostered by early native collectors who removed the feet before shipping the specimens to scientists or those interested in natural curiosities.

997. Did birds have a place in the ceremonies of primitive people? Medicine men and witch doctors often used feathers in their ceremonies and wore them as part of their costumes. John Bartram, in 1743, after watching an Indian religious ceremony near Onondaga, New York, wrote that a stick was placed before the cagelike hut in which the priest attempted to make visible a spirit which would reveal a desired fact. The spirit was supposed to take the form of a bird and perch upon the stick to deliver its information.

Ancient Egyptians worshiped the sacred ibis (now extirpated from that country), while Mayan Indians considered the quetzal sacred. Many primitive dances were based on the strutting actions of conspicuous birds known to the natives. Among American Indians crane, crow and turkey dances were copied for their ceremonies.

998. American Indians frequently used feathers to indicate their rank within the tribe. Have other people in recent history done likewise? In Hawaii where but few colorful birds lived, elaborate and very beautiful feather robes were worn by the nobility. Few of these robes still exist, most of them carefully preserved in museums, their value placed at $10,000 or more. Far Eastern rulers displayed peacock feathers as a sign of their power and position.

Today young ladies presented at the Court of St. James must wear in their hair three white ostrich plumes placed according to protocol.

999. Have birds ever played a decisive part in the history of mankind? Many times explorers and colonists who have changed the course of civilization have been saved from starvation and enabled to carry out their plans because birds offered an available food supply. In direct influence, the cackling geese of Rome are credited with having saved Roman civilization in 338 B.C. from falling before the barbarians by waking the city before the attack could be made.

1000. What is the first record of birds having an influence on American history?   On October 7, 1492, Columbus was threatened by the mutiny of his crew while still some 720 miles east of the North American mainland. A flight of migratory land birds helped Columbus to win the sailors from their determination to return immediately to Spain. Columbus turned the *Santa Maria* toward the southwest, followed the birds, and shortened his route to land by about 200 miles, making a landing at San Salvador instead of on the mainland.

1001. What was the most dramatic instance of help by birds in American Colonial history?   The colonization of Utah by the Mormons began in 1848. The first spring after they arrived, they were troubled by floods, then killing frosts and next came the crickets advancing in a solid phalanx and eating everything as they marched. One of the colonists, Priddy Meeks, wrote: "I heard the voice of fowls flying overhead that I was not acquainted with. I looked up and saw a flock of seven gulls. In a few minutes there was another larger flock . . . they came faster and more of them until the heavens darkened with them and lit down in the valley till the earth was black with them and they would eat crickets. . . ."

Now on top of a very tall slim pillar in Temple Square at Salt Lake City are perched two golden California Gulls, a monument to the birds that saved the Mormon colony from disaster. (See Question 964.)

1002. Aside from their enrichment of language, do birds figure in the daily life of many people today?   Birds appear on so many objects in constant use that they have a part in the daily life of most people. They appear on coins and the stamps of practically every country in the world. Usually such a bird is a characteristic species of the country that displays it. The Canada goose on Canadian airmail stamps is an example. However, one wildlife conservation stamp of the United States shows not a common species but the very rare whooping crane.

1003. Who were the first naturalists to carry on extensive studies of American birds?   An English naturalist and writer, Mark Catesby (1679?–1749), made the first important contribution to American ornithology in his two great folios, which include the *Natural History of Carolina.* After more than 200 years this is still an important publication.

Thomas Pennant (1726–1798), also an English naturalist, contributed *Arctic Zoology* toward increased knowledge about birds of the western world.

1004. What American observers of the eighteenth and nineteenth centuries contributed most toward ornithological knowledge?   William Bartram (1739–1823), a Philadelphia naturalist, not only contributed journals of his travels which included descriptions of birds, notes on their habits, and careful drawings, but he also added some scientific papers, collected for George Edwards of England, and was instrumental in turning Alexander Wilson to the study of ornithology.

Alexander Wilson (1766–1813), born in Scotland, was a poet, weaver, and in the United States a teacher. His was the earliest attempt to treat in words and paintings all of the birds of North America.

John James Audubon (1775–1851) was born in Les Cayes, Santo Domingo, now Haiti. He combined in one man the abilities of a great artist, explorer, field student and writer. His greatest published work is *The Birds of America.* (See Question 957.)

Following Audubon came John Cassin (1813–1868), Spenser Fullerton Baird (1823–1888), who became secretary of the Smithsonian Institution, Elliot Coues (1842–1899), and Robert Ridgway (1850–1929). Many others, not strictly ornithologists, contributed abundantly to the growing knowledge of American birds through their accurate observations and careful reporting. By 1880 the ranks of distinguished ornithologists in North America had become too numerous to mention here.

1005. When was the American Ornithologists' Union (A.O.U.) founded?   This organization of American ornithologists was founded in 1883 to further the study and knowledge about birds.

1006. When was the National Audubon Society founded?   This leading society for conservation was founded in 1905, though pioneer societies of this name were organized as early as 1886. (See Questions 951–953.)

1007. Is there a United States government agency concerned with birds?   The United States Fish and Wildlife Service under the Department of Interior is concerned with the conservation of our wildlife, including birds. Their foremost interest in birds lies in the conservation and use of game species. However, all birdbanding comes under the jurisdiction of this service, as do hunting regulations and the protection of migratory birds. (See Questions 824–829, 923–925.)

1008. Is there a Canadian equivalent to the United States Fish and Wildlife Service?   The Canadian Wildlife Service is a government branch quite similar to the United States Fish and Wildlife Service. These services often co-operate on matters of continental importance.

1009. Is there a Canadian organization similar to the National Audubon Society in its principles and influence in conservation matters?   The scope and principles of the Audubon Society of Canada (founded November 9, 1948) are similar to those of the National Audubon Society in the United States. (See Question 956.)

1010. What is the national bird of the United States?   The bald eagle, *Haliaeetus leucocephalus*.

1011. Is the bald eagle really bald?   The head of a bald eagle is completely covered with feathers. When this species is young it has a dark head. When mature, its entire head is clothed with white feathers that extend over the neck. At the same time its tail becomes white.

1012. Is the bald eagle protected by law?   All bald eagles are protected by law in the United States and its possessions. Nevertheless, it is a sad commentary on human nature that many are shot each year for no better reason than the fact that they present large targets for thoughtless or unsporting hunters.

A major part of the food of bald eagles is made up of injured birds or animals, or carrion, yet they illegally are destroyed in great numbers in Alaska where they are regarded as vermin. Unless more effective protection is given the bald eagle, the national symbol of the United States may become extinct on this continent. It is decreasing rapidly.

1013. What bird has most often been chosen to represent a country or indicate rank within a country or tribe? The eagle. The United States is represented by a specific species (see Question 1010). In past centuries various countries of Europe were represented by a conventionalized bird known as the war eagle. Eagle feathers were used by American Indians to denote their rank as warriors and chieftains, while some tribes of Indians used the eagle to represent their clan, tribe or totem.

1014. Why has the eagle played such a prominent part in the culture of so many people? The large size of the eagle and its reputation for bravery, whether deserved or not, caused many people to admire and respect it.

1015. Do eagles really carry away babies? Stories of babies carried away by eagles continue to appear in newspapers. None of these has been authentic. The average weight of a bald eagle is 13 pounds. Only a small baby could possibly be lifted by an eagle. Moreover, very small babies are seldom left unattended by wise parents. Occasionally captive eagles, mistreated and tormented beyond endurance, have attacked their tormentors with telling effect, for their claws are sharp and powerful. But in the wild, eagles are shy and are afraid to approach man.

1016. Have countries other than the United States chosen an official bird to represent them? So far as can be learned, very few countries have chosen a national bird. Among the few that have done so are the following:

Burma: peacock
Ecuador: condor
France: cock
Guatemala: quetzal
Mexico: caracara
United States: bald eagle

1017. What are the state birds?

Alabama	Flicker
Arizona	Cactus wren
Arkansas	Mockingbird
California	California quail
Colorado	Lark bunting
Connecticut	Robin
Delaware	Blue hen chicken
District of Columbia	Wood thrush *
Florida	Mockingbird
Georgia	Brown thrasher *
Idaho	Mountain bluebird
Illinois	Cardinal
Indiana	Cardinal
Iowa	Goldfinch
Kansas	Western meadowlark
Kentucky	Cardinal
Louisiana	Brown pelican
Maine	Black-capped chickadee
Maryland	Baltimore oriole *
Massachusetts	Black-capped chickadee
Michigan	Robin
Minnesota	Goldfinch *
Mississippi	Mockingbird
Missouri	Eastern bluebird *
Montana	Western meadowlark
Nebraska	Western meadowlark
Nevada	Mountain bluebird *
New Hampshire	Purple finch *
New Jersey	Goldfinch
New Mexico	Roadrunner *
New York	Eastern bluebird *
North Carolina	Cardinal
North Dakota	Western meadowlark *
Ohio	Cardinal
Oklahoma	Scissor-tailed flycatcher
Oregon	Western meadowlark *
Pennsylvania	Ruffed grouse
Rhode Island	Rhode Island red hen

South Carolina . . . . Carolina wren
South Dakota . . . . Ring-necked pheasant
Tennessee . . . . Mockingbird
Texas . . . . Mockingbird
Utah . . . . California gull *
Vermont . . . . Hermit thrush *
Virginia . . . . Cardinal
Washington . . . . Goldfinch *
West Virginia . . . . Cardinal
Wisconsin . . . . Robin *
Wyoming . . . . Western meadowlark

(* indicates unofficial status of bird. Those unmarked were made official by an act of legislation. State birds listed as unofficial are those chosen by garden clubs, school children or even by newspaper campaigns. They have not been given legal status by the governor or state legislature.)

1018. Once chosen, do state birds always remain the same? The people who make our laws often change those already in existence. A new group of legislators may change the state bird or make official a bird that was chosen by popular vote or by proclamation of the governor.

XV. DOMESTICATION, ODD FACTS AND ADAPTABILITY OF BIRDS

1019. What is the most valuable bird as far as man is concerned?
The domestic hen, developed from the jungle fowl of Asia, is the most valuable of birds as far as man is concerned. Both for its eggs and flesh, this bird is of tremendous importance throughout the world. It ranks among the top producers of income from agriculture in the United States. Since the use of wild bird plumage has been prohibited in the United States, many of the feathers from hens which were once a waste product are now dyed, clipped, curled and used for decoration.

1020. Why have so few species of birds been domesticated? It is not unusual to find species of birds native to various parts of the earth domesticated locally. But to be truly successful as a domestic bird, a species must be able to live in any part of the world inhabited by man. The bird must not only adapt itself to varied climates but must have a temperament that suits it to easy domestication, its flesh must be excellent and it must be highly fertile. Comparatively few species fit these demands. The domestic chickens, geese, ducks and turkeys (with peacocks, guinea fowl and pigeons on a slightly lower level) are the only species that fulfill the requirements for satisfactory domestic birds.

1021. Has man domesticated birds for any reason except to supply food? Ostriches are domesticated for their plumes and to a lesser degree for their skin. Canaries have become cage birds because of their pleasing songs. Various parrots have been domesticated because of their versatility of speech, interesting habits and brilliant plumage, while myna birds, closely related to starlings, are gifted imitators of human speech.

Cormorants have been domesticated in many parts of the world and used as fishermen. Their use in this respect has died out except in certain parts of the Orient where native fishermen continue to keep flocks of cormorants on leashes. At the fishing grounds a ring is placed around the neck of the cormorant to prevent it from swallowing the catch. Whenever a cormorant catches a fish it is hauled in by the leash and the fish is removed. Once it has made several catches, the ring is removed from its neck so it can feed itself.

1022. Are there thieves among birds? In Maine the attention of the authors frequently has been called to an osprey which has caught a fish. Usually loud calls from such an osprey indicated that its catch was wanted by a bald eagle or a great black-backed gull. Though the osprey screams with resentment when attacked by one of these birds, it is usually forced to surrender the fish to the attacker.

In Florida, laughing and Bonaparte's gulls perch on the heads of brown pelicans that have just made a catch. As the pelicans open their bills to shift the fish into position for swallowing, the gulls snatch the food. Frigate-birds and jaegers pursue terns carrying fish and usually succeed in making those birds drop their catch.

1023. Do any birds use tools? Gulls and crows drop clams and other foods encased in hard shells onto flat hard surfaces such as walls, roads and cliffs. In the Galápagos Islands a bird called the woodpecker finch feeds largely on insects in the ground or the bark of trees. It has a typical finch bill, short, thick and pointed. To compensate for the inadequate bill, it grips in this bill short twigs, thorns or cactus spines which it uses to poke into the crevices where it cannot reach, then seizes its prey as it rushes out.

1024. Why do birds, particularly grackles, redwings and some species of herons, perch on cows and other animals? While a bird may use the back of a mammal occasionally as a convenient perch, usually there is a deeper reason. Most birds that perch on the back of a mammal do so because insects have congregated there and provide an easy source of food.

W. H. Hudson wrote of having watched a deer stand quietly with enjoyment evident in each line of its body while a jackdaw explored it for ticks. Cattle egrets which habitually feed on insects stirred up by grazing cattle often feed on insects infesting the cattle themselves as the big ruminants lie chewing their cuds.

1025. What is anting? Many birds have been observed to place live ants in their feathers, a habit known as anting. No satisfactory explanation for this strange activity has been made. Some believe anting helps rid the birds of ectoparasites.

1026. Do birds place things other than ants in their feathers? Birds have rubbed themselves with cigarette stubs in which the glow of fire remained. Walnuts while still green and juicy are sometimes pierced by the bill, which is then thrust into the feathers. Leaves are sometimes rubbed on the feathers. Many liquids such as orange juice, vinegar and even beer have been rubbed on their feathers by birds. Moth balls, too, are said to have been rubbed over the plumage by some birds.

1027. What is the peck order or peck right? There is a definite social organization among flocks of birds. The flock is sorted out with the most dominant individual able to peck any other member of the flock, the next in order of dominance can peck any but the top bird and so on down the line to the subordinate individual pecked by all the flock but not permitted to peck any bird. This order may change because of hormone change within the birds, causing them to be less or more dominant.

1028. Do birds ever feed young birds not their own? Penguins frequently feed any young bird that begs for food. Three swifts often attend one nest and all three birds feed the young. In an area where there are many swallows nesting, such as a barn with several barn swallow nests, a collection of inhabited tree swallow boxes or a wall with many cliff swallow nests on it, it is not unusual to see a constant stream of adult swallows fly to a single nest to feed the young.

Kingbirds have been photographed feeding young phoebes. In the same way, records have been preserved of song sparrows feeding both young juncoes and robins.

1029. Why are birds not electrocuted when they perch on high-tension wires? In order for electricity to harm a living creature, there must be a ground. Wires strung along poles pass over glass or other insulating material which prevents the electricity from being grounded at the pole. When a bird perches on a high-tension wire there is no ground, therefore the bird is unharmed. However, if the bird perched close enough so that some part of its body touched the pole or another exposed wire, it would be electrocuted, for then a ground or circuit would be made.

1030. Can any passerine bird swim? Most passerine birds can swim for a very short distance if necessary. One group of land birds, the dippers (Cinclidae) to which the American water ouzel belongs, habitually feeds by walking along the bottoms of mountain streams or the shallow edges of lakes.

1031. Do water ouzels have webbed feet? Water ouzels do not have webbed feet. They are closely related to wrens, which they resemble in shape and posture. Their oil gland is ten times larger than that of their close relatives. Their nictitating membrane, which undoubtedly gives valuable protection to this water-loving bird, is white and therefore quite conspicuous.

1032. Do birds ever store food for future use? Jays frequently hide food and no doubt they often return and eat it. The California woodpecker is sometimes called the acorn woodpecker from its habit of feeding on acorns. They store these by drilling holes in tree trunks or in poles and inserting an acorn in each hole. Red-headed woodpeckers frequently store food in the same manner. Chickadees and nuthatches also have been known to store food.

1033. Are any birds poisonous to man? Apparently if birds feed on vegetable matter poisonous to man they too become poisonous to him. Forbush wrote of ruffed grouse in New England that became poisonous after feeding on the leaf buds of mountain laurel. Pigeons are said to feed at times on seeds that are poisonous and thus become poisonous to man.

In winter many finches feed regularly on the seeds of poison ivy. It would be interesting to know if they become poisonous, too, but finches are not game birds and are well protected by migratory bird laws, so it is doubtful that an investigation of this matter will be made.

1034. What are the chief sports in which birds have a leading part? It is claimed that more people in the world indulge in cockfighting than in any other sport. This sport is illegal in the United States. Nevertheless, it has a large following here.

Other sports concerned with birds are bird-watching, falconry, pigeon racing, upland-bird hunting, water fowl hunting and bird photography.

1035. What is the sport of falconry and where did it originate?
This is a sport sometimes called hawking, which involves the flying of falcons and hawks. The peregrine falcon and gyrfalcon are the most popular species of hawks used in this sport, though the golden eagle is also a favorite. While the game obtained is used for the table, the sport and recreation involved are the chief factors in the popularity of the sport. Falconry is believed to have originated in China about 2,000 B.C. From there it spread throughout Asia, North Africa, and Europe. Once the sport was confined by law to kings and the nobility. In Europe it was pursued with enthusiasm from about A.D. 850 until the middle of the seventeenth century. The sport has many enthusiastic followers in many parts of the world, including North America.

1036. Why is falconry opposed by conservationists? Conservationists oppose falconry by amateurs who rob the nests of peregrine falcons and other hawks. Most of these birds meet a quick death in the hands of people who do not know how to care for them. Few people have sufficient knowledge to feed and care for the hawks properly. Many are too slovenly to adhere to the strict regime essential to provide for the well-being of these high-strung birds. Only people who have served a stiff apprenticeship under competent falconers should attempt falconry on their own. All hawks capable of training for falconry are too beautiful and too few in numbers to be destroyed by untrained would-be falconers.

1037. How many people take part in water-fowl hunting? More than 2,000,000 duck stamps at $2.00 each are sold annually. While some of the stamps are bought by collectors, the majority of them are purchased by water-fowl hunters, thus giving clear evidence of the popularity of this sport.

1038. How many people in North America are active bird-watchers? It is estimated that more than a million people in the United States and Canada enjoy bird-watching as a sport or as part of scientific projects.

1039. Geographically, North America extends southward to Central America. Why do ornithologists consider the northern boundary of Mexico the southern extent of North America? The ornithologist's North America differs from that of the geographer because many birds of South and Central America are found in Mexico. The southern boundary of the United States forms a convenient line of demarcation between birds of the tropics and birds of the north.

1040. Why do birds sometimes stretch flat, with their wings spread as if dead? Birds, like humans, appear to enjoy sun baths. It is probable that all species of birds sun bathe occasionally. Photographers hidden in blinds frequently observe their subjects enjoying the sun. Birds may pause when feeding or pursuing other activities, lie flat with the head turned sideways, stretch their wings and tail, often closing their eyes and relaxing the feathers so they lie loosely. Ibises and herons often indulge in sun bathing on sandy beaches or the shell rims of islands. Evident enjoyment emanates from birds as it does from humans as they sun bathe.

1041. What is the best way to transport an injured wild bird to a person skilled in caring for such creatures? If the bird is fairly small, place it in a paper bag. The feathers will not be damaged and the bird cannot injure itself further in the bag. A large injured or sick bird should be placed in a box small enough so it cannot struggle. The feathers of hand-held birds usually suffer badly.

1042. Young birds often fall from the nest. What should be done when this happens? If the nest is undamaged and the parent birds are still attentive, the young birds should be replaced in the nest. Cover the nest gently with the hand until the young settle down and become calm and contented.

If the parent birds have disappeared, been killed or refuse to return to the young, it is possible to hand-raise many species of wild birds. It must be remembered that State and Federal laws concerning the possession of wild birds should be consulted and suitable arrangements made to meet the laws. Raising young birds is fairly arduous for they require large quantities of food offered at frequent intervals.

1043. What should be done with young, hand-raised birds when they are able to fly? It is best to release such birds as soon as they are able to feed themselves and fly acceptably for their mode of life.

Otherwise such birds become dependent on their foster parents and eventually fall easy prey to other creatures.

Because human emotions easily become involved, it is difficult to feed and care for young birds without making pets of them. However, the future of hand-raised birds is much brighter if no attention is devoted to them beyond simply supplying them with food, warmth and cleanliness.

1044. What food should be given birds that require human care for survival?   Zoo keepers frequently divide birds into two groups according to their food habits: soft-bills which include insect and fruit eating birds (warblers, catbirds, blackbirds, etc.) and hard-bills or seed eating birds (sparrows, finches, etc.). "Mockingbird food" available at most bird-food dealers and pet shops mixed with grated carrots, ant eggs (really pupa cases), chopped hard-boiled eggs, cottage cheese and various fresh fruits may be given soft-billed birds. The hard-billed birds may be given the same food when young but when well developed rape, millet, flax seed (especially good for sick or weak birds), sunflower and hemp seeds should be added.

1045. How can nourishment be given injured, sick, or young birds that refuse food offered to them?   Very young birds open their bills freely when approached and food may be placed deep in the throat. This is essential since the muscles concerned with swallowing are located far down in the throat of birds. Birds old enough to fear man must be force-fed. To do this the mandibles must be forced gently apart. The food, as with very young birds, must be placed deep in the throat. It is sometimes necessary to hold the bill closed with one hand while gently massaging the throat with the other to encourage swallowing or the food will be spit out. Until a bird is old enough to feed itself or accustomed enough to captivity to feed itself, it must be force-fed.

1046. Will the diet outlined above satisfy a hawk?   Hawks need an all-meat diet. Liver, heart and brains from the butcher supply vital elements. Roughage also is needed. This can be provided by trapping mice and other small rodents and offering these whole or divided into suitable pieces for small hawks. Freshly killed mammals found on highways may be collected for feeding hawks.

1047. If an injured bird is found, what should be done?   If a bird is injured too seriously to feed or protect itself it may be placed in a darkened box small enough so it cannot injure itself by struggling. If bones are newly broken, it is possible to set them. Wings, after setting, are bound against the body. Legs are fastened to splints. The bones of birds heal within a few days (some doctors say in four days); therefore if a bone is not set quickly, it is soon too late for it to mend. Successful repair work is done frequently by devoted amateurs but in general it is wise to have the help of a veterinarian when bone-setting or amputation is required.

1048. Is there a book the layman needing help concerning the care or feeding of wild birds may consult?   "The Book of Wild Pets" by Clifford B. Moore. (G. P. Putnam's Sons, New York) has a helpful section on the care and feeding of wild birds.

BIRD BOOKS FOR A HOME LIBRARY

Guides to Bird Identification

Cruickshank, Allan D. *Pocket Guide to the Birds.* Dodd, Mead & Co., N.Y.

Peterson, Roger Tory. *A Field Guide to Eastern Birds; A Field Guide to Western Birds.* Houghton Mifflin Co., Boston and N.Y.

Pough, Richard H. *Audubon Land Bird Guide; Audubon Water Bird Guide; Audubon Western Bird Guide.* Doubleday & Co., N.Y.

Zim, Herbert S., and Ira N. Gabrielson. *Birds, A Guide to the Most Familiar American Birds—A Golden Nature Guide.* Simon & Schuster, N.Y.

Bird Nests

Headstrom, Richard. *Birds' Nests—A Field Guide.* Ives Washburn, N.Y.

Where to Look for Birds

Pettingill, Olin Sewall. *A Guide to Bird Finding East of the Mississippi; A Guide to Bird Finding West of the Mississippi.* Oxford University Press, N.Y.

How to Study Birds

Hickey, Joseph J. *A Guide to Bird Watching.* Oxford University Press, N.Y.

Attracting Birds

Terres, John K. *Songbirds in Your Garden.* Thomas Y. Crowell Co., N.Y.

Illustrated Bird Books (with text)

Barruel, Paul. *Birds of the World—Their Life and Habits.* Oxford University Press, N.Y.

Murphy, Robert C., and Dean Amadon. *Land Birds of America.* McGraw-Hill, N.Y.

Rand, Austin L. *American Water and Game Birds.* E. P. Dutton & Co., N.Y.

General Ornithology

Allen, Arthur A. *The Book of Bird Life.* D. Van Nostrand Co., N.Y.
Armstrong, Edward A. *Bird Display and Behavior.* Oxford University Press, N.Y.
Fisher, James. *A History of Birds.* Houghton Mifflin Co., Boston and N.Y.
Wallace, George J. *An Introduction to Ornithology.* The Macmillan Co., N.Y.

Bird Photography

Cruickshank, Allan D. *Hunting with the Camera.* Harper & Bros., N.Y.

Migration

Broun, Maurice. *Hawks Aloft; The Story of Hawk Mountain.* Dodd, Mead & Co., N.Y.
Lincoln, F. C. *The Migration of American Birds.* Doubleday & Co., N.Y.

INDEX

All references are to question numbers

Accidental birds, 66, 798, 799
Adductor muscles, 192, 193
Aepyornis maximus (*see* Elephant bird)
Aesop, 975
Africa, 147, 327, 362, 456, 540, 722, 785, 849
Air sacs, 221-223, 225, 230, 231, 568
Alaska, 55, 148, 152, 686, 1012
Albatross, 90, 109, 179, 402, 403, 675, 719, 749, 775
  Laysan, 602
  royal, 711, 775
  wandering, 18, 147, 182
Albinism, 354, 355
Alcid, 359, 747, 754, 760
Allen, A. A., 653
Alps, 287
Altricial brids, 330, 676, 740, 742, 749, 766-779
America, North, 55, 71, 72, 90, 113, 136, 152, 162, 432, 576, 603, 653, 712, 713, 714, 716, 749, 788, 802, 816, 825, 831, 840, 848-851, 993
America, South, 145, 150, 152, 159, 171, 433, 455, 533, 641, 809, 850
American Ornithologists' Union, 16, 1005
Antarctic, 147, 646, 710
Anatomy, 172-306
Anhinga, 260, 364, 518
Ani, 426
  groove-billed, 641
  smooth-billed, 641
Anting, 1025
Apodiformes, 21
Apteria, 316
Arabia, 991
Archeopterex, 5

Arctic, 125, 147, 150, 280, 361, 686, 809
Argentina, 146, 148
Aristophanes, 976
Aristotle, 117, 720, 978
Aspect ratio, 109
Atlantic, 54, 128, 162
Attracting birds, 860-909
Audubon Christmas bird count, 806
Audubon, John James, 807, 823, 957, 1004
Audubon, National Society, 951-956, 1006
Audubon Society of Canada, 1009
Auk, 634, 680
  great, 814
Auklet, rhinocerus, 453
Australia, 145, 335, 427, 606, 668, 669, 690, 728, 993
Aves, 2, 19, 442

Baird, S. F., 1004
Baltic, 153
Banding of birds, 820-859
Banding permits, 826-828
Barbet, 629
  bearded, 327, 540
Bartram, John, 997
Bartram, William, 978, 1004
Bastard wing, 396, 397
Bathing, 903-907, 1040
Bats, 114
Baumgartner, Mrs. F. M., 832
Beals, M. V., 832
Beebe, William, 188
Bergstrom, E. A., 846
Bible, 115, 972, 974, 996
Bills of birds, 241, 442-461
Binocular vision, 505

A CATALOGUE OF SELECTED DOVER BOOKS
IN ALL FIELDS OF INTEREST

A CATALOGUE OF SELECTED DOVER BOOKS
IN ALL FIELDS OF INTEREST

THE DEVIL'S DICTIONARY, Ambrose Bierce. Barbed, bitter, brilliant witticisms in the form of a dictionary. Best, most ferocious satire America has produced. 145pp. 20487-1 Pa. $1.75

ABSOLUTELY MAD INVENTIONS, A.E. Brown, H.A. Jeffcott. Hilarious, useless, or merely absurd inventions all granted patents by the U.S. Patent Office. Edible tie pin, mechanical hat tipper, etc. 57 illustrations. 125pp. 22596-8 Pa. $1.50

AMERICAN WILD FLOWERS COLORING BOOK, Paul Kennedy. Planned coverage of 48 most important wildflowers, from Rickett's collection; instructive as well as entertaining. Color versions on covers. 48pp. 8¼ x 11. 20095-7 Pa. $1.50

BIRDS OF AMERICA COLORING BOOK, John James Audubon. Rendered for coloring by Paul Kennedy. 46 of Audubon's noted illustrations: red-winged blackbird, cardinal, purple finch, towhee, etc. Original plates reproduced in full color on the covers. 48pp. 8¼ x 11. 23049-X Pa. $1.50

NORTH AMERICAN INDIAN DESIGN COLORING BOOK, Paul Kennedy. The finest examples from Indian masks, beadwork, pottery, etc. — selected and redrawn for coloring (with identifications) by well-known illustrator Paul Kennedy. 48pp. 8¼ x 11. 21125-8 Pa. $1.50

UNIFORMS OF THE AMERICAN REVOLUTION COLORING BOOK, Peter Copeland. 31 lively drawings reproduce whole panorama of military attire; each uniform has complete instructions for accurate coloring. (Not in the Pictorial Archives Series). 64pp. 8¼ x 11. 21850-3 Pa. $1.50

THE WONDERFUL WIZARD OF OZ COLORING BOOK, L. Frank Baum. Color the Yellow Brick Road and much more in 61 drawings adapted from W.W. Denslow's originals, accompanied by abridged version of text. Dorothy, Toto, Oz and the Emerald City. 61 illustrations. 64pp. 8¼ x 11. 20452-9 Pa. $1.50

CUT AND COLOR PAPER MASKS, Michael Grater. Clowns, animals, funny faces . . . simply color them in, cut them out, and put them together, and you have 9 paper masks to play with and enjoy. Complete instructions. Assembled masks shown in full color on the covers. 32pp. 8¼ x 11. 23171-2 Pa. $1.50

STAINED GLASS CHRISTMAS ORNAMENT COLORING BOOK, Carol Belanger Grafton. Brighten your Christmas season with over 100 Christmas ornaments done in a stained glass effect on translucent paper. Color them in and then hang at windows, from lights, anywhere. 32pp. 8¼ x 11. 20707-2 Pa. $1.75

CREATIVE LITHOGRAPHY AND HOW TO DO IT, Grant Arnold. Lithography as art form: working directly on stone, transfer of drawings, lithotint, mezzotint, color printing; also metal plates. Detailed, thorough. 27 illustrations. 214pp.
21208-4 Pa. $3.00

DESIGN MOTIFS OF ANCIENT MEXICO, Jorge Enciso. Vigorous, powerful ceramic stamp impressions — Maya, Aztec, Toltec, Olmec. Serpents, gods, priests, dancers, etc. 153pp. 6⅛ x 9¼.
20084-1 Pa. $2.50

AMERICAN INDIAN DESIGN AND DECORATION, Leroy Appleton. Full text, plus more than 700 precise drawings of Inca, Maya, Aztec, Pueblo, Plains, NW Coast basketry, sculpture, painting, pottery, sand paintings, metal, etc. 4 plates in color. 279pp. 8⅜ x 11¼.
22704-9 Pa. $4.50

CHINESE LATTICE DESIGNS, Daniel S. Dye. Incredibly beautiful geometric designs: circles, voluted, simple dissections, etc. Inexhaustible source of ideas, motifs. 1239 illustrations. 469pp. 6⅛ x 9¼.
23096-1 Pa. $5.00

JAPANESE DESIGN MOTIFS, Matsuya Co. Mon, or heraldic designs. Over 4000 typical, beautiful designs: birds, animals, flowers, swords, fans, geometric; all beautifully stylized. 213pp. 11⅜ x 8¼.
22874-6 Pa. $5.00

PERSPECTIVE, Jan Vredeman de Vries. 73 perspective plates from 1604 edition; buildings, townscapes, stairways, fantastic scenes. Remarkable for beauty, surrealistic atmosphere; real eye-catchers. Introduction by Adolf Placzek. 74pp. 11⅜ x 8¼.
20186-4 Pa. $2.75

EARLY AMERICAN DESIGN MOTIFS, Suzanne E. Chapman. 497 motifs, designs, from painting on wood, ceramics, appliqué, glassware, samplers, metal work, etc. Florals, landscapes, birds and animals, geometrics, letters, etc. Inexhaustible. Enlarged edition. 138pp. 8⅜ x 11¼.
22985-8 Pa. $3.50
23084-8 Clothbd. $7.95

VICTORIAN STENCILS FOR DESIGN AND DECORATION, edited by E.V. Gillon, Jr. 113 wonderful ornate Victorian pieces from German sources; florals, geometrics; borders, corner pieces; bird motifs, etc. 64pp. 9⅜ x 12¼.
21995-X Pa. $2.75

ART NOUVEAU: AN ANTHOLOGY OF DESIGN AND ILLUSTRATION FROM THE STUDIO, edited by E.V. Gillon, Jr. Graphic arts: book jackets, posters, engravings, illustrations, decorations; Crane, Beardsley, Bradley and many others. Inexhaustible. 92pp. 8⅛ x 11.
22388-4 Pa. $2.50

ORIGINAL ART DECO DESIGNS, William Rowe. First-rate, highly imaginative modern Art Deco frames, borders, compositions, alphabets, florals, insectals, Wurlitzer-types, etc. Much finest modern Art Deco. 80 plates, 8 in color. 8⅜ x 11¼.
22567-4 Pa. $3.50

HANDBOOK OF DESIGNS AND DEVICES, Clarence P. Hornung. Over 1800 basic geometric designs based on circle, triangle, square, scroll, cross, etc. Largest such collection in existence. 261pp.
20125-2 Pa. $2.75

VICTORIAN HOUSES: A TREASURY OF LESSER-KNOWN EXAMPLES, Edmund Gillon and Clay Lancaster. 116 photographs, excellent commentary illustrate distinct characteristics, many borrowings of local Victorian architecture. Octagonal houses, Americanized chalets, grand country estates, small cottages, etc. Rich heritage often overlooked. 116 plates. 11⅜ x 10. 22966-1 Pa. $4.00

STICKS AND STONES, Lewis Mumford. Great classic of American cultural history; architecture from medieval-inspired earliest forms to 20th century; evolution of structure and style, influence of environment. 21 illustrations. 113pp.
20202-X Pa. $2.50

ON THE LAWS OF JAPANESE PAINTING, Henry P. Bowie. Best substitute for training with genius Oriental master, based on years of study in Kano school. Philosophy, brushes, inks, style, etc. 66 illustrations. 117pp. 6⅛ x 9¼. 20030-2 Pa. $4.50

A HANDBOOK OF ANATOMY FOR ART STUDENTS, Arthur Thomson. Virtually exhaustive. Skeletal structure, muscles, heads, special features. Full text, anatomical figures, undraped photos. Male and female. 337 illustrations. 459pp.
21163-0 Pa. $5.00

AN ATLAS OF ANATOMY FOR ARTISTS, Fritz Schider. Finest text, working book. Full text, plus anatomical illustrations; plates by great artists showing anatomy. 593 illustrations. 192pp. 7⅞ x 10¾. 20241-0 Clothbd. $6.95

THE HUMAN FIGURE IN MOTION, Eadweard Muybridge. More than 4500 stopped-action photos, in action series, showing undraped men, women, children jumping, lying down, throwing, sitting, wrestling, carrying, etc. "Unparalleled dictionary for artists," American Artist. Taken by great 19th century photographer. 390pp. 7⅞ x 10⅝. 20204-6 Clothbd. $12.50

AN ATLAS OF ANIMAL ANATOMY FOR ARTISTS, W. Ellenberger et al. Horses, dogs, cats, lions, cattle, deer, etc. Muscles, skeleton, surface features. The basic work. Enlarged edition. 288 illustrations. 151pp. 9⅜ x 12¼. 20082-5 Pa. $4.50

LETTER FORMS: 110 COMPLETE ALPHABETS, Frederick Lambert. 110 sets of capital letters; 16 lower case alphabets; 70 sets of numbers and other symbols. Edited and expanded by Theodore Menten. 110pp. 8⅛ x 11. 22872-X Pa. $3.00

THE METHODS OF CONSTRUCTION OF CELTIC ART, George Bain. Simple geometric techniques for making wonderful Celtic interlacements, spirals, Kells-type initials, animals, humans, etc. Unique for artists, craftsmen. Over 500 illustrations. 160pp. 9 x 12. USO 22923-8 Pa. $4.00

SCULPTURE, PRINCIPLES AND PRACTICE, Louis Slobodkin. Step by step approach to clay, plaster, metals, stone; classical and modern. 253 drawings, photos. 255pp. 8⅛ x 11. 22960-2 Pa. $5.00

THE ART OF ETCHING, E.S. Lumsden. Clear, detailed instructions for etching, dry-point, softground, aquatint; from 1st sketch to print. Very detailed, thorough. 200 illustrations. 376pp. 20049-3 Pa. $3.75

CONSTRUCTION OF AMERICAN FURNITURE TREASURES, Lester Margon. 344 detail drawings, complete text on constructing exact reproductions of 38 early American masterpieces: Hepplewhite sideboard, Duncan Phyfe drop-leaf table, mantel clock, gate-leg dining table, Pa. German cupboard, more. 38 plates. 54 photographs. 168pp. 8⅜ x 11¼. 23056-2 Pa. $4.00

JEWELRY MAKING AND DESIGN, Augustus F. Rose, Antonio Cirino. Professional secrets revealed in thorough, practical guide: tools, materials, processes; rings, brooches, chains, cast pieces, enamelling, setting stones, etc. Do not confuse with skimpy introductions: beginner can use, professional can learn from it. Over 200 illustrations. 306pp. 21750-7 Pa. $3.00

METALWORK AND ENAMELLING, Herbert Maryon. Generally coneeded best all-around book. Countless trade secrets: materials, tools, soldering, filigree, setting, inlay, niello, repoussé, casting, polishing, etc. For beginner or expert. Author was foremost British expert. 330 illustrations. 335pp. 22702-2 Pa. $3.50

WEAVING WITH FOOT-POWER LOOMS, Edward F. Worst. Setting up a loom, beginning to weave, constructing equipment, using dyes, more, plus over 285 drafts of traditional patterns including Colonial and Swedish weaves. More than 200 other figures. For beginning and advanced. 275pp. 8¾ x 6⅜. 23064-3 Pa. $4.50

WEAVING A NAVAJO BLANKET, Gladys A. Reichard. Foremost anthropologist studied under Navajo women, reveals every step in process from wool, dyeing, spinning, setting up loom, designing, weaving. Much history, symbolism. With this book you could make one yourself. 97 illustrations. 222pp. 22992-0 Pa. $3.00

NATURAL DYES AND HOME DYEING, Rita J. Adrosko. Use natural ingredients: bark, flowers, leaves, lichens, insects etc. Over 135 specific recipes from historical sources for cotton, wool, other fabrics. Genuine premodern handicrafts. 12 illustrations. 160pp. 22688-3 Pa. $2.00

THE HAND DECORATION OF FABRICS, Francis J. Kafka. Outstanding, profusely illustrated guide to stenciling, batik, block printing, tie dyeing, freehand painting, silk screen printing, and novelty decoration. 356 illustrations. 198pp. 6 x 9. 21401-X Pa. $3.00

THOMAS NAST: CARTOONS AND ILLUSTRATIONS, with text by Thomas Nast St. Hill. Father of American political cartooning. Cartoons that destroyed Tweed Ring; inflation, free love, church and state; original Republican elephant and Democratic donkey; Santa Claus; more. 117 illustrations. 146pp. 9 x 12. 22983-1 Pa. $4.00
23067-8 Clothbd. $8.50

FREDERIC REMINGTON: 173 DRAWINGS AND ILLUSTRATIONS. Most famous of the Western artists, most responsible for our myths about the American West in its untamed days. Complete reprinting of *Drawings of Frederic Remington* (1897), plus other selections. 4 additional drawings in color on covers. 140pp. 9 x 12. 20714-5 Pa. $3.95

EARLY NEW ENGLAND GRAVESTONE RUBBINGS, Edmund V. Gillon, Jr. 43 photographs, 226 rubbings show heavily symbolic, macabre, sometimes humorous primitive American art. Up to early 19th century. 207pp. 8⅜ x 11¼.
21380-3 Pa. $4.00

L.J.M. DAGUERRE: THE HISTORY OF THE DIORAMA AND THE DAGUERREOTYPE, Helmut and Alison Gernsheim. Definitive account. Early history, life and work of Daguerre; discovery of daguerreotype process; diffusion abroad; other early photography. 124 illustrations. 226pp. 6⅙ x 9¼.
22290-X Pa. $4.00

PHOTOGRAPHY AND THE AMERICAN SCENE, Robert Taft. The basic book on American photography as art, recording form, 1839-1889. Development, influence on society, great photographers, types (portraits, war, frontier, etc.), whatever else needed. Inexhaustible. Illustrated with 322 early photos, daguerreotypes, tintypes, stereo slides, etc. 546pp. 6⅛ x 9¼.
21201-7 Pa. $5.95

PHOTOGRAPHIC SKETCHBOOK OF THE CIVIL WAR, Alexander Gardner. Reproduction of 1866 volume with 100 on-the-field photographs: Manassas, Lincoln on battlefield, slave pens, etc. Introduction by E.F. Bleiler. 224pp. 10¾ x 9.
22731-6 Pa. $5.00

THE MOVIES: A PICTURE QUIZ BOOK, Stanley Appelbaum & Hayward Cirker. Match stars with their movies, name actors and actresses, test your movie skill with 241 stills from 236 great movies, 1902-1959. Indexes of performers and films. 128pp. 8⅜ x 9¼.
20222-4 Pa. $2.50

THE TALKIES, Richard Griffith. Anthology of features, articles from Photoplay, 1928-1940, reproduced complete. Stars, famous movies, technical features, fabulous ads, etc.; Garbo, Chaplin, King Kong, Lubitsch, etc. 4 color plates, scores of illustrations. 327pp. 8⅜ x 11¼.
22762-6 Pa. $6.95

THE MOVIE MUSICAL FROM VITAPHONE TO "42ND STREET," edited by Miles Kreuger. Relive the rise of the movie musical as reported in the pages of Photoplay magazine (1926-1933): every movie review, cast list, ad, and record review; every significant feature article, production still, biography, forecast, and gossip story. Profusely illustrated. 367pp. 8⅜ x 11¼.
23154-2 Pa. $7.95

JOHANN SEBASTIAN BACH, Philipp Spitta. Great classic of biography, musical commentary, with hundreds of pieces analyzed. Also good for Bach's contemporaries. 450 musical examples. Total of 1799pp.
EUK 22278-0, 22279-9 Clothbd., Two vol. set $25.00

BEETHOVEN AND HIS NINE SYMPHONIES, Sir George Grove. Thorough history, analysis, commentary on symphonies and some related pieces. For either beginner or advanced student. 436 musical passages. 407pp.
20334-4 Pa. $4.00

MOZART AND HIS PIANO CONCERTOS, Cuthbert Girdlestone. The only full-length study. Detailed analyses of all 21 concertos, sources; 417 musical examples. 509pp.
21271-8 Pa. $6.00

THE FITZWILLIAM VIRGINAL BOOK, edited by J. Fuller Maitland, W.B. Squire. Famous early 17th century collection of keyboard music, 300 works by Morley, Byrd, Bull, Gibbons, etc. Modern notation. Total of 938pp. 8⅜ x 11.
ECE 21068-5, 21069-3 Pa., Two vol. set $15.00

COMPLETE STRING QUARTETS, Wolfgang A. Mozart. Breitkopf and Härtel edition. All 23 string quartets plus alternate slow movement to K156. Study score. 277pp. 9⅜ x 12¼.
22372-8 Pa. $6.00

COMPLETE SONG CYCLES, Franz Schubert. Complete piano, vocal music of Die Schöne Müllerin, Die Winterreise, Schwanengesang. Also Drinker English singing translations. Breitkopf and Härtel edition. 217pp. 9⅜ x 12¼.
22649-2 Pa. $4.50

THE COMPLETE PRELUDES AND ETUDES FOR PIANOFORTE SOLO, Alexander Scriabin. All the preludes and etudes including many perfectly spun miniatures. Edited by K.N. Igumnov and Y.I. Mil'shteyn. 250pp. 9 x 12.
22919-X Pa. $5.00

TRISTAN UND ISOLDE, Richard Wagner. Full orchestral score with complete instrumentation. Do not confuse with piano reduction. Commentary by Felix Mottl, great Wagnerian conductor and scholar. Study score. 655pp. 8⅛ x 11.
22915-7 Pa. $11.95

FAVORITE SONGS OF THE NINETIES, ed. Robert Fremont. Full reproduction, including covers, of 88 favorites: Ta-Ra-Ra-Boom-De-Aye, The Band Played On, Bird in a Gilded Cage, Under the Bamboo Tree, After the Ball, etc. 401pp. 9 x 12.
EBE 21536-9 Pa. $6.95

SOUSA'S GREAT MARCHES IN PIANO TRANSCRIPTION: ORIGINAL SHEET MUSIC OF 23 WORKS, John Philip Sousa. Selected by Lester S. Levy. Playing edition includes: The Stars and Stripes Forever, The Thunderer, The Gladiator, King Cotton, Washington Post, much more. 24 illustrations. 111pp. 9 x 12.
USO 23132-1 Pa. $3.50

CLASSIC PIANO RAGS, selected with an introduction by Rudi Blesh. Best ragtime music (1897-1922) by Scott Joplin, James Scott, Joseph F. Lamb, Tom Turpin, 9 others. Printed from best original sheet music, plus covers. 364pp. 9 x 12.
EBE 20469-3 Pa. $6.95

ANALYSIS OF CHINESE CHARACTERS, C.D. Wilder, J.H. Ingram. 1000 most important characters analyzed according to primitives, phonetics, historical development. Traditional method offers mnemonic aid to beginner, intermediate student of Chinese, Japanese. 365pp.
23045-7 Pa. $4.00

MODERN CHINESE: A BASIC COURSE, Faculty of Peking University. Self study, classroom course in modern Mandarin. Records contain phonetics, vocabulary, sentences, lessons. 249 page book contains all recorded text, translations, grammar, vocabulary, exercises. Best course on market. 3 12" 33⅓ monaural records, book, album.
98832-5 Set $12.50

THE BEST DR. THORNDYKE DETECTIVE STORIES, R. Austin Freeman. The Case of Oscar Brodski, The Moabite Cipher, and 5 other favorites featuring the great scientific detective, plus his long-believed-lost first adventure — 31 New Inn — reprinted here for the first time. Edited by E.F. Bleiler. USO 20388-3 Pa. $3.00

BEST "THINKING MACHINE" DETECTIVE STORIES, Jacques Futrelle. The Problem of Cell 13 and 11 other stories about Prof. Augustus S.F.X. Van Dusen, including two "lost" stories. First reprinting of several. Edited by E.F. Bleiler. 241pp.
20537-1 Pa. $3.00

UNCLE SILAS, J. Sheridan LeFanu. Victorian Gothic mystery novel, considered by many best of period, even better than Collins or Dickens. Wonderful psychological terror. Introduction by Frederick Shroyer. 436pp. 21715-9 Pa. $4.00

BEST DR. POGGIOLI DETECTIVE STORIES, T.S. Stribling. 15 best stories from EQMM and The Saint offer new adventures in Mexico, Florida, Tennessee hills as Poggioli unravels mysteries and combats Count Jalacki. 217pp. 23227-1 Pa. $3.00

EIGHT DIME NOVELS, selected with an introduction by E.F. Bleiler. Adventures of Old King Brady, Frank James, Nick Carter, Deadwood Dick, Buffalo Bill, The Steam Man, Frank Merriwell, and Horatio Alger — 1877 to 1905. Important, entertaining popular literature in facsimile reprint, with original covers. 190pp. 9 x 12. 22975-0 Pa. $3.50

ALICE'S ADVENTURES UNDER GROUND, Lewis Carroll. Facsimile of ms. Carroll gave Alice Liddell in 1864. Different in many ways from final Alice. Handlettered, illustrated by Carroll. Introduction by Martin Gardner. 128pp. 21482-6 Pa. $1.50

ALICE IN WONDERLAND COLORING BOOK, Lewis Carroll. Pictures by John Tenniel. Large-size versions of the famous illustrations of Alice, Cheshire Cat, Mad Hatter and all the others, waiting for your crayons. Abridged text. 36 illustrations. 64pp. 8¼ x 11. 22853-3 Pa. $1.50

AVENTURES D'ALICE AU PAYS DES MERVEILLES, Lewis Carroll. Bué's translation of "Alice" into French, supervised by Carroll himself. Novel way to learn language. (No English text.) 42 Tenniel illustrations. 196pp. 22836-3 Pa. $2.50

MYTHS AND FOLK TALES OF IRELAND, Jeremiah Curtin. 11 stories that are Irish versions of European fairy tales and 9 stories from the Fenian cycle — 20 tales of legend and magic that comprise an essential work in the history of folklore. 256pp. 22430-9 Pa. $3.00

EAST O' THE SUN AND WEST O' THE MOON, George W. Dasent. Only full edition of favorite, wonderful Norwegian fairytales — Why the Sea is Salt, Boots and the Troll, etc. — with 77 illustrations by Kittelsen & Werenskiöld. 418pp. 22521-6 Pa. $4.00

PERRAULT'S FAIRY TALES, Charles Perrault and Gustave Doré. Original versions of Cinderella, Sleeping Beauty, Little Red Riding Hood, etc. in best translation, with 34 wonderful illustrations by Gustave Doré. 117pp. 8⅛ x 11. 22311-6 Pa. $2.50

MOTHER GOOSE'S MELODIES. Facsimile of fabulously rare Munroe and Francis "copyright 1833" Boston edition. Familiar and unusual rhymes, wonderful old woodcut illustrations. Edited by E.F. Bleiler. 128pp. 4½ x 6⅜. 22577-1 Pa. $1.50

MOTHER GOOSE IN HIEROGLYPHICS. Favorite nursery rhymes presented in rebus form for children. Fascinating 1849 edition reproduced in toto, with key. Introduction by E.F. Bleiler. About 400 woodcuts. 64pp. 6⅞ x 5¼. 20745-5 Pa. $1.00

PETER PIPER'S PRACTICAL PRINCIPLES OF PLAIN & PERFECT PRONUNCIATION. Alliterative jingles and tongue-twisters. Reproduction in full of 1830 first American edition. 25 spirited woodcuts. 32pp. 4½ x 6⅜. 22560-7 Pa. $1.00

MARMADUKE MULTIPLY'S MERRY METHOD OF MAKING MINOR MATHEMATICIANS. Fellow to Peter Piper, it teaches multiplication table by catchy rhymes and woodcuts. 1841 Munroe & Francis edition. Edited by E.F. Bleiler. 103pp. 4⅝ x 6.
22773-1 Pa. $1.25
20171-6 Clothbd. $3.00

THE NIGHT BEFORE CHRISTMAS, Clement Moore. Full text, and woodcuts from original 1848 book. Also critical, historical material. 19 illustrations. 40pp. 4⅝ x 6. 22797-9 Pa. $1.25

THE KING OF THE GOLDEN RIVER, John Ruskin. Victorian children's classic of three brothers, their attempts to reach the Golden River, what becomes of them. Facsimile of original 1889 edition. 22 illustrations. 56pp. 4⅝ x 6⅜.
20066-3 Pa. $1.50

DREAMS OF THE RAREBIT FIEND, Winsor McCay. Pioneer cartoon strip, unexcelled for beauty, imagination, in 60 full sequences. Incredible technical virtuosity, wonderful visual wit. Historical introduction. 62pp. 8⅜ x 11¼. 21347-1 Pa. $2.50

THE KATZENJAMMER KIDS, Rudolf Dirks. In full color, 14 strips from 1906-7; full of imagination, characteristic humor. Classic of great historical importance. Introduction by August Derleth. 32pp. 9¼ x 12¼. 23005-8 Pa. $2.00

LITTLE ORPHAN ANNIE AND LITTLE ORPHAN ANNIE IN COSMIC CITY, Harold Gray. Two great sequences from the early strips: our curly-haired heroine defends the Warbucks' financial empire and, then, takes on meanie Phineas P. Pinchpenny. Leapin' lizards! 178pp. 6⅛ x 8⅜. 23107-0 Pa. $2.00

THE BEST OF GLUYAS WILLIAMS. 100 drawings by one of America's finest cartoonists: The Day a Cake of Ivory Soap Sank at Proctor & Gamble's, At the Life Insurance Agents' Banquet, and many other gems from the 20's and 30's. 118pp. 8⅜ x 11¼. 22737-5 Pa. $2.50

THE MAGIC MOVING PICTURE BOOK, Bliss, Sands & Co. The pictures in this book move! Volcanoes erupt, a house burns, a serpentine dancer wiggles her way through a number. By using a specially ruled acetate screen provided, you can obtain these and 15 other startling effects. Originally "The Motograph Moving Picture Book." 32pp. 8¼ x 11.   23224-7 Pa. $1.75

STRING FIGURES AND HOW TO MAKE THEM, Caroline F. Jayne. Fullest, clearest instructions on string figures from around world: Eskimo, Navajo, Lapp, Europe, more. Cats cradle, moving spear, lightning, stars. Introduction by A.C. Haddon. 950 illustrations. 407pp.   20152-X Pa. $3.50

PAPER FOLDING FOR BEGINNERS, William D. Murray and Francis J. Rigney. Clearest book on market for making origami sail boats, roosters, frogs that move legs, cups, bonbon boxes. 40 projects. More than 275 illustrations. Photographs. 94pp.
20713-7 Pa. $1.25

INDIAN SIGN LANGUAGE, William Tomkins. Over 525 signs developed by Sioux, Blackfoot, Cheyenne, Arapahoe and other tribes. Written instructions and diagrams: how to make words, construct sentences. Also 290 pictographs of Sioux and Ojibway tribes. 111pp. 6⅛ x 9¼.   22029-X Pa. $1.50

BOOMERANGS: HOW TO MAKE AND THROW THEM, Bernard S. Mason. Easy to make and throw, dozens of designs: cross-stick, pinwheel, boomabird, tumblestick, Australian curved stick boomerang. Complete throwing instructions. All safe. 99pp.   23028-7 Pa. $1.75

25 KITES THAT FLY, Leslie Hunt. Full, easy to follow instructions for kites made from inexpensive materials. Many novelties. Reeling, raising, designing your own. 70 illustrations. 110pp.   22550-X Pa. $1.25

TRICKS AND GAMES ON THE POOL TABLE, Fred Herrmann. 79 tricks and games, some solitaires, some for 2 or more players, some competitive; mystifying shots and throws, unusual carom, tricks involving cork, coins, a hat, more. 77 figures. 95pp.   21814-7 Pa. $1.25

WOODCRAFT AND CAMPING, Bernard S. Mason. How to make a quick emergency shelter, select woods that will burn immediately, make do with limited supplies, etc. Also making many things out of wood, rawhide, bark, at camp. Formerly titled Woodcraft. 295 illustrations. 580pp.   21951-8 Pa. $4.00

AN INTRODUCTION TO CHESS MOVES AND TACTICS SIMPLY EXPLAINED, Leonard Barden. Informal intermediate introduction: reasons for moves, tactics, openings, traps, positional play, endgame. Isolates patterns. 102pp. USO 21210-6 Pa. $1.35

LASKER'S MANUAL OF CHESS, Dr. Emanuel Lasker. Great world champion offers very thorough coverage of all aspects of chess. Combinations, position play, openings, endgame, aesthetics of chess, philosophy of struggle, much more. Filled with analyzed games. 390pp.   20640-8 Pa. $4.00

DRIED FLOWERS, Sarah Whitlock and Martha Rankin. Concise, clear, practical guide to dehydration, glycerinizing, pressing plant material, and more. Covers use of silica gel. 12 drawings. Originally titled "New Techniques with Dried Flowers." 32pp. 21802-3 Pa. $1.00

ABC OF POULTRY RAISING, J.H. Florea. Poultry expert, editor tells how to raise chickens on home or small business basis. Breeds, feeding, housing, laying, etc. Very concrete, practical. 50 illustrations. 256pp. 23201-8 Pa. $3.00

HOW INDIANS USE WILD PLANTS FOR FOOD, MEDICINE & CRAFTS, Frances Densmore. Smithsonian, Bureau of American Ethnology report presents wealth of material on nearly 200 plants used by Chippewas of Minnesota and Wisconsin. 33 plates plus 122pp. of text. 6⅛ x 9¼. 23019-8 Pa. $2.50

THE HERBAL OR GENERAL HISTORY OF PLANTS, John Gerard. The 1633 edition revised and enlarged by Thomas Johnson. Containing almost 2850 plant descriptions and 2705 superb illustrations, Gerard's Herbal is a monumental work, the book all modern English herbals are derived from, and the one herbal every serious enthusiast should have in its entirety. Original editions are worth perhaps $750. 1678pp. 8½ x 12¼. 23147-X Clothbd. $50.00

A MODERN HERBAL, Margaret Grieve. Much the fullest, most exact, most useful compilation of herbal material. Gigantic alphabetical encyclopedia, from aconite to zedoary, gives botanical information, medical properties, folklore, economic uses, and much else. Indispensable to serious reader. 161 illustrations. 888pp. 6½ x 9¼. USO 22798-7, 22799-5 Pa., Two vol. set $10.00

HOW TO KNOW THE FERNS, Frances T. Parsons. Delightful classic. Identification, fern lore, for Eastern and Central U.S.A. Has introduced thousands to interesting life form. 99 illustrations. 215pp. 20740-4 Pa. $2.75

THE MUSHROOM HANDBOOK, Louis C.C. Krieger. Still the best popular handbook. Full descriptions of 259 species, extremely thorough text, habitats, luminescence, poisons, folklore, etc. 32 color plates; 126 other illustrations. 560pp. 21861-9 Pa. $4.50

HOW TO KNOW THE WILD FRUITS, Maude G. Peterson. Classic guide covers nearly 200 trees, shrubs, smaller plants of the U.S. arranged by color of fruit and then by family. Full text provides names, descriptions, edibility, uses. 80 illustrations. 400pp. 22943-2 Pa. $4.00

COMMON WEEDS OF THE UNITED STATES, U.S. Department of Agriculture. Covers 220 important weeds with illustration, maps, botanical information, plant lore for each. Over 225 illustrations. 463pp. 6⅛ x 9¼. 20504-5 Pa. $4.50

HOW TO KNOW THE WILD FLOWERS, Mrs. William S. Dana. Still best popular book for East and Central USA. Over 500 plants easily identified, with plant lore; arranged according to color and flowering time. 174 plates. 459pp. 20332-8 Pa. $3.50

DRIED FLOWERS, Sarah Whitlock and Martha Rankin. Concise, clear, practical guide to dehydration, glycerinizing, pressing plant material, and more. Covers use of silica gel. 12 drawings. Originally titled "New Techniques with Dried Flowers." 32pp. 21802-3 Pa. $1.00

ABC OF POULTRY RAISING, J.H. Florea. Poultry expert, editor tells how to raise chickens on home or small business basis. Breeds, feeding, housing, laying, etc. Very concrete, practical. 50 illustrations. 256pp. 23201-8 Pa. $3.00

HOW INDIANS USE WILD PLANTS FOR FOOD, MEDICINE & CRAFTS, Frances Densmore. Smithsonian, Bureau of American Ethnology report presents wealth of material on nearly 200 plants used by Chippewas of Minnesota and Wisconsin. 33 plates plus 122pp. of text. 6⅛ x 9¼. 23019-8 Pa. $2.50

THE HERBAL OR GENERAL HISTORY OF PLANTS, John Gerard. The 1633 edition revised and enlarged by Thomas Johnson. Containing almost 2850 plant descriptions and 2705 superb illustrations, Gerard's Herbal is a monumental work, the book all modern English herbals are derived from, and the one herbal every serious enthusiast should have in its entirety. Original editions are worth perhaps $750. 1678pp. 8½ x 12¼. 23147-X Clothbd. $50.00

A MODERN HERBAL, Margaret Grieve. Much the fullest, most exact, most useful compilation of herbal material. Gigantic alphabetical encyclopedia, from aconite to zedoary, gives botanical information, medical properties, folklore, economic uses, and much else. Indispensable to serious reader. 161 illustrations. 888pp. 6½ x 9¼. USO 22798-7, 22799-5 Pa., Two vol. set $10.00

HOW TO KNOW THE FERNS, Frances T. Parsons. Delightful classic. Identification, fern lore, for Eastern and Central U.S.A. Has introduced thousands to interesting life form. 99 illustrations. 215pp. 20740-4 Pa. $2.75

THE MUSHROOM HANDBOOK, Louis C.C. Krieger. Still the best popular handbook. Full descriptions of 259 species, extremely thorough text, habitats, luminescence, poisons, folklore, etc. 32 color plates; 126 other illustrations. 560pp. 21861-9 Pa. $4.50

HOW TO KNOW THE WILD FRUITS, Maude G. Peterson. Classic guide covers nearly 200 trees, shrubs, smaller plants of the U.S. arranged by color of fruit and then by family. Full text provides names, descriptions, edibility, uses. 80 illustrations. 400pp. 22943-2 Pa. $4.00

COMMON WEEDS OF THE UNITED STATES, U.S. Department of Agriculture. Covers 220 important weeds with illustration, maps, botanical information, plant lore for each. Over 225 illustrations. 463pp. 6⅛ x 9¼. 20504-5 Pa. $4.50

HOW TO KNOW THE WILD FLOWERS, Mrs. William S. Dana. Still best popular book for East and Central USA. Over 500 plants easily identified, with plant lore; arranged according to color and flowering time. 174 plates. 459pp. 20332-8 Pa. $3.50

THE STYLE OF PALESTRINA AND THE DISSONANCE, Knud Jeppesen. Standard analysis of rhythm, line, harmony, accented and unaccented dissonances. Also pre-Palestrina dissonances. 306pp. 22386-8 Pa. $4.50

DOVER OPERA GUIDE AND LIBRETTO SERIES prepared by Ellen H. Bleiler. Each volume contains everything needed for background, complete enjoyment: complete libretto, new English translation with all repeats, biography of composer and librettist, early performance history, musical lore, much else. All volumes lavishly illustrated with performance photos, portraits, similar material. Do not confuse with skimpy performance booklets.

CARMEN, Georges Bizet. 66 illustrations. 222pp. 22111-3 Pa. $3.00
DON GIOVANNI, Wolfgang A. Mozart. 92 illustrations. 209pp. 21134-7 Pa. $2.50
LA BOHÈME, Giacomo Puccini. 73 illustrations. 124pp. USO 20404-9 Pa. $1.75
ÄIDA, Giuseppe Verdi. 76 illustrations. 181pp. 20405-7 Pa. $2.25
LUCIA DI LAMMERMOOR, Gaetano Donizetti. 44 illustrations. 186pp.
22110-5 Pa. $2.00

ANTONIO STRADIVARI: HIS LIFE AND WORK, W. H. Hill, et al. Great work of musicology. Construction methods, woods, varnishes, known instruments, types of instruments, life, special features. Introduction by Sydney Beck. 98 illustrations, plus 4 color plates. 315pp. 20425-1 Pa. $4.00

MUSIC FOR THE PIANO, James Friskin, Irwin Freundlich. Both famous, little-known compositions; 1500 to 1950's. Listing, description, classification, technical aspects for student, teacher, performer. Indispensable for enlarging repertory. 448pp.
22918-1 Pa. $4.00

PIANOS AND THEIR MAKERS, Alfred Dolge. Leading inventor offers full history of piano technology, earliest models to 1910. Types, makers, components, mechanisms, musical aspects. Very strong on offtrail models, inventions; also player pianos. 300 illustrations. 581pp. 22856-8 Pa. $5.00

KEYBOARD MUSIC, J.S. Bach. Bach-Gesellschaft edition. For harpsichord, piano, other keyboard instruments. English Suites, French Suites, Six Partitas, Goldberg Variations, Two-Part Inventions, Three-Part Sinfonias. 312pp. 8⅛ x 11.
22360-4 Pa. $5.00

COMPLETE STRING QUARTETS, Ludwig van Beethoven. Breitkopf and Härtel edition. 6 quartets of Opus 18; 3 quartets of Opus 59; Opera 74, 95, 127, 130, 131, 132, 135 and Grosse Fuge. Study score. 434pp. 9⅜ x 12¼. 22361-2 Pa. $7.95

COMPLETE PIANO SONATAS AND VARIATIONS FOR SOLO PIANO, Johannes Brahms. All sonatas, five variations on themes from Schumann, Paganini, Handel, etc. Vienna Gesellschaft der Musikfreunde edition. 178pp. 9 x 12. 22650-6 Pa. $4.50

PIANO MUSIC 1888-1905, Claude Debussy. Deux Arabesques, Suite Bergamesque, Masques, 1st series of Images, etc. 9 others, in corrected editions. 175pp. 9⅜ x 12¼. 22771-5 Pa. $4.00

INCIDENTS OF TRAVEL IN YUCATAN, John L. Stephens. Classic (1843) exploration of jungles of Yucatan, looking for evidences of Maya civilization. Travel adventures, Mexican and Indian culture, etc. Total of 669pp.
20926-1, 20927-X Pa., Two vol. set $6.00

LIVING MY LIFE, Emma Goldman. Candid, no holds barred account by foremost American anarchist: her own life, anarchist movement, famous contemporaries, ideas and their impact. Struggles and confrontations in America, plus deportation to U.S.S.R. Shocking inside account of persecution of anarchists under Lenin. 13 plates. Total of 944pp.
22543-7, 22544-5 Pa., Two vol. set $9.00

AMERICAN INDIANS, George Catlin. Classic account of life among Plains Indians: ceremonies, hunt, warfare, etc. Dover edition reproduces for first time all original paintings. 312 plates. 572pp. of text. 6⅛ x 9¼.
22118-0, 22119-9 Pa., Two vol. set $8.00
22140-7, 22144-X Clothbd., Two vol. set $16.00 .

THE INDIANS' BOOK, Natalie Curtis. Lore, music, narratives, drawings by Indians, collected from cultures of U.S.A. 149 songs in full notation. 45 illustrations. 583pp. 6⅝ x 9⅜.
21939-9 Pa. $6.95

INDIAN BLANKETS AND THEIR MAKERS, George Wharton James. History, old style wool blankets, changes brought about by traders, symbolism of design and color, a Navajo weaver at work, outline blanket, Kachina blankets, more. Emphasis on Navajo. 130 illustrations, 32 in color. 230pp. 6⅛ x 9¼.
22996-3 Pa. $5.00
23068-6 Clothbd. $10.00

AN INTRODUCTION TO THE STUDY OF THE MAYA HIEROGLYPHS, Sylvanus Griswold Morley. Classic study by one of the truly great figures in hieroglyph research. Still the best introduction for the student for reading Maya hieroglyphs. New introduction by J. Eric S. Thompson. 117 illustrations. 284pp.
23108-9 Pa. $4.00

THE ANALECTS OF CONFUCIUS, THE GREAT LEARNING, DOCTRINE OF THE MEAN, Confucius. Edited by James Legge. Full Chinese text, standard English translation on same page, Chinese commentators, editor's annotations; dictionary of characters at rear, plus grammatical comment. Finest edition anywhere of one of world's greatest thinkers. 503pp.
22746-4 Pa. $5.00

THE I CHING (THE BOOK OF CHANGES), translated by James Legge. Complete translation of basic text plus appendices by Confucius, and Chinese commentary of most penetrating divination manual ever prepared. Indispensable to study of early Oriental civilizations, to modern inquiring reader. 448pp.
21062-6 Pa. $3.50

THE EGYPTIAN BOOK OF THE DEAD, E.A. Wallis Budge. Complete reproduction of Ani's papyrus, finest ever found. Full hieroglyphic text, interlinear transliteration, word for word translation, smooth translation. Basic work, for Egyptology, for modern study of psychic matters. Total of 533pp. 6½ x 9¼.
EBE 21866-X Pa. $4.95

BUILD YOUR OWN LOW-COST HOME, L.O. Anderson, H.F. Zornig. U.S. Dept. of Agriculture sets of plans, full, detailed, for 11 houses: A-Frame, circular, conventional. Also construction manual. Save hundreds of dollars. 204pp. 11 x 16.
21525-3 Pa. $6.00

HOW TO BUILD A WOOD-FRAME HOUSE, L.O. Anderson. Comprehensive, easy to follow U.S. Government manual: placement, foundations, framing, sheathing, roof, insulation, plaster, finishing — almost everything else. 179 illustrations. 223pp. 7⅞ x 10¾.
22954-8 Pa. $3.50

CONCRETE, MASONRY AND BRICKWORK, U.S. Department of the Army. Practical handbook for the home owner and small builder manual contains basic principles, techniques, and important background information on construction with concrete, concrete blocks, and brick. 177 figures, 37 tables. 200pp. 6½ x 9¼.
23203-4 Pa. $4.00

THE STANDARD BOOK OF QUILT MAKING AND COLLECTING, Marguerite Ickis. Full information, full-sized patterns for making 46 traditional quilts, also 150 other patterns. Quilted cloths, lamé, satin quilts, etc. 483 illustrations. 273pp. 6⅞ x 9⅝.
20582-7 Pa. $3.50

101 PATCHWORK PATTERNS, Ruby S. McKim. 101 beautiful, immediately useable patterns, full-size, modern and traditional. Also general information, estimating, quilt lore. 124pp. 7⅞ x 10¾.
20773-0 Pa. $2.50

KNIT YOUR OWN NORWEGIAN SWEATERS, Dale Yarn Company. Complete instructions for 50 authentic sweaters, hats, mittens, gloves, caps, etc. Thoroughly modern designs that command high prices in stores. 24 patterns, 24 color photographs. Nearly 100 charts and other illustrations. 58pp. 8⅜ x 11¼.
23031-7 Pa. $2.50

IRON-ON TRANSFER PATTERNS FOR CREWEL AND EMBROIDERY FROM EARLY AMERICAN SOURCES, edited by Rita Weiss. 75 designs, borders, alphabets, from traditional American sources printed on translucent paper in transfer ink. Reuseable. Instructions. Test patterns. 24pp. 8¼ x 11.
23162-3 Pa. $1.50

AMERICAN INDIAN NEEDLEPOINT DESIGNS FOR PILLOWS, BELTS, HANDBAGS AND OTHER PROJECTS, Roslyn Epstein. 37 authentic American Indian designs adapted for modern needlepoint projects. Grid backing makes designs easily transferable to canvas. 48pp. 8¼ x 11.
22973-4 Pa. $1.50

CHARTED FOLK DESIGNS FOR CROSS-STITCH EMBROIDERY, Maria Foris & Andreas Foris. 278 charted folk designs, most in 2 colors, from Danube region: florals, fantastic beasts, geometrics, traditional symbols, more. Border and central patterns. 77pp. 8¼ x 11.
USO 23191-7 Pa. $2.00

Prices subject to change without notice.
Available at your book dealer or write for free catalogue to Dept. GI, Dover Publications, Inc., 180 Varick St., N.Y., N.Y. 10014. Dover publishes more than 150 books each year on science, elementary and advanced mathematics, biology, music, art, literary history, social sciences and other areas.